S0-CJQ-988

COMMUNICATION AND AFFECT

Language and Thought

CONTRIBUTORS

FERGUS I. M. CRAIK
JAMES DEESE
ROY FREEDLE
PAUL A. KOLERS
ERIC H. LENNEBERG
MICHAEL LEWIS
MORRIS MOSCOVITCH
MARTIN T. ORNE
GREGORY RAZRAN

Symposium on Communication and Affect, 2d, Erindale
College, 1972.

Communication
and Affect

LANGUAGE AND THOUGHT

Edited by

PATRICIA PLINER   LESTER KRAMES
THOMAS ALLOWAY

Erindale College
University of Toronto
Mississauga, Ontario, Canada

ACADEMIC PRESS   *New York and London*   *1973*

A Subsidiary of Harcourt Brace Jovanovich, Publishers

COPYRIGHT © 1973, BY ACADEMIC PRESS, INC.
ALL RIGHTS RESERVED.
NO PART OF THIS PUBLICATION MAY BE REPRODUCED OR
TRANSMITTED IN ANY FORM OR BY ANY MEANS, ELECTRONIC
OR MECHANICAL, INCLUDING PHOTOCOPY, RECORDING, OR ANY
INFORMATION STORAGE AND RETRIEVAL SYSTEM, WITHOUT
PERMISSION IN WRITING FROM THE PUBLISHER.

ACADEMIC PRESS, INC.
111 Fifth Avenue, New York, New York 10003

United Kingdom Edition published by
ACADEMIC PRESS, INC. (LONDON) LTD.
24/28 Oval Road, London NW1

Library of Congress Cataloging in Publication Data

Symposium on Communication and Affect, 2d, Erindale
College, 1972.
    Communication and effect: language and thought.

    Bibliography: p.
      1.   Languages–Psychology–Congresses.   2.   Thought
and thinking–Congresses.   I.   Pliner, Patricia, ed.
II.   Krames, Lester, ed.   III.   Alloway, Thomas, ed.
IV.   Title.
BF455.S95 1972   153   72–9335
ISBN 0–12–558250–1

PRINTED IN THE UNITED STATES OF AMERICA

BF
455
.S92
1972

10/3/74 B+T 9,95/9,45

CONTENTS

Contents vii

Quasi-Controls as Procedures to Evaluate the Total
  Experimental Communication   179
Demand Characteristics as a Spoiler Variable   182
The Peculiar Nature of the Psychological Experiment and How It
  Affects Replication of Prior Research   184
Summary   188
References   189

Author Index   193
Subject Index   198

The editors have recently learned of the untimely death of Professor Gregory Razran, one of the contributors to this volume. In recognition of his extensive contributions to psychology, we would like to dedicate this volume to his memory.

LIST OF CONTRIBUTORS

Numbers in parentheses indicate the pages on which the authors' contributions begin.

FERGUS I. M. CRAIK (45), Erindale College, University of Toronto, Ontario, Canada

JAMES DEESE (9), Department of Psychology, The University of Virginia, Charlottesville, Virginia

ROY FREEDLE (127), Educational Testing Service, Princeton, New Jersey

PAUL A. KOLERS (21), Department of Psychology, University of Toronto, Ontario, Canada

ERIC H. LENNEBERG (1), Department of Psychology, Cornell University, Ithaca, New York and Department of Neurology, The New York Hospital, Cornell Medical School, White Plains, New York

MICHAEL LEWIS (127), Educational Testing Service, Princeton, New Jersey

MORRIS MOSCOVITCH (89), Erindale College, University of Toronto, Ontario, Canada

MARTIN T. ORNE (157), Unit for Experimental Psychiatry, Institute of the Pennsylvania Hospital and Department of Psychiatry, University of Pennsylvania, Philadelphia, Pennsylvania

GREGORY RAZRAN* (67), Queens College of the City University of New York, New York, New York

* Deceased.

ix

PREFACE

During the past three decades, behavioral psychologists have been devoting an increasing amount of attention to problems of language and thought. This interest has gone beyond the strict behavioristic approaches to rote memory and language acquisition viewed as conditioning, and has often involved the incorporation of cognitive theories into what nevertheless remains, at the observational level, an essentially behavioral enterprise.

This volume contains a series of papers dealing with this neobehavioristic approach to language and thought. The individual papers represent a broad spectrum of substantive topics that are linked by their common neobehavioristic methodology and by their subject matter dealing with human verbal and symbolic behavior.

Eric Lenneberg employs linguistic theory in an attempt to delineate the behavioral criteria for knowledge of a language. James Deese discusses the linguistic concept of marked and unmarked attributes and relates it to cognitive structure and affect. Paul Kohlers compares the pictoral and verbal modes of representing information. Fergus Craik proposes a "levels of processing" model of human memory. Gregory Razran discusses the evolution of human cognition and compares Soviet and Western approaches to this problem. Morris Moscovitch discusses some current empirical and theoretical approaches to the question of localization of language functions in the human brain. Michael Lewis and Roy Freedle describe the complex communication network between the human infant and mother. Finally, Martin Orne discusses the nature of implicit communications in experimental situations.

The papers in this volume were originally presented at the second of a series of annual symposia on Communication and Affect held at Erindale College, University of Toronto, in March 1972. This series of symposia has been generously supported by the College and represents a portion of the College's emphasis upon interdisciplinary programs.

We would like to take this opportunity to thank some of the many people whose efforts have contributed to the success of this series of symposia. Among them are I. M. Spigel, who proposed the idea of holding a series of symposia; J. T. Wilson and E. A. Robinson, Principal and Dean, respectively, of Erindale College, who arranged financial support; and Donald Thompson, who advised us in the selection of symposium participants. In addition, we would like to acknowledge the dedicated assistance of the College's nonacademic staff under the direction of Arthur Boorman, Arnold Miller, Georgie Anderson, and Stanley Wardle. Mrs. Doris Heckman, our secretary, also provided invaluable help with the necessary details of organizing and staging the symposium.

Finally, although their remarks do not appear in this volume, the discussants of the major papers made an important contribution to the symposium. Thus, we would like to thank M. G. Effran, B. Forrin, J. B. Gilmore, R. S. Lockhart, M. W. Milgram, N. P. Moray, and N. J. Slameka.

WHAT IS MEANT BY KNOWING A LANGUAGE?

Eric H. Lenneberg

Cornell University
and
The New York Hospital

There are many practical situations in which one may be in doubt as to whether a subject actually knows English or whether he is just doing something that superficially resembles speaking, without any real knowledge of English. The classical example of the latter is the parrot. Recently, two young female chimpanzees are said to have acquired skills that are, in the eyes of their trainers, like knowing English, though many observers continue to be skeptical (Ploog & Melnechuk, 1971). Even among humans, it is not always clear whether an individual in fact *knows* a natural language. Clinicians are often faced with patients whose language behavior is so deviant that serious doubts may be raised about their language capacities. Such borderline cases are valuable for our understanding of the nature of language. It is clear why this should be so; just as it is difficult for us to appreciate the vital nature of the atmosphere until we are deprived of it, it is difficult for us to see just what we do when we understand and speak a language until we are faced with malfunctioning of the mechanisms involved. Language is so intimately interwoven with our cognitive life, that we normally find it hard to imagine what "language-free cognition" would be like. (Yet such conditions exist among the congenitally deaf before formal instruction in language or sign communication has begun; Furth, 1966.) Let us start with some operational tests for language knowledge.

Suppose we train a subject (throughout this first section, *subject* stands for normal child, neurological patient, or experimental animal alike) to hand us an object placed before him upon being given a certain signal.

1

When the light goes on, he finds in front of him a box, an apple, or a bottle, for example; he learns that he is expected to pick the object up and give it to the experimenter. After he has learned this game, we start building up a vocabulary. Each object will have its own signal, say the spoken English word that corresponds to it, some graphic representation, or some tactual pattern — the sense modality is immaterial. As soon as the subject performs correctly on some 10 words, we begin to train him (by whatever means we can think of) to execute commands of the following type: When the light goes on, the subject will always find two objects in front of him, selected from among those whose "names" he seems to know. However, now he is no longer to hand the experimenter automatically whatever is in front of him, but must wait for special instructions. For instance, one instruction might be expressed by the word (graphic symbol, etc.) "and"; another by the word "or"; yet another by the phrase "the larger," etc. The first instruction is followed correctly only if the subject hands both objects; the second only if he hands one of the two objects; the third only if he picks up the larger; and so on. It is clear that each instruction is, in fact, a command to relate the two objects before him to one another. "Relate object O_1 to object O_2 'and-wise' ('or-wise,' 'comparatively bigger-wise,' etc.) before handing them to the experimenter!" is what the instructor is essentially saying to the subject.

What our next step in training ought to be is clear enough; since we only chose objects whose "name" the subject had learned previously, we should now leave all of the objects he knows permanently in front of him, but instruct him verbally which two objects are to be related in the specified way in the handing game. Natural languages abound with relational instructions of this sort. Virtually every utterance in English has (or implies) just about as many relational instructions as "names" of things. Therefore, if we want to test for language knowledge or the capacity for language knowledge, it is only reasonable to investigate the set of relations as carefully as the vocabulary. If our subject can name 10 objects, we should find out whether he can as easily learn to follow, say, 10 relational instructions. Prepositions lend themselves very nicely to this. In general, we would now be saying to the subject, "Relate word w_1 to word w_2 in manner phi." Or, in symbols,

$$(w_1, w_2)_\phi, \tag{1}$$

where ϕ is a potentially open set of relations, and w_1 and w_2 are elements from a potentially open set of object words.

So far, the task used in order to enable our subject to give evidence of his knowledge was completely fixed. It was a standing order to hand objects to the experimenter. Because of this standardization, the task did not have to enter into the language of instruction. It was no different in this respect from a lever-pressing "instruction" to a rat in a Skinner box, which is also transmitted to the rat without the use of English. The meaning of formula (1) was pegged to this standard instruction. But natural languages have no such fixed reference; one may change imperatives as freely as one changes shirts. It is a variable in its own right. Instead of the imperative "hand to experimenter," I might choose to train my subject to "look at," "point to," "avoid by escaping," "place," etc., and relate these imperatives to phrases of type (1). Formula (1) is thus revealed as incomplete; we simply did not bother to write down the imperative (or, more generally, the context of the formula) because, in the artificial situation that we created, it was constant. Now that we are about to add this sort of more variable instruction to our subject, we had better create a symbol that indicates the context for formula (1). Since we began with an imperative, "give," let us say that the context of the formula shall be symbolized by gamma; thus

$$[(w_1, w_2)_\phi \ w_3]_\gamma, \tag{2}$$

where gamma stands for any instruction on how to relate (1) to something else.[1] The Greek letter, as in formula (1), stands for a general set of relations; the imperative is one such. It relates the words to the listener and/or to the speaker in specific and complicated ways. Among the possible relational instructions are those that relate a statement to either people and their actions or to other statements. An example of the latter might be "The bottle or the apple is in the bigger box."

Notice that we are not particularly concerned here with just how the information is to be encoded, what physical form the signals to the subject must have, or how they are to be arranged sequentially. It is quite immaterial for this discussion whether the vehicle of communication is standardized English. The essential aspect of language that I wish to bring out is this: I have implied that there is a class of words that are the *names of objects* (table, chair, box); this was our class *w*. Furthermore, the constituents of this class are constantly being related to one another during discourse, and each such relation has its own name. Thus, the names of relations (Greek letters) seemed to constitute a second class of words — one that apparently was to be treated as distinct from the class *w*; let us call this

[1] In natural languages, the relations (Greek letters) are given either by "little words," by affixes, by word order, or by a combination of any one of these with the semantic relations expressed in the sequence of words as a whole. For instance, "fish like food" is fairly automatically construed as analogous to "monkeys like trees," but "fish" could also be construed as the imperative of "to fish," — an alternative that no one would choose, because it would result in a meaningless sentence. Or, it might be construed as any one of the following triple compounds: fish-like food, fish like-food (which has no meaning in English), or a phrase analogous to "food like fish."

second class *function words*. (Synonyms for the two classes are lexical items and operators or formatives; content words and functors.)

We would now like to show that this dichotomous classification is actually quite unsatisfactory, since it implies a formal distinction that is impossible to make precise when it comes to natural languages. This difficulty, which we shall illustrate presently, is undoubtedly due to an important feature of language. Proper appreciation of the nature of language depends upon the countenancing of this difficulty.

"Names of objects" is merely a convenient fiction, upheld at the risk of the erroneous impression of the existence of fixed, absolute (i.e., nonrelative) semantic items in the language system. In fact, words are themselves relations. This situation is most obvious in the case of kinship terms (aunt, cousin, mother, etc.). It is also obvious in most of those cases where the *w* constituent is an adjective (tall and dark; pretty or witty; etc.); these words can only be understood with respect to a reference base (tall with respect to grass, buildings, people). It is true even of such words as table, box, chair, etc. This may be seen from the fact that one and the same physical object may easily be labeled with any one of these three *names,* depending on the use that is being made of it. In other words, names of objects can only be said to be correct relative to given circumstances.

The extraordinary conclusion one must draw from this discussion is that virtually every aspect of language is *relational*. It is true of content words, of function words, and, of course, it is *a fortiori* true of the combination of words. Any kind of concatenation of words in any language and at any state of language development implies relations between the concatenated words. This is best illustrated by those concatenations that do not include a function word at all. In mature English they occur, for instance, in compounded nouns (cf. lady-driver, screw-driver, lady-killer, lady-bug; or house beautiful). Notice that each compound may either be expanded into a phrase of independent, but interrelated words, as is done, for example, in dictionary definitions, or may be replaced by a single-word contraction or synonym (e.g., lady-killer — *expansion*: someone who attempts to impress or overwhelm ladies; *contraction*: dandy). It is in compounds that we see most clearly how words come about; they are shorthand for something that can readily be "explained" in terms of a phrase or sentence — a whole composition of relations and interrelations. Compounds are halfway between an explicit relational structure (phrase or sentence) and a single symbol (word or morph) that summarizes or stands for this more complex composition. Thus a universal property of languages is that words or morphs may be analyzed as complex relations. Furthermore, there are substitution operations (transformations, if you like) by which any relational composition may be replaced by a single morph and, vice versa, any single morph may be replaced by an explicit relational composition. It is a reversible mapping:

$$\text{relational composition} \leftrightarrow \text{single morph.} \tag{3}$$

It will be useful to emphasize here the affinity in this respect between the structure of language and the structure of ordinary arithmetic. Everything we have said about a language such as English might as readily have been said about the much more specialized language of numbers. A short elaboration of this point might make it easier to illustrate just what is meant by phrases such as "learning or knowing a language."

In arithmetic, numbers may be seen as the content words; the symbols that instruct us what to do with numbers (such as addition or multiplication) may be seen to correspond to the function words (and, times, etc.). Arithmetic phrases are "one and two," "one times two," or, in more general form, they may be regarded as a pair of numbers n_1, n_2, together with an instruction of how to relate these. Formally

$$(n_1, n_2)_\phi. \tag{4}$$

Arithmetical sentences (One and two is three.) may then be represented as follows:

$$(1, 2) \xrightarrow{+} 3,$$
$$(1, 2) \xrightarrow{\sim} 1, \tag{5}$$
$$(1, 2) \xrightarrow{\cdot} 2.$$

Every content word in this language (i.e., number) stands for a host of inherent possible relational compositions (e.g., 3 is the same as $1 + 1 + 1$, $256 - 253$, etc.), and every composition may be replaced by a content word. In arithmetic, we call this sort of relating *computing,* and we know that this means to operate on something, to engage in certain specific activities. Notice that numbers are constructed by us; that is, they are the result of operations that we have performed. We do not pick them up ready-made, so to speak; nor does one recognize specific number of objects (if there are more than seven) in nature. The operations from which a number is derived may be iterated without limits, and thus an infinity of numbers is generated. Just as there is no end to numbers that are constructable by the iteration of a small number of operations, so there is no end to the words that we may construct by the iterated operations available through language. (For example, children in their earliest language stage often do not feel constrained by lack of lexical knowledge; they readily make up a word if society has not yet provided them with one, and it is not at all uncommon to be given, by the word-making child, an explicit definition of his neologism.) The infinity of "nameables" is, however, not so much reflected by the expandability of the lexicon, as by the mapping operation of (3). Every word has a given semantic field associated with it; these fields are "fuzzy" and overlap, and they may be arbitrarily expanded or contracted by the use of ever more general words or by becoming ever more detailed and explicit. Thus the semantic realm has properties that are somewhat similar to those of the number line (which is analogous to the semantic realm of the language of numbers). The semantic realm of language is also a continuum (not a collection of discrete items), and this continuum, just as the one called the number line, is a mental construct. (For further elaboration of this line of thinking, see Benacerraf & Putnam, 1964; Lenneberg, 1971; Piaget, 1971; Weyl, 1949.)

Nevertheless, language and arithmetic are both also tied to the real world. Tables and chairs, aunts and uncles, sins and blessings, may be counted, and consequently numbers refer to realities of various kinds; and physical things we sit at or on are unquestionably tables and chairs, respectively. There is no contradiction here between this statement and the previous one that the semantic realms of these languages are mental constructs. Inches or centimeters refer also to real things and, at the same time, are man-made constructs.

In order to understand the nature of language, it is first of all necessary to rid ourselves of the notion that its most important components are simply labels or "names." Language is relational in every aspect and at every term. Hence to teach someone to speak is essentially *to invite him to relate aspects of the environment in such and such a way.* The language community induces the child to treat what is before him in quantitative, qualitative, comparative terms; induces him to say something that relates an object to its use, or to the speaker, or to the listener, or to another object. In order for such an invitation to relate to be successful, the subject must have a natural inclination to deal with his environment in certain ways. He must be able to carry out operations upon what he sees or touches and be able to compute the sorts of relations that are reported on in language as well as in arithmetic.

The conception of language as a dynamic, computational *activity* is of particular importance in a psychobiological context. For instance, when we describe the natural, biological history of language development, we are really describing the gradual emergence of certain physiological processes that are the basis for computational activity. The nature of these processes becomes more and more specialized or distinct by an embryogenic process of differentiation, entirely comparable to the differentiation of cellular function and anatomic structure. Thus, the student of language acquisition would do well to keep in mind that he is describing the behavior of immature human beings, whose mentality is undergoing growth by maturation and differentiation. Children's early utterances are not simply erroneous adult sentences (such as an adult's first steps in a foreign language), but, in fact, reflect primitive, undifferentiated computational activities.

These remarks suffice to indicate that I think of language knowledge as a peculiar activity of the human brain. If we were to speak of these activities in strictly biological terms, we would stress their physiological aspects; if we were to speak about them to psychologists, we would probably refer to them as cognitive processes, and would be concerned with such things as specializations in the realm of perception, memory, and concept formation.

References

Benacerraf, P., & Putnam, H. *Philosophy of mathematics.* Englewood Cliffs, New Jersey: Prentice-Hall, 1964.

Furth, H. G. *Thinking without language: Psychological implications of deafness.* New York: Free Press, 1966.

Lenneberg, E. H. Of language knowledge, apes, and brains. *Journal of Psycholinguistic Research,* 1971, **1**, 1–29.

Piaget, J. *Biology and knowledge: An essay on the relations between organic regulations and cognitive processes.* Chicago: Univ. of Chicago Press, 1971.

Ploog, D., & Melnechuk, T. Are apes capable of language? *Neuroscience Research Progress Bulletin,* 1971, **9**, 59–700.

Weyl, H. *Philosophy of mathematics and natural science.* Princeton, New Jersey: Princeton Univ. Press, 1949.

COGNITIVE STRUCTURE AND AFFECT IN LANGUAGE

James Deese

The University of Virginia

There is almost no idea in the history of Western psychology that has been so widely agreed upon as the notion that psychological functions can be differentiated into cognitive, affective, and conative components. These are sometimes incarnated as intellect, emotion, and the will, or as cognition, affection, and motivation. The form varies, but the essentials remain the same. First pronounced in classical times, this doctrine, since Descartes, has been integrated into every aspect of psychology including the relations of physiology to psychology. The discovery of the autonomic nervous system and its associated central structures by Langley, Cannon, and others early in the twentieth century gave an almost indisputable physical basis for the notion that emotion is a separate entity. It is no accident that psychological interest in emotion has turned from the traditional questions concerning hedonic states to questions about the bodily expressions of the emotions. Indeed, at about the same time the autonomic system was described, the discovery of the conditioned reflex by Pavlov, and its psychological generalization by Watson, gave a basis for understanding all of the complex changes in emotional reactions in people both in normal and abnormal states without reference to conscious experience, thinking, or any of the traditional intellectual categories. Interest in the hedonic aspects of emotion surfaced again only in the 1950s with the discovery of central reinforcing effects.

Will is disguised in modern psychology as motivation. While there is less agreement about motivation than about emotional expression, it is commonly held that the study of motivation concerns itself with the instigators

9

of action (as, indeed, did the study of the will). In all of modern psychology, from the seventeenth century on, the structure of motivation has always been conceived to have some relation to the structure of emotion, but it has at the same time always been assured that it is necessary to talk about the two categories as distinct and independent components of mind, or, in a more contemporary context, as explanatory categories for the description of behavior.

In contemporary psychology, it is still the dominant tradition to take from British empiricism the stance toward questions of intellect, of memory, knowing, and the use of language that lays all intellectual activity to experience. Thus, while the contemporary behavioral psychologist finds little difficulty with the notion, say, that the peculiar character of the emotions is due to some innate organization in the hypothalamus and related structures, he still feels uncomfortable with any view that associates activities of knowing with anything innate. The modern experimental psychologist has, rather reluctantly, allowed the study of perception to be influenced by notions of innate determinants, but the degree of reluctance is revealed by the fact that the most important students of perception for an entire generation — the Gestalt psychologists — were never really fully and wholeheartedly accepted within English and American experimental psychology. But notions of innate structures in intellect, until very recently, have made almost no impression upon the psychology of thinking at all. The experimental psychology of thinking, with its heavy emphasis upon concept learning, etc., owes its dominant attitude to John Locke's notion of simple and compound ideas, empiricism in general, and associationism in particular.

Recently there has been a great challenge to the traditional empiricist position of experimental psychologists. That challenge has largely come from recent linguistic theorists, principally Chomsky. Chomsky, as well as many other linguists and psychologists, have argued that the human infant possesses a device which, abstractly considered, corresponds to a theory of language of an extraordinary degree of power. This device enables the infant to discover, or, more accurately, to invent for himself the language of the community into which he was born. The arguments arising from these views have deeply divided psychological students of intellectual processes. However, most students of the development of language have adopted, in modified form, the rationalism advocated by Chomsky.

Questions raised by this revival of rationalism in the psychology of thinking brought me a few years ago to reconsider the appropriateness of the traditional tripartite division of psychology. The division is most useful when one wishes to ascribe some unique quality to each of the three aspects of mind. Much of the interest of seventeenth- and eighteenth-century philosophers in the problems of mind arises from the view that thinking is the activity which makes it fully possible for men to understand the world of nature. In short, the interest is epistemological. It is essential to have a rational mind (separate from the passions — to use Descarte's term) if there is to be a sharp metaphysical distinction between mind and matter. The metaphysical distinctions associated with the notion of mind have tended to disappear ever since Kant, so that not even many philosophers now take stock in the notion that we can know about the world independently of the categories imposed by our minds. Those categories are viewed as being psychologists, in a certain sense, arbitrary and biologically they might just as well be described as motivational and intellectual. I do not believe that there is much startling in this view, but some of its implications have not been fully understood by psychologists.

If we grant that thinking, like emotion and motivation, have some biologically determined innate components, and if we are willing to foreswear any special metaphysical or epistemological properties assigned to the nature of human thought that would enable us to transcend our intellectual limitations in understanding nature, we may then easily abandon the notion of separate intellectual, affective, and conative components of the mind. From the viewpoint of cognition, this entails the possibility of regarding affect not as something attached to, associated, or correlated with the various schemata that comprise cognitive activity, but as inherently a part of the intellectual structure that determines the act or judgment.

Having said this much by way of introduction, I must now confess that it is not my purpose to present a comprehensive account of how communication and the cognitive structures underlying communication are suffused with affective components. In short, I have no general theory to offer at this point. However, the general proposition that affectivity is inherently a part of intellectual categories leads me to explore some of those categories themselves. I shall try to illustrate how affective components are inherent in cognitive structures through some case histories or examples that I regard as revealing the complete interdependence of linguistic, cognitive, and affective features of language.

One of the most basic principles in linguistic analysis is that of minimal contrast. Minimal contrast occurs at any linguistic level when two elements differ by a single feature and that feature is relevant to a linguistic distinction. For example, the initial segment /b/ in *bill* is in minimal contrast to the segment /p/ in *pill* because (1) they differ by a single feature and (2) there is a linguistic distinction (the words have different meanings in English). The segments /p^0/ and /p$^+$/ are not in minimal contrast in English (though they are in some languages). Whether or not we aspirate in English after a stop has no linguistic significance, and whether or not we actually do it is conditioned by the phonemic environment of the stop in question.

Thus, we do aspirate when the stop is initial (as in *pill*), but we do not aspirate when the stop is part of a consonant cluster (as in *spill*).

Minimal contrast occurs at levels other than the phonemic. Thus, within the semantic field of English kinship terms, *brother* and *sister* are in minimal semantic contrast. They have the same semantic values for generation and consanguinity, but they contrast in sex, and the contrast is semantically relevant in the English lexicon. Of course, any given pair of lexical items selected at random is likely not to be in minimal contrast of any sort, for the members of such a pair will differ in many features. Whereas this is true at many linguistic levels it is particularly true in semantic contrasts, for which feature analysis has severe limitations. Moreover, my point is that the principle of minimal contrast is a very general one. Some psychologists have argued that the principle of minimal contrast is only an exemplification of an underlying cognitive category. I so argued, for example, in a sketch of a theory of semantics which asserts that the psychological characteristics underlying semantic distinctions are composed of a small number of formal categories to which content or information is assimilated (Deese, 1969). One of these categories is defined by minimal contrast. In this conception, any particular semantic usage is determined by some underlying abstract cognitive structure such as grouping, contrast, scaling, analogy, spatial modeling, etc., applied to some perceptual representation of events in the world. As one of a number of such structures, the principle of contrast would, at first glance, appear to have no inherent affective characteristic. However, another general linguistic principle seems to operate in many if not all examples of minimal contrast. While a formal analysis of the principle does not in any way imply an affective component, in fact, it leads to a striking interpretation of minimal contrast as a psychological category possessing an inherent, affective interpretation.

The additional principle is that of marking. When applied to the principle of minimal contrast, it has the effect of asserting that contrasts are not symmetrical. Marking occurs when some feature is added to a basic form in order to produce a new form that differs from the old *only by the single added feature*. The new form is said to be the marked form of the old, and the old is generally described as the unmarked form. The two forms are in minimal contrast. In theory, marking could occur by a process of subtracting or eliminating some manifest or overt feature, though I know of no such examples. However, the anthropologist, Greenberg (1966) has discovered some cases in many different languages in which the marked–unmarked distinction is not overtly signaled in the language. It remains in these cases a covert distinction.

Plurality illustrates overt marking in English. We add a special form to all nouns in order to make them into plurals. Thus *friend* is the unmarked form with respect to plurality and *friends* the marked form. Tense provides another example. Ordinarily (there are some differences of opinion here) the past tense is regarded as the marked form in contrast with the unmarked present.

An interesting and important example of covert marking occurs in certain English adjectives (and in those of other languages, according to Greenberg). Many, though not all adjectives occur in pairs, and these pairs appear to be in some minimal contrast in a clear semantic sense. They differ in meaning in but a single respect; they are the (+) and (−) value of some semantic dimension named by the feature. The difference in meaning between members of a given pair hinge on a single morphological feature that is added to the unmarked member of the pair. Thus, in English, such pairs as *conscious–unconscious* or *moral–immoral* occur. The marker in this case is one of a small number of prefixes that can appear before an adjective. Not all adjectives form such pairs. The color words in English (and in other modern European languages) or the words descriptive of emotional states (*angry, jealous,* etc.) do not seem to occur in pairs. There are some adjectives, however, that are not overtly marked as being paired, but which seem to have all the semantic properties of such pairs. Examples of covertly marked pairs include *good–bad, deep–shallow, tall–short.* According to Greenberg, one member of such pairs is marked and the other unmarked. *Shallow,* for example, is marked and *deep* is unmarked. The criteria Greenberg uses to distinguish between the marked and unmarked members are based upon contextual neutralization. One criterion of contextual neutralization is nominalization. The unmarked member of the pair will provide the name of the dimension. Thus, the name of the *deep–shallow* dimension is depth. Another criterion is provided by the fact that the unmarked member of the pair, when part of a question, does not bias the expected answer. Thus it is possible to ask "How old is the baby?" as the usual form of the question (*old* is the unmarked member of the *old–young* pair). It turns out that the following points hold:

(1) Unmarked members come into English with their current meaning at an earlier date than marked members as determined by the Oxford English Dictionary.

(2) Unmarked members are more likely to occur, according to the Thorndike–Lorge count (Thorndike & Lorge, 1944).

(3) Children, on the average, correctly use unmarked members before they use marked members.

All of this seems to have little to do with the inherent affectivity of linguistic structures. However, such is not the case. It turns out that affectivity is deeply intertwined with the principle of marking. Hamilton and Deese

(1971), in an investigation of the psychological correlates of marking, first discovered this fact in connection with a study of a series of pairs of adjectives not overtly marked in English. We assembled 27 pairs of adjectives that met the contextual neutralization criteria of marking. We discovered that naive subjects could sort these adjectives into two categories with a very high degree of agreement and that, furthermore, these categories corresponded perfectly to the marked–unmarked distinction. These subjects knew nothing of the marking principle, of course, and the only instruction given to them was to sort the adjectives into two pairs of opposites. Afterward we inquired as to the basis for the sorts made by our subjects. Uniformly they responded with descriptions that could only be coded as "evaluative." Such adjectives as *active, agile, clean, bright, deep, fresh, generous, good, proud,* and *safe* are marked (+) for evaluation, while the adjectives *clumsy, dirty, shallow, stale, stingy, bad, humble,* and *dangerous* are, in general, marked (−) for evaluation. Any technique of measurement, such as the semantic differential, will reveal the presence of the evaluation feature in all of these marked pairs. Almost any example of overtly marked adjective-pairs will reveal the same process at work. *Friendly, moral, legible,* and *secure* are all evaluatively (+) with respect to *unfriendly, immoral, illegible,* and *insecure.* Furthermore, the correlation of evaluation with marking is not limited to adjectives. Past tense verbs are, in a sufficiently large sample, evaluatively negative with respect to their present tenses. A cross-cultural semantic differential investigation (Tanaka, Oyama, & Osgood, 1963) reveals the same effect. Furthermore, evaluatively positive nouns are about equally (+) or (−) in the singular and the plural, whereas negatively evaluative nouns are much more (−) in the plural than in the singular.

Critics of male chauvinism will not be surprised to discover that nearly all terms that refer to feminine characteristics in contrast to masculine characteristics are marked. Thus *woman* is marked with respect to *man* and *female* with respect to *male.* Perhaps it is because the *official* control of language is in the hands of men that such is the case. Not all caste systems (such as that differentiating the status of men and women) need be indicated by marking for, as we shall see, there are many other devices, largely metaphorical in nature, for giving an inherent evaluative character to caste and other such differences. However, many differentiations of status do exhibit the marked–unmarked correlation with evaluation.

Thus, there appears to be an inherent correlation between the principles of marking and a negative affective component in lexical entries. There are several plausible reasons for the relation. Osgood's (Boucher & Osgood, 1969) "Pollyanna" hypothesis is one, and Zajonc (1968) has advanced a notion that is the exact opposite of the "Pollyanna" hypothesis. Both of these notions depend upon the fact that frequency of usage is correlated with affectivity (and, as we have just seen, so is marking). Osgood supposes that we are all natural optimists and that whatever it is we have to say about one another and the world, it tends to be good rather than bad. Zajonc also assumes that we are natural optimists, but he takes a different view as to what the optimism produces. He argues that we tend to look on whatever happens frequently as being good simply as a way of adjusting to the world. My notion is that we tend to be conservative pessimists. We like things as they are, and any deviant or unusual state, or anything outside of our own ego characteristics tend to be judged as evaluatively $(-)$. Marked linguistic elements are attached to new distinctions and new words in the language, and hence, on the average, marked elements are negative. Since there is a correlation between marking and age of lexical entries in the language and also a correlation between marking and the age at which children will correctly use items, this seems to be an instance of linguistic ontogeny recapitulating linguistic phylogeny.

For my purposes here, however, it is not directly relevant why there is an intrinsic relation between marking and affectivity, only that it occurs and that it is intrinsic — that is to say that it is not "learned" as such, but is inherently part of the way in which we view the world.

There are other, perhaps broader aspects of an intrinsic relation between affectivity and cognitive structures. The further examples I have chosen to discuss are in conceptual and methodological contrast with the preceding one. They are psychological in the sense that they do not rely upon linguistics, and they do depend upon more diffuse kinds of evidence. The preceding example illustrated the relation between affect and cognition when the cognitive structure is embedded in the language, while the one I am about to describe is intended to be much more general — to reflect cognitive structure prior to or independent of language.

I believe that semantic relations are essentially psychological and not linguistic in nature. Any attempt to characterize semantic relations — whether abstract or not — requires more information than can be provided by purely linguistic categories. Linguistic theory has, for this reason, always found it difficult to assimilate semantic structures to the formal structure of language — to make semantics a part of linguistics. I assert this despite the long tradition of describing categories in the form of semantic statements ("a noun is the name of a thing," etc.) and the recent interest in generative semantic theory. I believe that the correct solution to the problem is to regard linguistic structures as independent of semantic structures, but coded onto them in (what ideally) would be some one-to-one relation.

Whether they are so coded or not, semantic structures depend both upon human perception of the world and nonlinguistic intellectual processes and must be so treated.

It is convenient and of the utmost theoretical importance to regard semantic structures as being coded onto linguistic structures at two levels at least. One of these levels corresponds to the semantic structure of *propositions* which embody relations among events in perception or conceptions of the world. The other corresponds to the level of concepts or semantic entities which enter into such propositions. It is convenient, though not necessary, to suppose that propositions are paired with some basic syntactic structure in a given language, such as that language's base phrase markers. For example, the English base phrase marker *Noun Phrase + Aux + T Verb + Noun Phrase* might be paired with the propositional meaning "some concept X acts in some way Y upon some concept Z." How specific such a meaning would be would depend upon the extent to which syntactic features enter into the characterization of the basic categories, for example the nouns which serve as heads of the various noun phrases. If, for example, both subject and predicate noun phrases are marked $(+)$ with respect to the feature *concrete* the propositional meaning corresponding to the phrase marker might be characterized as "object X does something Y to object Z," a meaning which is much more specific.

Semantic structures would have to be paired also with the specific lexical items inserted into syntactic structures. It is at this level that I am mainly concerned, though a strong case can be made that intrinsic affective elements entering into syntactic structures as well as lexical structures. In this connection, I only mention that Johnson (1967) was able to demonstrate what everyone feels to be the case, namely that the passive construction in English is genuinely less active and potent (on the semantic differential) than active constructions generally. However, I shall pass over these possibilities in order to consider cases additional to that provided by marking for intrinsic, affective components entering into semantic structures at the level of concepts and lexical selection.

The information coded onto lexical entries represents, I have argued (Deese, 1969), the impression of experience upon one of a small number of cognitive categories. Experience itself, of course, is in turn the result of the impression of perceptual categories upon the information received by the senses. Cognitive categories and perceptual categories have developmental histories, as the work of Piaget tells us. However, they are universal and must in whole or part reflect the work of processes innate to the human species.

One of the most ubiquitous of the cognitive categories derives directly from our perceptual experience of space. An extraordinarily wide variety of interpretations placed upon abstract, symbolic, and even personal events requires the use of space as a model or metaphor. Explicit spatial imagery represents the obvious case. But there is also implicit application of spatial models and metaphors. These are not quite so obvious, and perhaps they are more important because they are more pervasive. The great practical appeal of graphical representation in science and technical writing provides an example that, while specialized, is particularly significant. There is really little excuse for the presentations of graphs of the familiar sort (in Cartesian coordinates, for example), for all the information in them can, usually with greater precision, be presented in equations or in tabular form. Graphs, however, yield a unique conceptual interpretation to the human mind, one that uses spatial relations as metaphors for very abstract representations or representations of events that have no inherent spatial property. There is nothing spatial, to use a psychological example, about either IQ or SES.

Not only do spatial models and metaphors pervade our conceptual structures, but certain spatial relations have inherent and universal affective significance. One of the most consistent results to emerge from cross-cultural comparisons of spatial metaphor is that the evaluative feature is coded onto the up–down dimensions with complete consistency. The *specific* concepts in a culture which make use of the spatial metaphors of *up* and *down* or *high* and *low* show little consistency, but the evaluative feature is almost perfectly consistent. For example, Maori, Malay, and many English usages agree that *high* and its various synonyms are to be reserved for important personages. In addition, Maori, but not Malay, uses words for high to denote the state of being thrilled or excited (see Deese, 1969). Contemporary English dialects use the term in a variety of ways to indicate excitement, derived either from a drug state (in more familiar American dialects) or from righteous anger, in certain less familiar dialects. However, in all cases the contrast is with a form that is evaluatively negative. To be *down* is to be depressed. Sky gods are superior to, stronger than, and ethically better than the earth gods or dwellers beneath the earth.

Asch (1958), in his study of metaphors, points to the existence of a number of universal agreements between spatial configurations and affective features. For example, the concept *straight* is universally used to code meanings that are (+ evaluation). De Soto and his colleagues (De Soto, London, & Handel, 1965) point out that it is good to be "upright" or "on the level" and bad to be "oblique," "slanted," or "biased." They also remind us that the medieval concept of the Great Chain of Being and the post-Darwinian concept of the phylogenetic or evolutionary scale have in common a reduction of a series of similar complex relations (a partial ordering embedded in a tree) to a single spatial dimension, and they both have evaluative implications in insisting upon a distinction between "higher" and "lower" beings.

The experiments by De Soto and his colleagues on spatial paralogic reveal the effect of spatial metaphors on the ability to solve problems in abstract reasoning. Linear syllogisms are easier to solve when the problems require people to think in a consistent direction. For example, the problem: "Harry is worse than Joe; Joe is worse than Al. Is Harry worse than Al?" is easier to solve than the problem: "Harry is worse than Joe; Al is better than Joe. Is Harry worse than Al?" Not only is such the case, but problems are easier to solve when they are stated in the direction implied by the unmarked state – that is, when the problems are in the "better than" rather than the "worse than" direction. These investigations were able to demonstrate directly that most people work, within the spatial metaphor, from top to bottom when thinking "better than" and from the bottom to the top when thinking "worse than."

A careful analysis of any conceptual category into which semantic or lexical information is encoded reveals that one can always find cases in which affective dimensions inherently are part of the cognitive structure formed within the conceptual category. Thus space, particularly when it is used metaphorically, has its inherent affective component. Since an astonishing number of our abstractions are spatial metaphors, abstractions are particularly vulnerable to the affectivity inherent in lexical concepts. Even such abstractions as hierarchical representations – the partial ordering achieved with branching trees – is metaphorically expressed in a way in which affectivity intrudes. Thus "higher nodes" "dominate" "lower nodes."

I have barely commented on the way in which affectivity is inherently a part of the conceptual structure of propositions. At this point I make only an additional brief mention of the problem to illustrate that at the propositional level, as well as at the conceptual level, affectivity is inherent in intellectual operations. The simplest way to make that point is to refer to what Shneidman (1969) calls psychologic. Psychologic, in Shneidman's definition, consists of those covert and overt aspects of personality that are a piece with an individual's style of thinking. The extreme example is given by schizophrenic intellectual style. A thorough case history of a schizophrenic will contain the kind of information that enables us to interpret what a schizophrenic means when he says something bizarre. An example that Shneidman borrows from von Domarus and Arieti is that of the man who says "I am Switzerland." What he is really saying is "I am free." However, in that individual's logical system a particular may stand for an abstraction. Switzerland is a free country, so saying "I am Switzerland" is equivalent to saying "I am free." Schizophrenic thinking. in this case, provides an unusual and bizarre example, but such idiosyncratic application of propositional logic occurs in normal thinking as well. Indeed, it is the rule rather than the exception. In the tradition, I suppose, initiated by the classical experiments of Woodworth and Sells (1935), it is the fashion to regard such aberrations of propositional logic as exactly that — aberrations. However, they are only aberrations when compared with the propositions that would generate, say, the correct syllogism. A detailed analysis of actual human thinking reveals that propositions of the "I am Switzerland" sort are the basis for the "illogical" reasoning. It is not that the subjects in "atmosphere effect" experiments cannot "correctly" reason through the syllogisms they try to solve, it is that they are busy working on other propositions which make use of the same terms, propositions that may be only partly articulated, if at all.

All this appears to make a shambles of objectivity. Indeed, I think there is little objectivity in ordinary thinking and communication and perhaps even extraordinary thinking, when it appears in ordinary language. The invention of various abstract symbol systems in intended to give a generality to various logical systems, but also achieves the function of providing some kind of norm against which it is possible to measure ordinary thinking and thus establish some kind of objectivity. I have argued elsewhere (Deese, 1969) that such empty symbol systems are alien to human thinking and may be used only with enormous difficulty. Hence they are reserved for special occasions, often purely demonstrable, and for special subjects, such as mathematics. In the meantime, our usual abstractions — those with which we really think — are cast in the form of spatial metaphors, or reflect the psychological correlates of linguistic marking, or show the influence of animate, often human relations used to carry the meaning of those things we like to think are not concrete, animate or human. The conceptual categories of the sophisticated users of a language, such as English, may not be all that different from the conceptual categories of the users of a language which suffices for conditions of primitive living. Lévi-Strauss has implied as much, and the data supplied by Casagrande and Hale (1967) provides evidence on the form of conceptual categories of an Amerind language, Papago, which shows many of the characteristics of an intrinsic relation between affect and thought.

References

Asch, S. E. The metaphor: A psychological inquiry. In R. Tagiuri & L. Petrullo (Eds.), *Person perception and interpersonal behavior.* Stanford: Stanford Univ. Press, 1958. Pp. 86–94.

Boucher, J., & Osgood, C. The Pollyanna hypothesis. *Journal of Verbal Learning and Verbal Behavior,* 1969, **8**, 1–8.

Casagrande, J. B., & Hale, K. L. Semantic relationships in Papago folk definitions. *Studies in Southwestern Linguistics.* The Hague: Mouton, 1967.

Deese, J. Conceptual categories in the study of content. In G. Gerbner (Ed.), *Communication and content.* New York: Wiley, 1969.

De Soto, C., London, M., & Handel, S. Social reasoning and spatial paralogic. *Journal of Personality and Social Psychology,* 1965, **2**, 513–521.

Greenberg, J. H. *Language universals.* The Hague: Mouton, 1966.

Hamilton, H. W., & Deese, J. Does linguistic marking have a psychological correlate? *Journal of Verbal Learning and Verbal Behavior,* 1971, **10**, 707–714.

Johnson, M. G. Syntactic position and rated meaning. *Journal of Verbal Learning and Verbal Behavior,* 1967, **6**, 240–246.

Shneidman, E. S. Logical content analysis: An explication of styles of "concludifying." In G. Gerbner (Ed.), *Communication and content.* New York: Wiley, 1969.

Tanaka, Y., Oyama, T., & Osgood, C. E. A cross-cultural and cross-concept study of the generality of semantic space. *Journal of Verbal Learning and Verbal Behavior,* 1963, **2**, 392–405.

Thorndike, E. L., & Lorge, I. *The teacher's word book of 30,000 words.* New York: Teachers College, Columbia Univ., 1944.

Woodworth, R. L., & Sells, S. B. An atmosphere effect in formal syllogistic reasoning. *Journal of Experimental Psychology,* 1935, **18**, 451–460.

Zajonc, R. B. Attitudinal effects of mere exposure. *Journal of Personality and Social Psychology,* 1968, **9** (Monograph supplement), 1–32.

SOME MODES OF REPRESENTATION

Paul A. Kolers

University of Toronto

Of the many ways available to man for representing information, pictures and words are perhaps the most commonly used. Despite their commonness, our understanding of what we actually do when we acquire information from pictures and from written words, and what they are as objects is still imperfect. Many of the claims that have been made about them are overstated, as I shall show by describing some similarities in the way we acquire information from these two modes of representation. Having illustrated these similarities, I shall then point out some notable differences between the two.

One of the main sources of controversy is the assertion that the reading of words is restricted to a serial scan of text, the eyes proceeding regularly across the lines of print and down the columns of the page, but the perception of pictures is based on holistic, immediate, simultaneous processing. In other words, it is alleged that to read a sentence we move our gaze along its physical boundary, scanning the letters serially, but we see a picture all at once. Let us examine these two claims by appealing to evidence.

Suppose that words were read serially, letter by letter. What would be the consequences? In one experiment (Kolers & Katzman, 1966), the letters of words were flashed one by one on the same part of a viewing screen, simulating the input that would be received if the eyes looked at words letter by letter. The subjects for the test were college students; their task in one condition was to name the letters that had been presented and, in another, to name the word the letters spelled. The sequences were always six letters long, the average length of English words. The duration for which the letters were presented was varied and subjects' success in naming

21

either letters or words was scored. The finding was quite straightforward: The likelihood of naming all six letters correctly, and the likelihood of naming the word they spelled both increased with an increase in the duration for which the letters were presented, as one might expect. However, the duration of exposure required for 90% success in naming either letters or words was approximately .33 sec. That is, each letter of a six-letter word had to be presented for about .33 sec if the subject was to name all of its letters or the word itself perfectly. This comes out to a reading rate of about one word every 2 sec, or 30 words per minute, a rate that is actually about one-tenth the reading rate of normal college students. Thus if one did read serially, letter by letter, he would be restricted to a rate far lower than we customarily measure. This is one piece of evidence that suggests that normal reading does not proceed serially, letter by letter.

Suppose we assume that we do not read letter by letter, but read word by word. We have some reason to think that the maximum rate would still be about 3 per second, although now three words rather than letters; but this comes to only 180 words per minute, still significantly less than the average reader's rate. Moreover, we would have to assume that the eyes fixated on each word, proceeding serially along the line of print. When we look at the record made by movements of the eyes of skilled readers as they read lines of print, however, we find no such evidence. Judd and Buswell (1922) photographed the eyes of students reading various passages, some of them easy, others difficult. The vertical lines in Fig. 1 show the sequence of fixations made by a subject reading a fairly easy

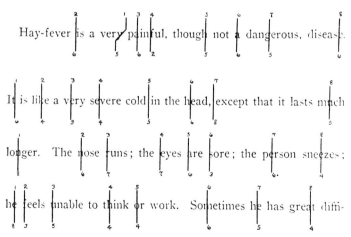

Fig. 1. Eye fixations in reading text. The numbers above the vertical lines show the sequence of fixations; the numbers below show the duration of each fixation in units of 40 msec. (From Judd and Buswell, 1922.)

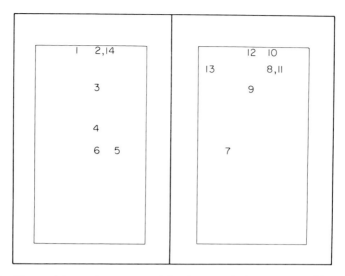

Fig. 2. The position and sequence of fixations made by a very rapid reader on two pages of a book. (Adapted from Thomas, 1962.)

passage. The numbers above the lines indicate the sequence of looks, the numbers below indicate the duration of the looks in units of about 40 msec. Two features may be brought out: the irregularity of the sequence of looks, and the irregularity in the loci of fixation. The irregularity of sequence is shown by the fact that the eyes do not always move from left to right;

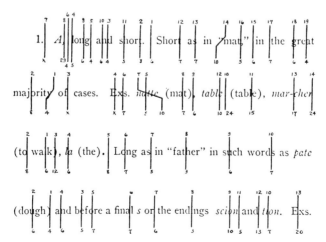

Fig. 3. Fixations of a student studying a grammar. (From Judd and Buswell, 1922.)

rather, they sometimes move leftward within a line. The irregularity of loci of fixation is shown by the fact that the distance between fixations is not the same from line to line, nor do the eyes fixate on every word. Moreover, when the fixations do fall upon a word, the part fixated is sometimes the beginning, sometimes the ending, and sometimes the middle. We may assume, when the reader fixates the beginning of a word, that he scans it, internally, in some serial order. If that were the case, then when he fixated the end of the word he would either have to scan it backward, or make some other internal adjustment to appreciate where its beginning was; the same sort of internal adjustment he would have to make when he fixated the middle of a word. Hence, even at this relatively trivial level of operation, the reader must be thought to be doing something other than scanning individual words serially in a fixed way.

There is another source of evidence: the records of people who read very rapidly — sometimes called speed readers. This evidence indicates that the eye movements of speed readers are such that a single reader does not read different pages in the same way, nor do two different readers read the same page in the same way (Taylor, 1957). Great irregularity in the positioning of looks characterizes both conditions. The most dramatic evidence along this line comes from records obtained by Thomas (1962), who photographed the eyes of a super speed reader, the lady dean of a college, whose reading rate is about thirty times faster than normal. Figure 2 illustrates the sequence of her looks while she read what is illustrated as two pages of a book. It is reported that in general the motions of her eyes proceeded in a counterclockwise direction; in the pages illustrated she read down the middle of the left-hand page, across, and up the middle of the right-hand page, a performance which refutes altogether the idea that reading needs to proceed serially, letter by letter or even word by word. Of course this performance is out of the normal range, but the fact that it can occur at all must be taken into account by any serious theory of reading.

The fixational movements of the eyes in reading are not always the same; they also vary with the nature of the material. Judd and Buswell (1922) illustrate the sequence found when a student was reading, not a light essay, but a fairly detailed French grammar (Fig. 3). Here, compared to the earlier sequence (Fig. 1), the distance between fixations is smaller, and much more inspection of details is engaged in. Moreover, the sequence of looks is even more irregular than that illustrated in Fig. 1, the eyes moving back and forth within a line of print.

These two lines of evidence indicate that reading could not typically go forward on a letter by letter or even on a word by word basis. First, if it did, we could not read as rapidly as we do, and second, direct measurements of the eyes' fixations provide no evidence of serial reading. So much for the first assertion, that reading is necessarily serial.

Reading Pictures

Consider now the second assertion, which is that pictures are perceived holistically — simultaneously, all at once. This argument is derived from assertions made 40–50 years ago by Gestalt psychologists, who were concerned with the notion that perception is immediate and direct. Evidence supporting the idea was adduced from many sources, chief among them the perceptual consequences of brief presentations. It has been found in many studies that flashes lasting only thousandths of a second can still be identified correctly, especially when the flashes are of shapes, such as squares, triangles, or even faces. This evidence proves very little, however, beyond the fact (albeit an important fact) that the knowledgeable subject can identify objects that he knows something about on the basis of remarkably brief flashes. But, in fact, the flashes can be words as well as pictures, as Cattell (1885) showed many years ago, and still be identified correctly. When the pictures are of unfamiliar objects, or are very detailed, only the barest outline or schematic description follows a brief flash; but if the number of flashes or their duration is increased, subjects can read out from the picture correspondingly more details (Helson & Fehrer, 1932). To put it another way, not all the information in a picture is apprehended at once; rather, the information in a picture is processed in time, and the more familiar or simpler the picture is, the more readily its content can be identified or described.

This aspect of picture perception, in which information is apprehended over time, is found not only with pictures that are flashed, it is also found when the subject is allowed to examine a picture while movements of his eyes are photographed. Here again I refer to data by Buswell (1935), who showed subjects the print by Hokusai illustrated in Fig. 4. They looked at it for some seconds; the parts at which they looked are indicated in a low-contrast copy of the print in Fig. 5. These are the results for 42 subjects. Notice that not all parts of the picture received fixations — that is, the fixations are not distributed homogeneously around the picture, for some regions receive many and other regions receive few. Here we see that a picture is not perceived on the basis of a single look, nor are all of its features perceived at once; rather, the eyes fixate on different regions of the picture, much as the eyes fixate on different regions of text.

The bias in regions fixated is brought out even more sharply in some figures provided by Yarbus (1967). Seven different people each looked for 3 min at the painting shown in the upper left panel of Fig. 6. The motions of their eyes are indicated by the black contour lines in the other panels. The seven people looked in ways that are individually different, but by and large their fixations were concentrated on the same regions of the picture. Thus they seem to agree on what parts of a picture contain the information of greatest interest, although they do show some variability in their judgments. In all cases, however, they are looking at different parts of the picture at different times. These movements of the eyes are shown more vividly in a series of measurements which each lasted 5 sec (Fig. 7). Here in finer detail than before is evidence for sampling or reading movements, by means of which different parts of the picture are brought to the center of attention over time, much as the different parts of a sentence are brought to attention over time (Fig. 3). This evidence therefore seems to show conclusively that pictures are not apprehended holistically or immediately, but are read over time, much as written words are read.

A curious aspect of this perceiving is its implicit contradiction of our subjective experience. Our subjective sense when we look at a picture, a page of a book, or even at the world about us, is that we see the whole scene all at once; but the data indicate that we are examining those scenes only in small pieces, and over time. What seems to be the case is that the perceptual experience of wholeness is something that we create within ourselves, filling in or supplementing the information we actually obtain from our looks. In other words, we seem to examine objects for details, but supply ourselves with their perceptual context. It may be that we can supply certain aspects of a picture more readily than certain aspects of a page of print. If that is the case, it might explain why we often think that we have seen a whole picture when in fact we have concentrated our looks upon selected regions, but rarely think we can see a whole page of text clearly. But whether this is so or not, the evidence does remain clear that we examine pictures, reading them over time, in a manner broadly similar to the way we examine printed words. Neither kind of examination is typically strictly serial, progressing linearly in one direction, as a typewriter carriage moves. Reading print need not be a serial process, nor is reading pictures a simultaneous process.

Fig. 4. Hokusai's "The Wave" was presented in color to 42 subjects for their inspection (top page 27). (From Buswell, 1935.)

Fig. 5. All the fixations made during a few seconds' inspection of "The Wave" are shown as black dots on this low-contrast copy of the painting (bottom page 27). (From Buswell, 1935.)

Fig. 4

Fig. 5

27

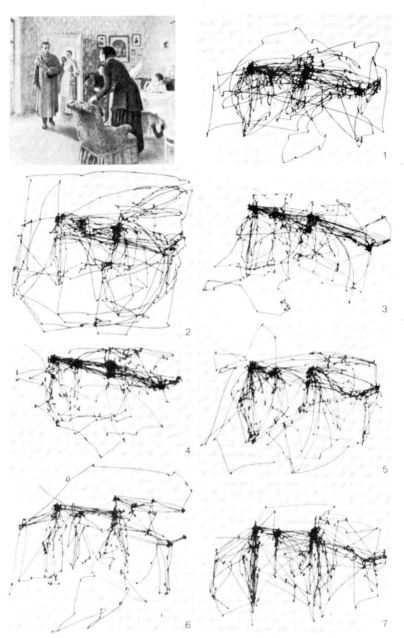

Fig. 6. Eye fixations of seven observers of the painting in the upper left panel. (From A. L. Yarbus, *Eye Movements and Vision*. New York: Plenum Publishing Corp., 1967.)

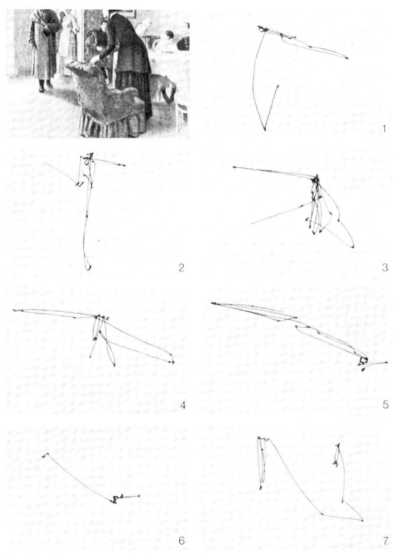

Fig. 7. Eye movements during successive five-second intervals, made by a single observer. (From A. L. Yarbus, *Eye Movements and Vision*. New York: Plenum Publishing Corp., 1967.)

29

Information Seeking

What I have shown so far, therefore, is that there is a marked similarity in the logistical aspects of gathering information from words and pictures: The eyes scan different parts of both kinds of displays, acquiring information from a series of fixations. The information acquired is based on samplings taken from the display, samplings which may be described as quantal or discrete; while our perceptual experience is whole or continuous. (We are, indeed, remarkably unaware of the movements our eyes make while we read or look.) In some still unknown way, our visual system fills in or supplements the discrete inputs to create the subjective sense of continuity. The means by which this transformation occurs of discrete input into continuous perception has been studied in several ways, but the mechanisms are not yet fully known (Kolers, 1972). I will skip over the details, therefore, although I would like to point out that the means by which these transformations are effected may constitute one of the most challenging problems in the study of perception, for they seem to be at the heart of the question of how physiological events are given psychological reality.

Even though the logistical operations of the eyes' movements are similar, we must wonder what sorts of information are acquired with them. In reading text, the main information acquired is grammatical — the semantic content of words and their syntactic relations. In some experiments in which we required subjects to read text of such a kind that they made many mistakes, an analysis of their errors proved to be quite illuminating. The greatest number of errors, more than 80%, were recognizable English words substituted for what was printed (Kolers, 1970). We analyzed these reading errors in respect to a grammatical feature, their part of speech. Table 1 shows as columns the part of speech of the word that was misread, and as rows the part of speech of the word substituted for it as a misreading. The values along the main diagonal show the correspondence, the percentage of times the subject substituted the identical part of speech for the word he misread. For example, 76% of the time that a noun was misread, a noun was substituted for it, 82% of the time a verb was misread, a verb was substituted for it, and so on. Not only were these regularities preserved, but many kinds of substitution were not made, such as a noun for a pronoun or conjunction, a preposition for an article or an article for a preposition, and so on. Thus, the subjects misreading a word were nevertheless faithful to this grammatical feature of the printed words. In another analysis we located where in a sentence an error occurred, irrespective of its part of speech. For this analysis we divided the sentences into fifths, so that a sentence 10 words long is composed of five two-word fifths, a sentence 25 words long is composed of five five-word fifths, and

TABLE 1

Part of Speech of Words Substituted for Words That Had Been Misread[a, b]

	Printed							
Said	Noun	Verb	Adjec-tive	Adverb	Pro-noun	Prepo-sition	Con-junc-tion	Arti-cle
Noun	76	4	18	4	0	5	0	0
Verb	3	82	0.5	6	2	7	10	0
Adjective	16	2	57	12	14	4	2	5
Adverb	2	3	10	45	6	4	2	6
Pronoun	0.5	4	2	10	56	2	12	16
Preposition	1	2	6	12	0	73	10	5
Conjunction	1	2	1	4	18	6	66	22
Article	0.5	0	7	8	4	0	0	45
Number of errors	180	163	160	61	31	61	40	25

[a] All values in percent.

[b] Table 7-4, Three stages of reading, in *Basic Studies on Reading,* edited by Harry Levin and Joanna P. Williams, © 1970 by Basic Books, Inc., Publishers, New York.

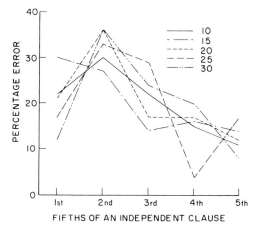

Fig. 8. Location of errors in respect to length of a sentence. Different lines show number of words in clause; see key. (Figure 7-3, three stages of reading, in *Basic Studies on Reading,* edited by Harry Levin and Joanna P. Williams, © 1970 by Basic Books, Inc., Publishers, New York.)

so on. Figure 8 shows the location of errors of reading as a function of such fifths of a clause. The errors tend to be at a maximum in the region of the second fifth of the sentence; and as the greatest number of sentences used were declarative, this means the errors were at a maximum in the region of the main verb. Moreover, the errors taper off sharply with succeeding fifths of the sentence, showing that the more of a sentence one has read correctly, the greater the likelihood that he will read the remainder correctly. The maximizing of errors in the region of the main verb suggests, in turn, that perceiving the nature of the relation between the noun phrases forming the beginning and end of a sentence is more difficult than perceiving the words being related.

From these and other analyses, we know now that in reading text subjects look for and are sensitive to certain formal, syntactic relations that hold the sentence together, and of course to the words being related. In other words, they look for the formally specifiable aspects of the written language. They do this moreover not in any deliberate conscious way; indeed, many college students cannot explicitly tell a conjunction from an adverb or a relative pronoun. The likelihood is virtually zero that they make a conscious decision about where in the sentence to misread, assess the part of speech of the word they have decided to misread, and then deliberately substitute another word of the same grammatical category. Rather than being conscious, their performance is part of the more or less automatic processing of text that characterizes skilled reading.

But as words are what is being read, what else could one misread than words? The point is not that misreadings of words occur when one is reading words; rather, it is that powerful and unsuspected regularities characterize the misreadings. The subjects do not haphazardly say any old thing when they misread; they preserve certain formal characteristics of the language they are reading. The errors that they make are consistent with the notion that the readers are seeking, and sometimes even creating, the words whose relations contain the information of interest. A similar process characterizes looking at pictures.

The evidence here comes from some other figures provided by Yarbus, again based on recordings of movements of the eyes made while people looked at objects or at pictures of them. Their looks trace out the contours of the objects examined (Fig. 9), as shown by the black lines in the low-contrast reproductions, they concentrate on eyes and mouth (Figs. 10 and 11), and they inspect unfamiliar or rare details (Fig. 12). In other words, the looks provide information about the spatial relations or structural details connecting the objects examined, as well as information about certain features we have learned are important, such as eyes and mouth, or rare details. Whether spatial arrangement of the parts of a picture is the pictorial analogue of the syntax of a sentence is a rather wide-open question. To draw the analogy fully would require redefining "syntax" at a more abstract level of analysis, more general than its strictly grammatical interpretation. The reason is that pictures lack syntax, as the term is ordinarily used (Goodman, 1968), a point to which I shall return. For the present,

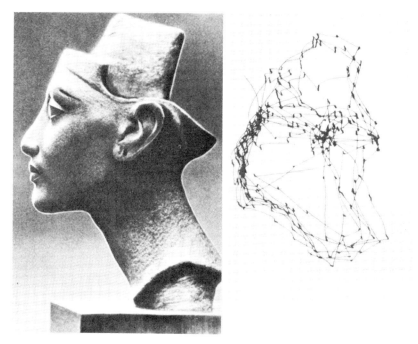

Fig. 9. Eye tracks made while looking at the figure at left are shown in a low-contrast copy at right. (From A. L. Yarbus, *Eye Movements and Vision.* New York: Plenum Publishing Corp., 1967.)

we can see that the eyes do not examine all parts of a picture, but concentrate upon certain areas, especially those that contain information appropriate to an interpretation of the picture.

This emphasis upon the semantic component of a pictorial display is illustrated vividly by some other data of Yarbus. In this case, the subject was again tested with the painting used earlier (Fig. 6), but now was given a question to answer prior to inspecting the picture. The picture examined is entitled "An unexpected visitor" and is shown in the top left panel of Fig. 13. The panel numbered "1" shows the eye tracks made during 3 min of uninstructed observing. The fixations concentrate on the figure rising from the chair, the figure entering the room, and the figures in the doorway. Large regions of the picture are left unexamined. In successive panels, movements of the eyes are shown when the subject was required to answer different questions. In panel 2, he was asked to estimate the financial circumstances of the family; in 3, to estimate the ages of the persons pictured; in 4, to guess what the people had been doing prior to the visitor's arrival; in 5, to remember what clothes the people were wearing;

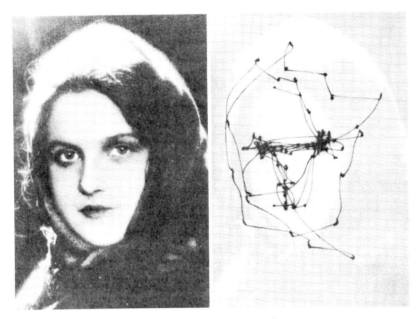

Fig. 10. Eye tracks of a single observer. (From A. L. Yarbus, *Eye Movements and Vision.* New York: Plenum Publishing Corp., 1967.)

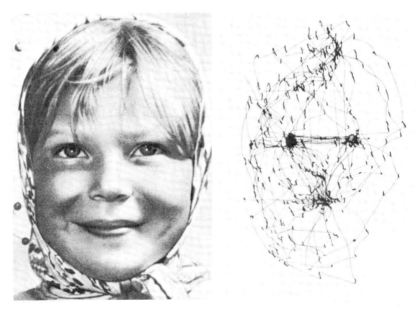

Fig. 11. Eye tracks made while looking at another figure. (From A. L. Yarbus, *Eye Movements and Vision.* New York: Plenum Publishing Corp., 1967.)

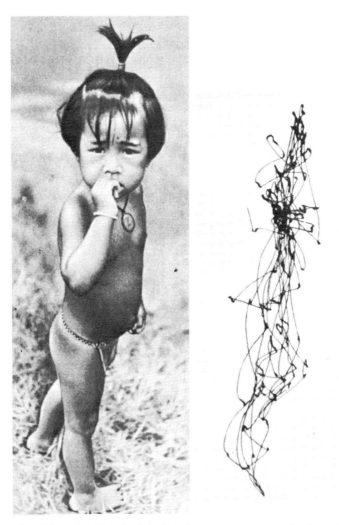

Fig. 12. The unfamiliar detail in the picture captures some fixations. (From A. L. Yarbus, *Eye Movements and Vision.* New York: Plenum Publishing Corp., 1967.)

in 6, to remember the placement of the people and of the objects in the room; and in 7, to estimate the length of time the visitor had been away.

The eye tracks differ from panel to panel, in each case concentrating upon regions of the picture that contain the information that is useful to answering the question. The eyes seek the regions of semantically rich information, searching for it in a pictorial array in a manner not seriously different from the searching movements that characterize the reading of a

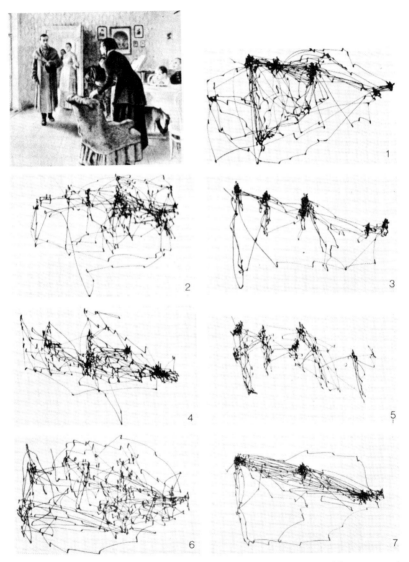

Fig. 13. Eye tracks from a single observer who was asked different questions about the painting in the upper-left panel. (From A. L. Yarbus, *Eye Movements and Vision.* New York: Plenum Publishing Corp., 1967.)

grammar (Fig. 3), or that we can imagine ourselves engaging in when examining a text for particular pieces of information or instruction.

Some Differences between Pictures and Words[1]

Having seen that the logistical and information-gathering operations are fairly similar in looking at pictures and in reading text, we must make some inquiry about what distinguishes these two kinds of representation, for pictures and text clearly are different at a certain level of description. The major difference between them is actually not in what they are, but in the rules we have available for interpreting them. I shall summarize the following discussion in four statements.

(1) A mark is a mark.
(2) A picture is a semantically interpreted mark.
(3) A word or a sentence is a syntactically interpreted picture.
(4) A notation is a rigorously defined (that is, unambiguous) word. What does this mean?

1. A mark is a mark. This statement establishes an identity relation. It says only that any mark on a surface is a mark on a surface. By "mark" I mean a range of perceptible events that includes random squiggles, letters of the alphabet, paintings, and so on. They may be interpreted or not.

2. A picture is a semantically interpreted mark. Of all possible kinds of marks the ones that we can interpret are called pictures. The rules for interpretation may be formally established, as is the case for the marks that we call Arabic numerals, or individual letters of the alphabet or ampersands. The rules may be informal, as is the case with most modern or abstract paintings whose interpretation has not yet been formalized, or cartoons or caricatures, or arrows or simple line drawings. All objects have assignable meanings, of course. But these objects lack syntax, or rules of joining. Individual numerals are only that, as is an arrow used to point direction, or the picture of a chair. There is nothing about a picture that allows one ever to say that it is "ungrammatical." The picture may be badly composed or poorly drawn, but those are features of craftsmanship, not of syntax. One might in some metaphorical way say that a face has a syntax, in the sense that a nose is usually placed below and between two eyes and above a mouth, so that certain orderings are present. But a picture of a face need not preserve these relations, as our comic book artists

---

[1] Here especially I have borrowed from the illuminating treatment of symbol systems in Goodman (1968).

display every day, and as Picasso and Braque demonstrated 60 years ago. Radical departures from the customary ordering relations still left configurations that were interpretable as faces, a fact that child psychologists have newly discovered and exploited when using radical distortions of the normal arrangement of a face to study the infant's response to "faces." Hence, a picture is semantically interpretable, but is syntactically free.

3. A word is a syntactically interpreted picture. When formal ordering rules are applied to semantically interpreted objects, the result is strings of items that stand in formally specifiable relations to each other. We can describe a word as misspelled when it does not abide by the conventions established for its representation; and we can speak of a sentence as ungrammatical when its components, the individual word classes, do not stand in the agreed upon syntactic relations. A sentence may be semantically opaque or semantically empty; but in both cases its words will abide by certain syntactic rules that govern their relation. Contrasted with this is a picture, in which any color or any shape can be placed anywhere in the display and the result still be a picture. Hence, a fundamental difference between pictorial representation and linguistic representation of information depends not upon interpretability, but upon the presence or absence of formally required relations between parts.

Both pictures and words can be ambiguous as to interpretation, of course. To overcome this feature of ambiguity, we must have recourse to other rules. We may use either words, or pictures that have been given precise reference (as in circuit schematics or architectural drawings, for example), but do so always with particular requirements in mind. Using the marks in this way we have a notation (Goodman, 1968).

4. A notation comprises rigorously differentiated words, unambiguous in reference and structure (that is, "appearance"). Terms used in technical discourse, in mathematics, physics, and even in some fields of psychology are notational. The words of natural language and most pictures are almost never used notationally, however. In summary, then, a notation is composed of words, but not all words are notational; a word is a picture, but not all pictures are words; and a picture is a mark, but not all marks are pictures.

An important difference between pictures and words as sources of information, therefore, is based not on their temporal characteristics (one allegedly serial and the other simultaneous), nor even upon the way they are read (one necessarily linear and the other free), but upon the presence or absence of rules governing construction of the items and complementary rules governing interpretation. Pictures are freely open to many interpretations because they are rich in semantic information, but deficient in syntactic regularities; any part can be seen as "modifying" any other.

Sentences are more constrained by the rules of syntax, and notations are even more constrained.

It is perhaps worth pointing out here, as an aside, that in the long history of argumentation regarding the best way to teach reading, an argument that in its present form dates back at least to the time of Aristotle (Mathews, 1966), two views have been in conflict. Their modern names are the "phonics" and the "whole word" approaches. The people favoring the whole word method argue that children should be taught to recognize words as so many pictures: graphic designs having a certain shape and configuration. The teachers use flash cards and other forms of brief exposure in an effort to quicken the recognitive processes. Those advocating the phonics approach, on the other hand, emphasize the sound significates or sound classes that letters are thought to represent. In light of what has already been said, it should be clear that written words are both pictorial or graphemic displays — they are marks on a page having certain spatial features — and they are linguistic displays, for the marks are interpretable as words. Hence the argument between the whole word and the phonics approaches is an argument between those advocating that words be recognized by the pictures that they make, and those advocating that words be recognized by the sounds the pictures are thought to represent. As written words are both pictorial and linguistic objects, neither group of advocates has had the whole story. Indeed, it is still not certain that anyone has the whole story, but what is certain is that written words are symbols; hence, children, in being taught to read, might profitably be taught something about the idea of representation itself and something about the role of symbols in that process. The whole word and the phonics approaches are primarily means to an end; but too often these means become ends in themselves. They are, that is to say, merely techniques for inculcating a skill, and as such may be more or less effective. Neither of them captures reading as a symbol-manipulating activity any more than finger scales capture the skilled playing of a sonata.

Some Uses

Pictures and words, because of some of their formal characteristics, are useful in different ways. Pictures are especially good at depicting spatial arrangements, and therefore any conceptualization that can be given a spatial representation. Graphs, for example, give a sense of a function more readily than a table of numbers or a paragraph can; Venn diagrams illustrate the relations between parts and wholes in logical relations more compactly and more neatly than do words. Similarly, a drawing of a circuit and a map of terrain are far more easily interpreted than are the corresponding words, for both represent spatial arrangements. When saying this we assume, however, that the interpreters are pictorially literate; that they know how to read pictures and maps. It is an old, but incorrect idea that pictures are read universally and only words are parochial (Kolers, 1969). The error is clearly revealed by recent experiences in countries in which the safety precautions to be followed in a gold mine, or the details of inserting and using an intrauterine device have been conveyed for illiterate persons as a series of pictures in comicbook fashion. The programs have not been especially successful, however, for the users have not known how to read the pictures; whether to read them from left to right or right to left, bottom to top or top to bottom, or even why a 2-inch-high drawing having a certain shape should be called a man or a woman, nor why the reader should identify himself with this 2-inch-high drawing. Thus, literacy is required for pictorial interpretation as much as for textual interpretation. But assuming the literacy is present, pictures are good at representing spatial and even, through another convention, temporal relations. Hence, our tendency to write flow charts or flow diagrams to represent sequences of actions or events. Pictures are so useful in identifying objects and their spatial relations, that for these tasks a picture may indeed be worth a thousand words. But if qualifications, commentary, or other subtleties govern interpretation, pictures fail miserably. If pictures are good for identifying, words are necessary for qualifying, commenting upon, or explaining. Neither pictures nor words are the royal road to information processing.

In various studies of perception and memory, the claim has been made that pictures provide for better, more detailed, or faster encodings than words do, but in other studies the opposite has been found. In fact sometimes pictures are recognized more readily than words, and sometimes words are recognized more readily than pictures (Kolers, 1969). The allegations of superiority are, unfortunately, sometimes based on an incomplete analysis of the stimuli used in the tests. It is well known that the perceptibility of a word increases with its familiarity: more commonly used words are recognized more readily than are rarer words. Surely the same sort of relation would hold for pictures. Indeed, in one experiment I required subjects to recognize "pictures" of the kind shown in Fig. 14. The task was to identify at a later time and by number the "picture" in B that matched the corresponding "picture" in A. The subjects performed the task very poorly, at only the chance level. In another condition of the same experiment they were required to identify analogous "pictures" as illustrated in Fig. 15. Performance was far better. The "pictures" in the first set were sentences written in the Devanagari alphabet; they were presented

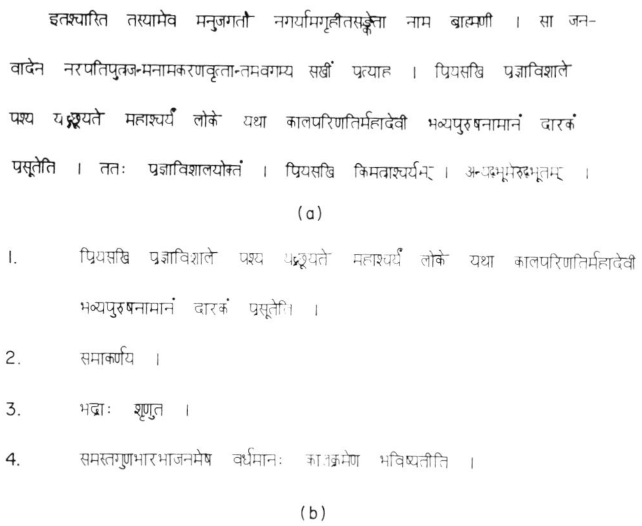

इतश्चारित तस्यामेव मनुजगतौ नगर्यामगृहीतसङ्केता नाम ब्राह्मणी । सा जन-

वादेन नरपतिपुत्रज-मनामकरणवृत्ता-तमवगम्य सखीं प्रत्याह । प्रियसखि प्रज्ञाविशाले

पश्य यच्छ्रूयते महाश्चर्यं लोके यथा कालपरिणतिर्महादेवी भव्यपुरुषनामानं दारकं

प्रसूतेति । ततः प्रज्ञाविशालयोक्तं । प्रियसखि किमत्राश्चर्यम् । अन्यथ्याप्रेछभूतम् ।

(a)

1. प्रियसखि प्रज्ञाविशाले पश्य यच्छ्रूयते महाश्चर्यं लोके यथा कालपरिणतिर्महादेवी

भव्यपुरुषनामानं दारकं प्रसूतेति ।

2. समाकर्णय ।

3. भद्राः शृणुत ।

4. समस्तगुणभारभाजनमेष वर्धमानः कालक्रमेण भविष्यतीति ।

(b)

Fig. 14. One kind of picture whose details many readers have difficulty in remembering.

to subjects ignorant of that system of writing. The second set were approximate transliterations of the same sentences presented to English-reading subjects. From other control tests, we were led to infer that it is familiarity with the kinds of pictures used, familiarity with the system of symbols, and not merely the availability of a kind of phonemic representation for the roman characters, that accounted for the difference in performance. In

Itascasti tasyameva manujagatau nagaryamagrhitasamketa nama brahmani. Sa janavadena narapati putrajanmanama-karanavr-ttantamavagamya sakhim pratyaha. Priyasakhi prajnavisale pasya yacchruyate mahascaryam loke yatha kalaparinatirmahadevi bhavyapurusanamanam darakam prasuteti. Tatah prajnavisalayoktam.

(a)

1. Priyasakhi prajnavisale pasya yacchruyate mahascaryam loke yatha kalaparinatirmahadevi bhavyapurusanamanam darakam prasuteti.
2. Samakarnaya.
3. Bhadrah srnuta.
4. Samastagunabharbhajanamesa vardhamanah kalakramena bhavisyatiti.

(b)

Fig. 15. A related picture that creates fewer problems for readers of the roman alphabet.

general one can expect that familiarity with pictures will affect their ease and speed of encoding, in a manner not too different from that for words.[2]

Suppose now that in some test we compared the ease of encoding pictures of objects — say pipe, book, pencil — and the ease of encoding their linguistic representations. How shall we draw a pipe or a book? Shall we have a photograph, a cartoon, a line drawing? And among these, what sort of pipe and what sort of picture? How shall we arrange the contrast, the shading, the figural detail? These are important questions, for as we modify the picture by adding or eliminating detail we can make it harder or easier to recognize, and make the pipe the "same one" as before or a different one. But if we present the *word* "pipe," we may write it in capital letters, small letters, or a mixture of the two; in Garamond or Gothic or sans serif font, and in all cases our word is the same linguistic object. The reason for this difference, of course, is that our pictures cannot be notated, but our words can. It is a trivially easy matter, therefore, by appropriate manipulation of stimulus conditions, to make the pictures harder to encode and recall or easier; and to make words more readily encodable than pictures or poorer. Thus this aspect of representation must be taken into account before statements are made regarding the relative poorness or superiority of pictures and words as objects for recognition.

A second aspect has to do with familiarity as already mentioned. Some representations are far more familiar to us as pictures, others are far more familiar as words. Thus, before asserting that pictures or words are the superior perceptual or memorial object, one would have to show that their internal representations are equal, so that one would be measuring speed of access or efficiency of representation rather than only familiarity. These are difficult points to show, and their not yet having been shown weakens the claims made for the necessary superiority of one or the other mode of representation.

Similarly, whether we have acquired information through our eyes or our ears, and our relative experience with these modes of encoding, surely must affect whether hearing or seeing is the more efficient strategy. We cannot any longer believe that all information that we have acquired is stored in a common "dictionary" in our heads; rather, we believe that the means by which information was encoded can affect our subsequent access and retrieval. By means of encoding, I mean not only the modality — pictures or words, eyes or ears; I mean rather the rules used for interpreting

[2] A picture can be a "copy" of an object – a realistic drawing – but a word never can; this aspect of visual similarity may play some role in perception so as to make it easier to learn to read a picture than to learn to read a word. For the skilled reader of words and pictures this difference in the ontogenesis of his skill is likely to be irrelevant. See Kolers (1963) for a related problem in learning languages.

and storing the information. Coming back to pictures and words, we can say that they differ not so much by virtue of what they are, for they are both only marks on a surface; they differ more by virtue of the rules governing their construction and the rules we use for their interpretation. The rules for creating and interpreting words are more formal and elaborate than are the rules for encoding pictures. It may be, therefore, that the greater number of rules governing the construction and interpretation of words makes for more work in their interpretation, whereas the greater plasticity in the construction of pictures makes it easier to interpret them. But one could state the opposite case just as well, to argue that the greater plasticity available in the construction and interpretation of pictures makes for more work. Unfortunately, we cannot yet say which is true. The role that formal rules of representation play in our acquisition, interpretation, and retrieval of information remains still to be studied, and must be studied before we can fully justify any claims made for ease of representation or interpretation as a function of kind of display.

Acknowledgments

Some of the ideas expressed were first discussed at Project Zero, Harvard Graduate School of Education. Preparation of this paper was supported in part by a grant from the Ontario Mental Health Foundation (OMHF No. 382) and in part by a grant from the National Research Council of Canada (A 7655).

References

Buswell, G. T. *How people look at pictures.* Chicago: Univ. of Chicago Press, 1935.

Cattell, J. McK. Über die Zeit der Erkennung und Benennung von Schriftzeichen, Bildern und Farben. *Philosophische Studien,* 1885, **2**, 635–650. Translated in *James McKeen Cattell, Man of Science.* Lancaster, Pennsylvania: Science Press, 1947.

Goodman, N. *Languages of art.* Indianapolis: Bobbs-Merrill, 1968.

Helson, H., & Fehrer, E. V. The role of form in perception. *American Journal of Psychology,* 1932, **44**, 79–102.

Judd, C. H., & Buswell, G. T. Silent reading. *Supplementary Educational Monographs,* 1922, **23**.

Kolers, P. A. Interlingual word associations. *Journal of Verbal Learning and Verbal Behavior,* 1963, **2**, 291–300.

Kolers, P. A. Some formal characteristics of pictograms. *American Scientist,* 1969, **57**, 348–363.

Kolers, P. A. Three stages of reading. In H. Levin & J. P. Williams (Eds.), *Basic studies on reading.* New York: Basic Books, 1970.

Kolers, P. A. *Aspects of motion perception.* Oxford: Pergamon, 1972.

Kolers, P. A., & Katzman, M. T. Naming sequentially presented letters and words *Language and Speech,* 1966, **9**, 84–95.

Mathews, M. *Teaching to read.* Chicago: Univ. of Chicago Press, 1966.

Taylor, E. A. The spans: perception, apprehension, and recognition. *American Journal of Ophthalmology,* 1957, **44**, 501–507.

Thomas, E. L. Eye movements in speed reading. In R. G. Stauffer (Ed.), *Speed reading: Practices and procedures,* Volume 10. Newark: University of Delaware Reading Study Center, 1962. Pp. 104–114.

Yarbus, A. L. *Eye movements and vision.* New York: Plenum, 1967.

A "LEVELS OF ANALYSIS" VIEW OF MEMORY

Fergus I. M. Craik

Erindale College, University of Toronto

Information-processing models of human memory are typically described in terms of a series of stores. The salient features of such models were summarized by Murdock (1967) and incorporated in his "modal model." Murdock suggested that incoming information is first held in a modality-specific sensory store. This store has a large capacity, but the information in it decays rapidly and is thus irretrievably lost unless the subject attends to the stored items. Attended items are then passed on to a limited-capacity short-term store (STS) where they are maintained by rehearsal or displaced by further inputs. Rehearsal performs the additional function of transferring information about the items to a permanent or long-term store (LTS), where capacity is apparently unlimited and forgetting follows the laws of "interference." This scheme is illustrated in Fig. 1. Although different in points of detail, the general features of the modal model are endorsed by the work of Broadbent (1958), Waugh and Norman (1965), and Atkinson and Shiffrin (1968).

The modal model focuses attention on such questions as the capacity, coding, and forgetting characteristics of the various memory stores; that is, on how many items each store can hold, the nature of the items, and how the items are lost from storage. Further issues which demand clarification are the registration and retrieval characteristics of each store and the nature of the transfer of information from one store to the next. Also, the model implies various assumptions about the human memory system — for example, that information necessarily flows from the sensory stores via STS to LTS and that the system is discontinuous from one memory compartment

45

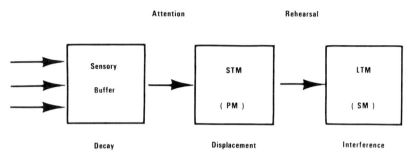

Fig. 1. A generalized multistore model of memory (Murdock's "modal model"). (After Murdock, 1967.)

to another. The latter implication may be contrasted with the argument that memory is better thought of as a continuum (Melton, 1963; Murdock, 1972).

In this chapter, I question the continuing usefulness of a "stores" or "box model" approach and suggest an alternative framework for the study of human memory. First, the limitations and inconsistencies of the modal model will be discussed under the headings of capacity, coding, and retention.

Capacity

Limited capacity is apparently not a critical feature of either the sensory store or LTS. Capacity is held to be large in the former (e.g., Kintsch, 1970, pp. 149–153) and unlimited in the latter store (e.g., Broadbent, 1971, p. 362). On the other hand, limited capacity is one of the major defining characteristics of STS (Broadbent, 1958, 1971). When the various estimates of STS capacity are examined, however, a variety of very different results are found. For example, recent estimates of STS capacity from free recall studies have yielded values of between two and four words (Baddeley, 1970; Murdock, 1972). However, measures of memory span (which have also been taken to reflect the limited capacity of STS) are typically between five and nine items depending on whether the items in question are words, letters, or digits (Crannell & Parrish, 1957). Finally, if the words in a span test form a sentence, subjects can accurately reproduce strings of 20 words (Craik & Masani, 1969). Thus if capacity is a critical feature of STS operation, a box model must account for this very wide range of capacity estimates.

Coding

A second reason for distinguishing discrete stages in memory concerns the apparently different types of coding which take place in the different stores. For example, in the short-term retention of speech, Conrad (1964) and Baddeley (1966) showed that STS coding was predominantly acoustic, whereas LTS coding was largely semantic in nature. This conclusion has been supported by subsequent work (e.g., Kintsch, 1970, pp. 182–193), but more recently the adequacy of acoustic–semantic coding differences as a basis for the STS–LTS distinction has been questioned. First, it has been shown that STS coding can be either acoustic or articulatory (Levy, 1971; Peterson & Johnson, 1971). Shulman (1971) used the more general term "phonemic" to describe this more flexible view of STS coding. Furthermore, papers by Kroll and his colleagues (Kroll, Parks, Parkinson, Bieber, & Johnson, 1970; Parkinson, Parks, & Kroll, 1971) have shown that STS can be visual in certain situations, and Gilson and Baddeley (1969) have demonstrated short-term retention of tactile stimuli. There is also some possibility that STS can deal with semantic information (Shulman, 1971).

Thus the type of coding observed appears to depend heavily on the material presented and the usefulness to the subject of the various dimensions of stimulus information. The subject can apparently choose to hold in STS the type of information which will be most useful to him when he is asked to retrieve the items. Although this is a reasonable view, it does imply that STS is more complex than was formerly supposed — apparently it can retain a wide variety of physical codes. Again the attractive simplicity of the multistore model may be questioned, and the possibility of an alternative explanatory framework considered.

Retention Characteristics

The different rates of forgetting displayed by items held in different stores provide a third source of evidence in favor of the multistore formulation. Apparently, information is lost very rapidly from the sensory store (Crowder & Morton, 1969; Sperling, 1960), in 5–20 sec from STS (Peterson & Peterson, 1959), and very slowly, if at all, from LTS (Atkinson & Shiffrin, 1968; Shiffrin & Atkinson, 1969). Presumably, each store should exhibit constant characteristics when different types of material and different paradigms are used, but again there is evidence that this constancy is not found.

For example, the durability of the memory trace for visual material appears to depend strongly on the particular material and experimental situation. Sperling (1960) estimated that visual sensory information persisted for approximately .5 sec; Posner (1969) found evidence for visual persistence of 1.5 sec; recent studies by Murdock (1971), Phillips and Baddeley (1971), and by Kroll, Parks, Parkinson, Bieber, and Johnson (1970) have yielded estimates of 6, 10, and 25 sec, respectively. Estimates are even longer in recognition memory for pictures (Shepard, 1967; Haber, 1970). While it is possible to attribute these very different estimates to the functioning of different visual stores, it may be more useful to envisage a continuum of visual processing with more durable retention resulting from deeper or more elaborate processing.

In any event, it seems that the distinguishing characteristics of the sensory store, STS and LTS, depend very much on the paradigm and on the material used. In particular, when visual material is considered, it is difficult to draw clear dividing lines between "sensory," "short-term," and "long-term" retention. Although the multistore formulation has been useful in providing guide lines for memory research, it may be that some workers are now taking the stores too literally in attempting to specify *the* capacity, *the* type of coding, and *the* retention characteristic at each stage. Such questions may not lead to fruitful insights about the organization of memory and, indeed, may constrain rather than stimulate further theorizing. In the following section, an alternative framework for human memory research is suggested.

A "Levels of Analysis" Framework

In the normal course of perceiving spoken and written speech, the incoming words are first analyzed in terms of their physical features and these analyzed features are then matched against more symbolic, abstract semantic features. Several theorists have now postulated a hierarchy of levels or stages of analysis running from the early analysis of physical features to later, more complex analyses of semantic features (e.g., Selfridge & Neisser, 1960; Treisman, 1964; Sutherland, 1968). Beyond the level at which letters and words are recognized, further processing of the input can occur through the generation of associations and images. While these levels of analysis are most clearly conceived in the case of speech, it is likely that all incoming patterns are subject to an analogous series of analyses.

It is suggested that the memory trace is one product of these perceptual processes, and that trace persistence is a positive function of the depth of analysis. As more analyses are carried out on a stimulus, so the resulting memory trace becomes more durable. Since the organism is normally concerned only with the extraction of meaning from stimuli, there is little need for the products of preliminary analyses to be stored in memory — in fact, it is probably advantageous to the organism if the results of these initial operations are rapidly expunged from the system. Thus it seems reasonable to speculate that the products of early physical analyses are very transient — the organism has no need to store them — while the products of later, more semantic analyses are stored so that the organism may profit by the experience and modify its future actions accordingly.

The hierarchy of perceptual analyses is seen as being essentially continuous from one level to the next, thus memory, also, is viewed as a continuum from the transient products of early analyses to the long-lasting results of later processing. While it is possible to draw a box called "sensory memory" around the memory traces resulting from initial analyses and a box labeled "long-term memory" around the results of later analyses, this procedure may constrain, rather than stimulate, further theorizing. Instead, it is suggested that the rate of forgetting depends on how deeply the stimulus was processed, with slower forgetting rates associated with deeper processing.

Such hierarchies of analysis presumably exist in many perceptual modalities. Auditory inputs may first be analyzed in terms of gross physical features — frequency, amplitude, waveform, etc. — but with successive stages of analysis becoming less dependent on stimulus features and more dependent on structures laid down through past learning. Later auditory analyses might concern recognition of a tune or a particular voice, or the evocation of a whole incident from the past. Similar processing schemes presumably exist in vision (from an analysis of lines, angles, brightness, etc. to an analysis of complex pictorial material) and also in speech (from an analysis of phonemes and graphemes to an analysis of sentences and arguments).

The scheme just outlined suggests that perceptual analysis follows an invariable sequence of steps from physical to semantic analysis. However, much recent evidence points to the probability that more meaningful analyses are carried out first and that the results of analyses which should logically occur early in processing are not available to consciousness until later (Macnamara, 1972). For example, although syllables appear to be larger and more meaningful units of speech than phonemes, Savin and Bever (1970) found that subjects could detect syllable targets faster than phoneme targets. Thus, the implication is that long practice may modify the order in which operations are performed, or that some stages drop out, either altogether or at least from conscious awareness. So far as this chapter is concerned, the point is that trace persistence is postulated to be a function of cognitive depth, where "depth" is defined in terms of the meaningfulness extracted from the stimulus rather than in terms of the number of analyses performed upon it.

Again, the term "depth of processing" implies a linear series of operations, whereas it seems more plausible that after a stimulus has been recognized, further processing does not occur as a sequence of necessary steps, but rather as one or several of many possible options. That is, after a word has been recognized, further processing may consist of the formation of images, associations or stories depending on the subject's biases or expectations. Thus, deeper processing depends on the strategy adopted by the subject. Further processing might be better described as "spread" rather than "depth" of encoding, but the latter term will be retained, since it conveys the flavor of the argument.

With these qualifications, greater depth usually implies more processing of the stimulus. Thus, with any one type of material it will take more time to carry out the further operations required for deeper levels of analysis. When material is held constant, processing time is a correlate of depth of analysis and thus of subsequent memory performance. However, the relationship between processing time and memory will probably not hold up across different types of memorized material. Some stimuli are more easily processed than others: for example, pictorial stimuli may be rapidly processed to a deep level and yield a persistent memory trace. On the other hand, relatively meaningless stimuli, such as nonsense shapes or unrelated letters, may be processed for a longer time, but yield a more transient memory record.

It will be important to specify more precisely the criteria of depth of analysis and the factors that lead to deeper processing and thus to better memory. Three classes of factors may be suggested: (1) stimulus salience or intensity; (2) the amount of processing devoted (or the amount of attention paid) to the stimulus; and (3) the item's meaningfulness or compatibility with the analyzing structures. The first two factors may be thought of as pushing the stimulus in from outside, while the third factor is better regarded as pulling the stimulus down from within the organism (see Broadbent, 1971). The present approach is concerned in part with specifying interactions and trading relations between these three classes of variables.

Although, in the present formulation, memory is viewed basically as a product of perceptual analysis, it is further suggested that the subject may retain stimuli in a second fashion — by maintaining processing at one level of analysis. The maintenance of processing at one level in any perceptual modality thus acts to prolong the perceptual experience of the stimulus in that modality. Processing is maintained by continuing to attend to some aspects of the stimulus, and I suggest that this process is equivalently described as "rehearsal of the item," "keeping the item in consciousness," or "storing the item in primary memory." Waugh and Norman's (1965) term "primary memory" (PM) will be used to describe this second reten- tion mechanism, and it should be noted that the term is used here in the original James (1890) sense of continued attention to the item or keeping the item in consciousness. When attention is diverted from the item it will be lost from PM and will be forgotten from memory at the rate appropriate to its level of analysis.

While it is suggested that PM retention is equivalent to rehearsal of the item, it is possible that this type of rehearsal — maintaining information at one level of processing — merely prolongs the item's high accessibility with- out leading to the formation of a more permanent memory trace. This "Type I processing" (repetition of analyses which have already been carried out) may be contrasted with "Type II processing," which involves further processing of the stimulus to a deeper level. Type II processing is equivalent to "elaborative encoding" (Tulving & Madigan, 1970), and only this second type of continued processing should lead to improved memory performance by the present view. To the extent that the subject utilizes Type II processing, memory will improve with total study time, but when he engages only in Type I processing, the "total time hypothesis" (e.g., Cooper & Pantle, 1967) will break down.

It should be noted that the present scheme maintains the distinction between a short-term storage mechanism and long-term memory, but that the short-term retention mechanism (PM) is seen, not as a store, but as the strategy of continued attention to some aspects of the stimulus. The main features of the levels of analysis formulation are shown in Fig. 2.

To summarize, it is suggested that memory is better described as a

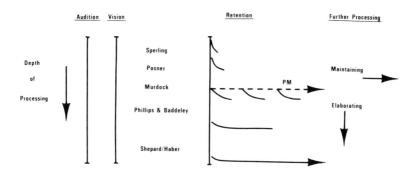

Fig. 2. Some features of a "levels of analysis" view of memory.

function of depth of processing or level of analysis, rather than as a function of various stores. Deeper or more elaborate processing leads to the formation of a more persistent trace. Information may also be maintained by continued processing at one level, but such maintenance will not by itself lead to permanent registration. When attention is diverted from the stimuli held in this manner (that is, maintained in PM), information about the stimuli is lost at a rate which depends on the level of analysis which the stimuli have achieved. These ideas are developed more fully by Craik and Lockhart (1972).

Five experimental studies are now briefly described. The first two experiments illustrate the point that when attention is diverted from material held in PM, the material is rapidly lost. This point may seem obvious, but both Reitman (1971) and Atkinson and Shiffrin (1971) have recently concluded that diversion of attention from PM is not sufficient for PM forgetting and that verbal material is only lost from PM through displacement by further verbal items.

Experiment I

Experiment I is an unpublished study by Gregory Mazuryk of Erindale College. He used the Brown–Peterson paradigm in which the subject is presented with a few items to remember; he then attempts to recall them after a retention interval filled with a distracting task. In Mazuryk's experiment, the interpolated task consisted of a continuous series of piano notes recorded at one note per second. Each note was drawn at random from four possible pitches; the subject's task was to press one of four telegraph keys — one key corresponded to each pitch. Thus the interpolated task could be described as "nonverbal shadowing." Subjects reported it to be very attention demanding.

In outline, each trial consisted of presenting five words (concrete nouns) to the subjects visually. This presentation was followed by one of three instruction words which defined the interpolated activity: SILENT, TONE, or PRESS. "Silent" indicated that no tones would occur and that the subject was free to rehearse the words throughout the silent retention interval. "Tone" indicated that the piano notes would be played back from a tape-recorder, but that the subject could ignore them — again he was free to rehearse. Finally, "Press" indicated that the subject was to shadow the tones by pressing the relevant keys — he was also asked to hum the notes as they were presented. This last instruction was an attempt to engage the subject's articulatory apparatus to some extent and thus prevent him from articulating the presented words. The subject continued to perform the task (or to rehearse) until a recall light appeared after either 1, 3, 6, 9, or 20 sec. The retention interval was not known in advance. Each of the 16 subjects was given 75 scored trials after practice — 5 replications at each retention interval for each interpolated activity. The different activities and retention intervals were presented to each subject in a unique random sequence.

The results of the study are shown in Fig. 3. The data shown are number of words correct, without regard to order of recall. The figure shows that while the silent and tone conditions led to no forgetting over the retention interval, the necessity to divert attention from the stored words in the press condition led to substantial forgetting. Thus apparently material is lost from PM when attention is demanded elsewhere — regardless of whether the interpolated task is verbal or nonverbal in nature. This conclusion will be discussed after a brief description of the next experiment which makes the same point.

Experiment II

Experiment II is an unpublished free recall study carried out by Michael and Olga Watkins in London. In free recall, the last few words presented are recalled extremely well, and this phenomenon (the recency effect) is usually interpreted as demonstrating short-term store (or PM) recall. In Watkins and Watkins' study, a list of 15 words was followed either by immediate recall or by recall after 20 sec of an attention-demanding nonverbal task.

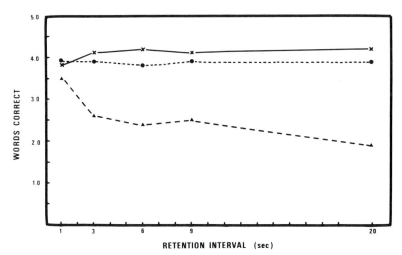

Fig. 3. Forgetting rates as a function of the nature of the interpolated task: (×) silent; (●) tone; (▲) press.

The task in question was tracking the target of a pursuit rotor. The issue is again whether the necessity to perform the interpolated task causes forgetting from PM and so reduces the magnitude of the recency effect.

Four groups of 10 subjects performed the task. The words were presented either auditorily or visually, and recall was either immediate or following 20 sec of pursuit rotor activity. Each group performed only one modality-recall combination and subjects in each group received 10 trials. The results are shown in Fig. 4.

Again, the implication is that an attention-demanding task is sufficient to cause PM forgetting, since the recency effect is greatly reduced for auditory input and virtually eliminated for visual input.

Possibly the main difference between the Watkins' results and those of previous workers (Reitman, 1971; Atkinson & Shiffrin, 1971) is the degree to which the interpolated task forced attention away from the items to be remembered. Both previous investigations used a signal-detection task as the interpolated activity, which may not have required such persistent monitoring as the tasks used in the Watkins' experiments. In support of this argument, Crowder (1967) reported a similar experiment in which a self-paced continuous reaction-time task was used as the interpolated task. He found that this demanding, but nonverbal task caused substantial forgetting of items held in PM.

Experiments I and II are thus taken to support the suggested conception

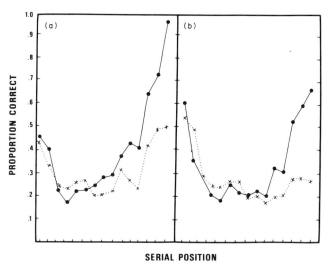

Fig. 4. Free recall performance as a function of input modality and interpolated task: (●) immediate recall; (×) pursuit rotor. (a) Auditory presentation. (b) Visual presentation.

of PM as involving continued attention to some aspects of the remembered items. If attention is diverted from this holding or rehearsal function, the items are rapidly lost.

Experiment III

The third experiment represents an attempt to document the distinction between Type I and Type II processing. It will be remembered that Type I processing simply involves maintenance of the products of analysis at one level, while Type II processing involves deeper, more elaborate processing of the item. According to the levels of analysis viewpoint, only the second type of continued processing ought to lead to an increase in memory performance.

Craik (1970) reported an experiment in which subjects were given a series of immediate free recall (IFR) trials followed by a "final free recall" (FFR) trial. On this final trial, subjects attempted to recall all words from all previous lists. It was found that while the serial position curve from IFR trials yielded the usual large recency effect, the analogous curve from the FFR trial gave rise to a negative recency effect — that is, words presented at the ends of lists were least well recalled in FFR. This finding was interpreted as showing that words originally retrieved from PM (the IFR recency effect) were not well registered in the long-term store. A second possible explanation of the negative recency effect is that terminal words in presentation lists are simply not rehearsed so often as words from the earlier parts of the list. In support of this proposition, Rundus (1971) asked subjects to rehearse aloud, and demonstrated that terminal words were rehearsed less frequently than earlier words.

However, arguing from a levels of analysis viewpoint, I would suggest that it is not simply the number of rehearsals which is important, but also the type of rehearsing which the subject carries out (Jacoby & Bartz, 1972; Watkins, 1972). If he subjects the last few words in a list to Type I processing only, the words will be maintained in PM and thus easily retrieved in IFR. Since the words have not been processed to a deep level, no durable traces will be formed and their probability of retrieval on the final trial will be low.

Experiment III was an attempt to decide whether it is amount of processing or type of processing which is the major factor in long-term recall. By stressing the importance of the last four words in each list, and interpolating an unfilled interval between presentation and free recall, it was hoped that subjects would rehearse the final words as often as words from the beginning of the list. There should be no need to process the last words to a deep level, however, since the subjects' only task as far as they knew, was to recall the items in IFR. The question is whether extra rehearsal of this type would lead to increased performance in FFR — the present formulation predicts that it would not.

Subjects were presented with a series of 12-word lists. They were told that recall would either be immediately after presentation or would be delayed for 20 sec. In the second case, the delay was unfilled and the subject was instructed to rehearse. On any trial, he did not know whether IFR would be immediate or delayed until the recall light came on. Subjects were tested individually and were told that all rehearsals must be spoken aloud. They were free to rehearse any words they wanted, but it was most important always to recall the last four words. Specifically, in the delayed IFR condition, they should ensure recall of the last four words by continuing to rehearse them. Subjects were given six immediate and six delayed lists. Words were presented visually at a 3-sec rate. After all 12 lists had been presented and recalled, the subject was unexpectedly given the FFR task.

Figure 5 shows that the delayed IFR condition had the required effect of boosting the number of rehearsals given to the last four words. The figure also shows that while the recency effect in IFR was more or less maintained in the delayed condition, the extra rehearsals had no facilitating effect on recall of these items in FFR.

The conclusion drawn from this study is that if the subject rehearses merely by maintaining the products of a relatively early analysis (for example, by maintaining a phonemic code), his rehearsals will not lead to improved memory performance.

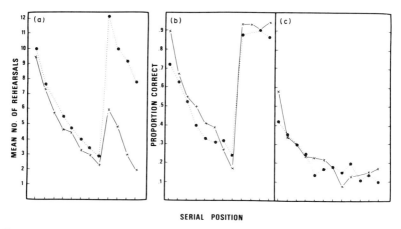

SERIAL POSITION

Fig. 5. Number of rehearsals, immediate free recall, and final free recall, with and without an unfilled delay: (×) immediate IFR; (●) delayed IFR. (a) Rehearsals. (b) Immediate recall. (c) Final recall.

The final two experiments to be described were attempts to obtain more direct evidence on the usefulness of the levels approach. In both experiments, subjects first performed a perceptual reaction-time task whose purpose was to lead to different words being analyzed to different levels. The first prediction was that deeper analyses would take longer to carry out and the second prediction was that deeper analysis would yield better performance on a subsequent unexpected memory task.

Experiment IV

Experiment IV, also unpublished, was carried out by Karl Egner of Erindale College. The 20 subjects were tested individually. Each was told that the experiment was concerned with how quickly he could make various types of decisions about single words presented briefly in a tachistoscope. Before each word was presented, the subject was asked one of five different questions about the word. The questions were:

(1) Is there a word present?
(2) Is the word in capital letters/lower case?
(3) Does the word rhyme with _____?
(4) Is the word a member of the following category: _____?
(5) Does the word fit into the following sentence: _____?

It was argued that the different questions would necessitate processing to a progressively deeper level as the questions went from (1) to (5).

The subject was given eight questions at each level — four leading to "yes" and four leading to "no" responses. There were 40 trials and question type was randomized. Two seconds after the question had been asked auditorily, the word was presented in the tachistoscope for 200 msec. The subject answered "yes" or "no" orally, and his vocal response stopped a timer that had been started at word onset. After all 40 trials had been presented, the subject was given a sheet with 80 words on it — the original 40, plus 40 distractors of a similar type. He was asked to check those words he recognized from the perceptual task.

The top panel of Fig. 6 shows the decision latencies for the five levels of questions. As predicted, it took progressively longer for subjects to answer the deeper, more semantic questions. "Yes" and "no" decisions took about the same time to make, except possibly at the sentence level where "no" decisions took longer. The lower panel shows the proportion of words recognized at the various levels. Only "yes" words are represented at level 1 since "no" at that level meant that no word had been presented. Apart from a

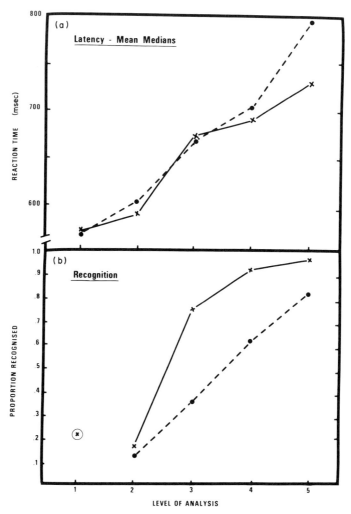

Fig. 6. Latency and recognition performance as a function of level of analysis: (×) yes; (●) no. (a) Latency, mean medians. (b) Recognition.

slight inversion between levels 1 and 2, recognition accuracy increased dramatically with level of analysis – accuracy was approximately six times better for sentences than for case decisions. Unexpectedly, "yes" decisions led to consistently better recognition than "no" decisions – perhaps because the subject was more able to regenerate the original questions from the target word, and this additional information facilitated recognition (Morris Moscovitch suggested this explanation).

In any event, the results are in good agreement with a levels of analysis view – deeper decisions about words required more time, and subsequent recognition performance was a function of the initial processing depth.

Experiment V

Finally, Experiment V was a recall version of Experiment IV, carried out in collaboration with Endel Tulving. Again, each subject was given an initial perceptual decision-making task followed by an unexpected recall test. The words used were common nouns of four to eight letters, exposed for 200 msec in a tachistoscope. Three types of questions were asked in this experiment:

(1) Is the word in capital letters/lower case?
(2) Does the word rhyme with _____?
(3) Does the word fit into the following sentence: _____?

Again, it was predicted that type (3) questions would require deeper analysis of the word than type (2) and (1) questions; more time would be required for the deeper analyses and that memory performance would be best for type (3) questions and poorest for type (1).

Each subject was given 108 trials on the perceptual task; 36 words (12 at each level) were presented once only during the series and these words always led to a "no" response (for example, the presented word did not rhyme with the example given). Also, 36 further words were presented twice – these words all yielded "yes" responses. The subject was warned that some words might be exposed twice, but of course did not know when this repetition would occur. In fact all repetitions occurred after 20 intervening items had been presented. When a word came up for the second time, the question asked was either *identical* to the question for its first appearance (for example, "does the word rhyme with train?"); or was a different question at the *same level* (for example, for the target word "book" – "the ____ was on the table" and "the girl looked at the ____"); or was a *different level* question (for example, "does the word rhyme with pocket?" and "is the word in capital letters?"). If C represents case decisions, R rhyme decisions, and S sentence decisions, then the nine possible combinations of questions are:

Identical repetitions	CC	RR	SS
Same level repetitions	CC′	RR′	SS′
Different level repetitions	CR	CS	RS

(where the different level repetitions include, for example, both *CR* and *RC* orders of presentation). Four examples of each combination were included.

The point of the repetition conditions was to explore the effect of encoding variability on subsequent recall. From previous studies, it was expected that the necessity to encode the word differently on its second exposure would increase its likelihood of being recalled (Bevan & Dukes, 1967).

On each trial, the subject was first presented with a question auditorily. Two seconds later the word appeared in the tachistoscope for 200 msec and the subject responded "yes" or "no" by pressing one of two response keys. After a subject had completed the perceptual task, he was unexpectedly asked to recall as many target words as he could from the task, in any order. He was given 5 min of written recall for this memory task.

Figure 7 shows decision latencies for the various conditions. Again, in general, latencies increased from C to R to S, although the picture is complicated by repetitions. For example, it is plausible that with identical repetitions, latencies should be facilitated more at the deeper levels where the question predicts the target word with greater accuracy. Figure 8 shows that this effect occurred.

The proportion of words recalled from the different treatment conditions is shown in Fig. 8. For the "no" responses, identical repetitions and same level repetitions, recall is influenced strongly by the level of analysis necessary in the perceptual task. Again, memory performance is increased by a factor of six between the case and sentence levels. Performance in the identical repetition group is much better than in the "no" group, but it is unclear how much this is a "yes/no" difference and how much the difference is due to the second presentation in the repetition group. Performance with same level repetitions was somewhat higher than with identical repetitions — giving a small amount of support to the encoding variability hypothesis. Performance in the "different levels" group is rather difficult to explain — perhaps it is sufficient to comment that with different levels of analysis on the two exposures, recall performance is more or less intermediate between recall performance on the two contributing levels.

In general, Experiment V is in good agreement with a levels of analysis viewpoint. Although subjects were not expecting the recall task, memory performance was impressively high and was obviously influenced by the nature of the decision made in the perceptual task. I should point out that similar results to those found in Experiments IV and V have been reported by Jenkins and his colleagues (Hyde & Jenkins, 1969; Johnston & Jenkins, 1971) and by Schulman (1971).

Conclusions

In summary, a "levels of analysis" or "depth of processing" framework is suggested for the study of human memory. The main difference (and

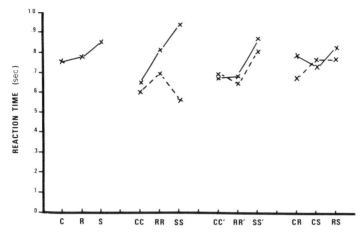

Fig. 7. Latency as a function of condition (Experiment V).

possibly advantage) in the levels approach compared to the multistore models, lies in the questions which one is led to ask. Some problems become more interesting and relevant while others become less so. In the former category, we want to know to what extent memory is simply a function of depth of encoding and to what extent further notions like retrieval cues, accessibility, and interitem organization are necessary. Also, how such broad factors as amount of attention paid to the stimulus and the compatibility of the stimulus with cognitive structures, interact in the analyzing process.

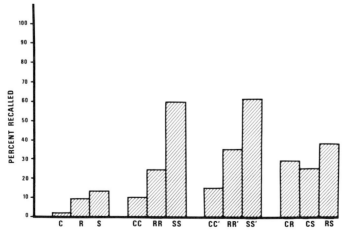

Fig. 8. Recall as a function of condition (Experiment V).

The questions of coding, capacity, and retention are less relevant in distinguishing different types of memory. By the present argument, primary memory coding depends on the processing modality which is being attended to. Capacity increases with processing depth, since we can make greater use of learned rules at deeper levels of analysis — thus, memory span in an unknown foreign language is only two or three words while sentence span in our own language is nearer 20 words. Third, it is suggested that retention is also a function of depth of processing.

Is this new framework different from the multistore approach in any important way or is it the same mixture served up differently? Obviously there are similarities, but there are also real differences, in my view. Problems of coding, capacity, and retention are less central in distinguishing types of memory. Also, it is less important to think of information being transferred from one stage of memory to the next. In fact, by the present view, information in LTS does not necessarily "pass through" STS as it does in most store models. By the present view, since memory is a by-product of an essentially perceptual system, STS is "off to the side" in the route an item takes from the environment to LTS, and whether we maintain the item at the STS level is very much an optional strategy rather than a structural feature.

In answer to Melton's (1963) question of whether memory is a continuum or a dichotomy, I would answer "in some ways both." The underlying perceptual analyzing systems are better described as continuous within any one modality, and memory is a continuum from the transient products of early analyses to the long-lasting products of later analyses. However, superimposed on this system is a second way in which we may retain stimuli — by continuing to attend to certain attributes of the stimuli. We do this (that is, keep items in PM) in cases where deeper processing is not necessary, when a rapid interaction with environmental stimuli is required and when it is necessary to hold on to the more literal aspects of stimuli because they are not particularly meaningful at a lower level.

Many of these ideas are vague and imprecise; it might be considered retrograde to propose a more general framework at this point. My view is that box models were also originally very general and very heuristic, but that they have since been taken too literally and thus many of the questions now asked may not be useful. So, as a personal preference, I am choosing to step back to a more general model which will encourage me to ask what I hope are more relevant questions.

Acknowledgments

The ideas outlined in this paper have benefited from discussions with several colleagues — especially Robert S. Lockhart and Michael J. Watkins. The author is also grateful for useful editorial comments.

The work was supported by Grant No. A8261 from the National Research Council of Canada.

References

Atkinson, R. C., & Shiffrin, R. M. Human memory: A proposed system and its control processes. In K. W. Spence and J. T. Spence (Eds.), *The psychology of learning and motivation,* Vol. II. New York: Academic Press, 1968. Pp. 89–195.

Atkinson, R. C., & Shiffrin, R. M. The control of short-term memory. *Scientific American,* 1971, **225**, No. 2, 82–89.

Baddeley, A. D. Short-term memory for word sequences as a function of acoustic, semantic and formal similarity. *Quarterly Journal of Experimental Psychology,* 1966, **18**, 362–365.

Baddeley, A. D. Estimating the short-term component in free recall. *British Journal of Psychology,* 1970, **61**, 13–15.

Bevan, W., & Dukes, W. F. Stimulus variation and recall: The role of belongingness. *American Journal of Psychology,* 1967, **80**, 309–312.

Broadbent, D. E. *Perception and communication.* New York: Pergamon Press, 1958.

Broadbent, D. E. *Decision and Stress.* New York: Academic Press, 1971.

Conrad, R. Acoustic confusions in immediate memory. *British Journal of Psychology,* 1964, **55**, 75–84.

Cooper, E. H., & Pantle, A. J. The total-time hypothesis in verbal learning. *Psychological Bulletin,* 1967, **68**, 221–234.

Craik, F. I. M. The fate of primary memory items in free recall. *Journal of Verbal Learning and Verbal Behavior,* 1970, **9**, 143–148.

Craik, F. I. M., & Lockhart, R. S. Levels of processing: A framework for memory research. *Journal of Verbal Learning & Verbal Behavior,* 1972, **11**, 671–684.

Craik, F. I. M., & Masani, P. A. Age and intelligence differences in coding and retrieval of word lists. *British Journal of Psychology,* 1969, **60**, 315–319.

Crannell, C. W., & Parrish, J. M. A comparison of immediate memory span for digits, letters and words. *Journal of Psychology,* 1957, **44**, 319–327.

Crowder, R. G. Short-term memory for words with a perceptual–motor interpolated activity. *Journal of Verbal Learning & Verbal Behavior,* 1967, **6**, 753–761.

Crowder, R. G., & Morton, J. Precategorical acoustic storage. *Perception & Psychophysics,* 1969, **5**, 365–373.

Gilson, E. Q., & Baddeley, A. D. Tactile short-term memory. *Quarterly Journal of Experimental Psychology,* 1969, **21**, 180–184.

Haber, R. N. How we remember what we see. *Scientific American,* 1970, **222**, No. 5, 104–112.

Hyde, T. S., & Jenkins, J. J. The differential effects of incidental tasks on the organization of recall of a list of highly associated words. *Journal of Experimental Psychology,* 1969, **82**, 472–481.

Jacoby, L. L., & Bartz, W. H. Rehearsal and transfer to LTM. *Journal of Verbal Learning & Verbal Behavior,* 1972, **11**, 561–565.

James, W. *Principles of psychology.* New York: Holt, 1890.

Johnston, C. D., & Jenkins, J. J. Two more incidental tasks that differentially affect associative clustering in recall. *Journal of Experimental Psychology,* 1971, **89**, 92–95.

Kintsch, W. *Learning, memory, and conceptual processes.* New York: Wiley, 1970.

Kroll, N. E. A., Parks, T., Parkinson, S. R., Bieber, S. L., & Johnson, A. L. Short-term memory while shadowing. Recall of visually and aurally presented letters. *Journal of Experimental Psychology,* 1970, **86**, 220–224.

Levy, B. A. Role of articulation in auditory and visual short-term memory. *Journal of Verbal Learning & Verbal Behavior,* 1971, **10**, 123–132.

Macnamara, J. Cognitive basis of language learning in infants. *Psychological Review,* 1972, **79**, 1–13.

Melton, A. W. Implications of short-term memory for a general theory of memory. *Journal of Verbal Learning & Verbal Behavior,* 1963, **2**, 1–21.

Murdock, B. B., Jr. Recent developments in short-term memory. *British Journal of Psychology,* 1967, **58**, 421–433.

Murdock, B. B., Jr. Four-channel effects in short-term memory. *Psychonomic Science,* 1971, **24**, 197–198.

Murdock, B. B., Jr. Short-term memory. In G. H. Bower (Ed.), *The psychology of learning and motivation,* Vol. V. New York: Academic Press, 1972. Pp. 67–127.

Parkinson, S. R., Parks, T., & Kroll, N. E. A. Visual and auditory short-term memory: The effects of phonemically similar auditory shadow material during the retention interval. *Journal of Experimental Psychology,* 1971, **87**, 274–280.

Peterson, L. R., & Johnson, S. T. Some effects of minimizing articulation on short-term retention. *Journal of Verbal Learning & Verbal Behavior,* 1971, **10**, 346–354.

Peterson, L. R., & Peterson, M. J. Short-term retention of individual verbal items. *Journal of Experimental Psychology,* 1959, **53**, 193–198.

Phillips, W. A., & Baddeley, A. D. Reaction time and short-term visual memory. *Psychonomic Science,* 1971, **22**, 73–74.

Posner, M. I. Abstraction and the process of recognition. In G. H. Bower and J. T. Spence (Eds.), *The psychology of learning and motivation,* Vol. III. New York: Academic Press, 1969. Pp. 152–179.

Reitman, J. S. Mechanisms of forgetting in short-term memory. *Cognitive Psychology,* 1971, **2**, 185–195.

Rundus, D. Analysis of rehearsal processes in free recall. *Journal of Experimental Psychology,* 1971, **89**, 63–77.

Savin, H. B., & Bever, T. G. The nonperceptual reality of the phoneme. *Journal of Verbal Learning & Verbal Behavior,* 1970, **9**, 295–302.

Schulman, A. I. Recognition memory for targets from a scanned word list. *British Journal of Psychology,* 1971, **62**, 335–346.

Selfridge, O. G., & Neisser, U. Pattern recognition by machine. *Scientific American,* 1960, **203**, No. 2, 60–68.

Shepard, R. N. Recognition memory for words, sentences, and pictures. *Journal of Verbal Learning & Verbal Behavior,* 1967, **6**, 156–163.

Shiffrin, R. M., & Atkinson, R. C. Storage and retrieval processes in long-term memory. *Psychological Review,* 1967, **76**, 179–193.

Shulman, H. G. Similarity effects in short-term memory. *Psychological Bulletin,* 1971, **75**, 399–415.

Sperling, G. The information available in brief visual presentations. *Psychological Monographs,* 1960, **74**, No. 11 (Whole No. 498).

Sutherland, N. S. Outlines of a theory of visual pattern recognition in animals and man. *Proceedings of the Royal Society, Series B,* 1968, **171**, 297–317.

Treisman, A. Monitoring and storage of irrelevant messages in selective attention. *Journal of Verbal Learning & Verbal Behavior,* 1964, **3**, 449–459.

Tulving, E., & Madigan, S. A. Memory and verbal learning. *Annual Review of Psychology,* 1970, **21**, 437–484.

Watkins, M. J. The characteristics and functions of primary memory. Unpublished Ph.D. thesis, University of London, 1972.

Waugh, N. C., & Norman, D. A. Primary memory. *Psychological Review,* 1965, **72**, 89–104.

SYMBOLING AND SEMANTIC CONDITIONING: ANTHROPOGENY

Gregory Razran[1]

Queens College of The City University of New York

Elsewhere (Razran, 1971, 1972) a view was set forth that higher animals have evolved four ascending varieties of cognitive learning reflected in (*a*) sensory preconditioning, (*b*) learned stimulus configuring, (*c*) insight or eduction, and (*d*) oddity learning. Cognitive status was accorded the first two varieties since, among other evidence, they become manifest to a significant degree only in birds and mammals; it was accorded to the last two because they are demonstrably even more difficult evolutionary attainments (Krushinsky, 1960; Warren, 1960). The respective generalities of the learning varieties were said to be: (*a*) the uncovering of existing and obvious spatial and temporal relations, (*b*) the formation of more or less enduring suprasummative unitary configurations, (*c*) the discovery of new and unobvious relations, and (*d*) the formation of more or less enduring concepts.

Learning to *configure* was held to be the key objective schema of the varieties and was equated with learning to *perceive*. (Concepts were considered "configures of configures" or "percepts of percepts.") Moreover, it was hypothesized that this learning is an outcome of integrated proprioceptive and interoceptive sequences of interacting sensory-orienting reactions and that perception is thereby a recode of direct primary information that an organism receives — a second-signal system, Pavlov's second being

[1] Deceased.

67

really a third [cf. traditional "motor theories of consciousness," Dunlap, 1914; Lange (a Russian), 1888, 1914; Max, 1937; Washburn, 1916]. The learned configures were termed neurocognitive in the sense that they are putatively neural, typically also phenomenal, but not behavioral events — specifically, that their *sui generis* neural patterns preexist, postexist, and presumably govern their specific phenomenal imagery; but, while they are equally outcomes of specific antecedent behavior and affect specific subsequent behavior, they are not themselves effector reactions. Nonconfigured conditioning of behavioral (and neural) reactions, fully evident in bony fish, higher-animal decorticates, and unaware human subjects (Ayrapet'yants, 1952; Hefferline, Keenan, & Hartford, 1959) was, on the other hand, judged to be nonperceptual, as were the conditioned *chaining* of reactions and *conditioned* modifications of percepts. Note that cognitive learning is predicated on organized perceptual organization. Unorganized sensory cognition or bare consciousness is granted genetic but not immediate pragmatic learning efficacy, which, more generally, disputes its total abrogation by Gestaltists and its total severance from perception by Gibson (1966), let alone the traditional creeds that perception is merely a complex cumulation of the essences of sensations.

My present view of animal learning is thus a long way from my early avowals (Razran, 1933, 1935) that such learning is all ultimately reducible to simple conditioning. The basic tenets upheld now and intimated for some time on the basis of subsequent evidence are:

(*a*)   Higher animals have evolved a superstructure of cognitive–perceptual learning functioning vis-à-vis simple conditioning in accordance with principles of evolutionary novelty along with that of continuity.

(*b*)   The essence of the superstructure is the formation of percepts, and its neural substratum is the evolution of newer afferent systems.

(*c*)   Its restricted neural base vis-à-vis the massive one of conditioning precludes, however, its being overriding in the learning of subprimates, and is further limited by the longer latency of the evocation of perceptual reactions.

(*d*)   No mechanism other than perception need be invoked to account for its several ascending levels of concrete manifestation.

In fine: *Higher-animal learning is an evolved hierarchical dyad of conditioning and perceiving,* similar in ultimate origination — both associative in the sense of involving juxtaposed interactions of reactions — but widely different in outcome. Pavlov's "associations form and govern gestalten [*Wednesdays,* 1949, Vol. 3, p. 46; original date, November 23, 1935]" should, however, be extended to "once formed, gestalten govern and form associations." Compare Tolman (1959): "Although I became convinced that the whole in some way governs its parts, these wholes, I felt, were acquired by learning and were not autochthonously given [p. 95]."

On the other hand, my view of human learning has changed less radically: Its birth cry was there in the 1930s. My very first series of experiments proclaimed, contrary to then prevalent dicta, the basic role of cognition in conditioning and added the theoretic that through *"the individual's experience, the sum-total of his symbolic 'past' has gradually become dominant over his somatic and visceral 'present'* [Razran, 1935, p. 120; italics in the original]." And later, as over a course of almost 40 years I became increasingly committed to the general doctrine of emergent evolutionary levels of learning, I came to weigh more and more the special thesis that man's symboling is a *sui generis* realm of learning, in addition to the conditioning–perceiving dyad – again, in accordance with evolutionary novelty along with that of continuity. Recent laboratory delvings, both East and West, into the quality of the developmental dynamics of learning in early human ontogeny has bolstered my pinpointing the man–brute divide, even as animal ecology, ethology, and behavioral genetics led me increasingly closer to the generalization that the *unlearned contains and models all that is learned, even as the learned modifies and models all that is unlearned and may through natural selection alter its very basis of genic pools.*

Having bared my general tack of the learning mind, I am now ready to probe my specific topic – a comprehensive systematic question and a much qualified answer. The question is: Does evidence of semantic conditioning disclose basic mechanisms of symboling? The answer is that, in the main, it does only when the conditioning is nonperceptual and/or the evoked reaction involuntary. Otherwise, when subjects perceive the CS–US relations and the reactions are under voluntary control (which to me means symbolic control), obtained results may be not objective disclosures of underlying symbolic structure but outcomes of its prior functions, which is what Maltzman, working for years with the perception-ridden GSR (Cook & Harris, 1937; Dawson & Grings, 1968; Dawson & Satterfield, 1969) has come to conclude (Maltzman, 1971; see also Maltzman, 1968; Maltzman, Langdon & Feeney, 1970). But, obviously, this does not pertain either to studies (like mine; Razran, 1939a and later) in which perceptual relations were invariably masked or in which CRs are not readily controllable.

Moreover, there is a mass of East–and West evidence that man's perceptual and symbolic learning does not always subordinate concomitant operation of laws of simple conditioning – either because, for some reason, available perception is not used or because, for some reason, it is dominated by conditioning – so that conventional perceptual–symbolic learning may, at times, corroborate conditioning evidence of semantic structure. Maltzman's (1971) position that "the principles of conditioning developed in

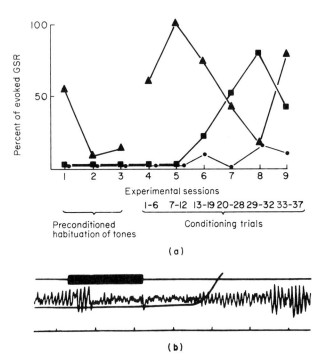

Fig. 1. (a) Sample GSR conditioning of one of ten subjects to a tone 10 dB below liminal awareness in Gershuni's laboratory: (▲) reactions to the control supraliminal tone; (■) reactions to the subliminal tone; (●) spontaneous reactions. Note that the subliminal tone evoked no preconditioning reaction (needed no habituation), and that the subliminal conditioning, appearing after 12 CR training trials and reaching its peak at 30, was first manifested in response to the supraliminal control tone. (From Chistovich, 1949.) (b) Sample conditioning of GSR and occipital–parietal alpha blocking in one of six subjects to a tone 6 dB below liminal awareness. Lines from above: administration of tone, alpha blocking GSR, and time in seconds. (From Gershuni, 1955.) But there are no equivalent semantic experiments in GSR conditioning.

animal studies cannot be applied in any straightforward fashion to conditioning, simple or semantic, in normal humans possessing speech, or, more accurately, the ability to think" [p. 90]" is not in my book. Nor is there valid evidence for his attempt to coordinate thinking and semantic generalization with the operation of (*a*) the orienting reflex, which is primarily a correlate of liminal consciousness (Gershuni, 1949; Sokolov, 1958) and may even be noncognitive (Makarov, 1959) and of (*b*) Ukhtomski's "dominance," which is a general concept of neurobehavioral interaction (Fedoseyev, 1963, p. 756; Razran, 1971). It should also be noted here that two Soviet experimenters (Chistovich, 1949; Gershuni, 1955) convincingly conditioned the GSR of 16 subjects to sounds 10 and 6 dB below awareness. The results, presented in Fig. 1, would hold, one supposes, also with subliminal verbal stimuli and consequent semantic testing — which, unfortunately, has so far not been tried.

Put differently, whereas the experimental base of true-blue — that is, noncognitive semantic conditioning is regrettably narrow, its unique evidence suggests a theory of symboling that coheres with my general evolutionary doctrine of learning, and that for the moment will be only intimated as predicating "a *sui generis* learned matrix of emergent neurocognitive semantic configures specially related to special behavioral reactions." Elaboration and defense of the theory will follow consideration of five selected samples of such evidence (with apologies for the Russians' single-subject style of presenting results and the small number of subjects in some of my studies.

Evidence

1. Semantic versus Phonetic (and Phonetographic) Generalization

Figure 2 (from Shvarts, 1954) best illustrates, perhaps, the distinctiveness of the two types of generalizations. The figure is a sample record of the vasoconstrictive CRs of nine subjects with a 10°C thermal stimulus as the US, auditory presentation of the Russian word *dom* house as the CS, and the Russian word *dym* [smoke] and English word *house* [the meaning of which the subjects knew very well] as the generalization stimuli. The first, second,

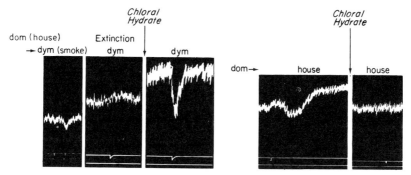

Fig. 2. Developmental dynamics of phonetographic and semantic CR generalization and the effects of chloral hydrate on each. (From Shvarts, 1954.)

and third panels from the left show, respectively, that the generalization to *dym* appeared in early stages of CR training, disappeared in the later stages, and reappeared after injections of chloral hydrate. In contrast, the fourth and fifth panels disclose, respectively, that the generalization to *house* appeared first when the CR was fairly well established and disappeared after the chloral hydrate injections. Similar results were obtained by the experimenter with conditioned lowering of light sensitivity, different conditioned and generalization words (such as *doktor* [physician], *diktor* [announcer], and *vrach* [physician]), and with four other subjects. The simple logic that semantic learning is a capstone of human learning was thus borne out with the systematic addition that it is a *superstructure* and not a *supercedure* of nonsemantic learning. Add to this corroborative data of the indubitable prevalence of semantic generalization in normal states of normal adults, its positive correlation with age and intelligence and negative correlation with pathological states and temporary disturbances (Luria & Vinogradova, 1959; Peastral, 1961; Razran, 1939b, 1949a, b, c; Riess, 1946; Shicko, 1969; Vinogradova & Eysler, 1959). How fruitful it would be to initiate studies relating the roles of the two levels of generalization to ontogenetic linguistic acquisition!

2. *Generalization along Logical Association Categories*

Razran (1949b, c, d, e) found such generalization in the salivary conditioning of 47 college students, using nine categories and 25 different word pairs. The means of percentages of generalization to generalization words (more than to control[2] words) in terms of the relations of the *generalization words to the conditioned words* were: *supraordinates,* 43; *contrasts,* 43; *coordinates,* 39; *whole–parts,* 38; *part–whole,* 36; *predicatives,* 35; and *subordinates,* 24; differences over 10% were, as a rule, statistically significant at $p < .01$. Note that, except for *contrasts, coordinates,* and, to an extent *predicatives,* the categories must obviously be reversed with respect to the relations of the *conditioned words to the generalization words,* and that the use of the former or latter designation depends on whether the generalization is effected during original CS training or subsequent GS (generalization stimulus) testing.[3] A. Ya. Fedorov and V. D. Volkova reported related data in Krasnogorsky's laboratory (Krasnogorsky, 1954).

[2] Feather (1965) is in error stating that I did not use *control* words; see Razran (1949c, p. 252, line 3), among others.

[3] See Cramer (1970) for recent data and some discussion of the problem, and notice that the former designation was used in my original reports of the experiments and the latter in a 1952 summary of them.

And Whitmarsh and Bousefield (1961), using the word pairs of one of my three experiments (Razran, 1949b), found a product-moment correlation of .70 "significant at less than .0001 level of confidence" between their predicted index of associative generalization in 600 subjects and the extent of my subjects' salivary generalization.

3. Conditioned Response Semantics and Grammar

Table 1 (from Razran, 1952) presents the results of a pilot study in which four American students were conditioned to salivate at the sight of three five-word Russian sentences, the meanings of which they learned beforehand, and then were tested for relative generalization to each word as percentages of the generalization to all five words. As may be seen, the amount of generalization reflected the grammatical and not lexical character of the words: 35, 30, and 46% to *predicative verbs*; 9, 18, and 14% to *subjects*; 27, 26, and 28% to *direct objects*; and 11, 13, and 12% to the *qualifying adjectives* of the *objects*. The differences between the *predicative verbs* plus the *direct objects,* and the *subjects* plus the *qualifying adjectives* were statistically significant with $p < .01$. Moreover, no differences to speak of, in the conditionability of the individual words were found in a control group[4] of four subjects so that the obtained differences in the experimental group were obviously a function of sentence membership.

Two other experiments in the category were performed by El'kin (1955, 1957) in the Soviet Union. In the first experiment, 30 university students were conditioned to withdraw their fingers (electric shock as the US) at the spoken sentences *Student vyderzhal ekzamen* [the student/passed/the examination], *Vklyuchayu tok* [I am turning on/the shock] and *Rukopis' prochitana* [the manuscript was read]. The relative generalizations to the single words in the first sentence were 7% to *Student,* 58% to *vyderzhal,* and 35% to *ekzamen* (respective absolute generalizations of 10, 87, and 52%) and thus correspond roughly to my findings. However, the generalizations of the second sentence were 100% to both words and of the third none to either — putative evidence of differing semantic word–sentence relationships. In the second experiment, blinking (US, air puff) was the CR, nine two- to five-word sentences the CSs, and 25 10- to 16-year-old school children the subjects. The main results show that the generalization was greatest to the *predicate verbs* and that when the word order in the

---

[4] The use of a control group was regrettably omitted in page 280 of my book (Razran, 1971) as was, in addition, the words "of relative" before "transfer" on lines 6 and 10 of the same page. Moreover, there is an error on the use of the control group on the original 1952 report of the experiment.

TABLE 1

Mean Percentage of *Relative Generalization of Conditioned Salivation in Four College Students from Three Five-Word Russian Sentences to the Individual Words (Grammatical Parts) of the Sentences,*[a], [b] *Subjects were told the meanings of the sentences and words but misinformed about the purpose of the experiment.*

Sentences	Mean percentage of relative generalization to:					
	Qualifier of subject	Subject	Predicative verb	Indirect object	Qualifier of direct object	Direct object
Ya dal yemu novy myach [I gave him a new ball.]		Ya [I] 9%	Dal [gave] 35%	Yemu [him] 18%	Novy [new] 11%	Myach [ball] 27%
Belokuraya devochka nashla zolotoye pero [The blond girl found a golden pen.]	Belokuraya [The blond] 13%	Devochka [girl] 18%	Nashla [found] 30%		Zolotoye [golden] 13%	Pero [pen] 26%
Ona khochet kupit' sery kashelyok [She wants to buy a gray purse.]		Ona [she] 14%	Khochet kupit' [wants to buy] 46%		Sery [gray] 12%	Koshelyok [purse] 28%

[a] Subjects were told the meanings of the sentences and words but misinformed about the purpose of the experiment.

[b] From G. Razran, Experimental semantics. *Transactions of the New York Academy of Sciences*, 1952, **14**, 171–177.

sentences was reversed (which in inflected Russian is still grammatical and conveys the same meaning) generalization decrements were found only in the 10- to 12-year-old group but not in the older group.

4. Sentenial versus Propositional Generalization

Razran's (1949a, 1952) pilot results, presented in Table 2 are, also regrettably, the only ones in the category. Four college students were conditioned to salivate at the sight of sentences "Poverty is degrading," "Roosevelt will be elected," and "Socialism is desirable," and tested for generalization to seven variations of each sentence. The variations, involving similarity in words, meanings, or both, yielded three generalization sentences affirming the propositions (or total meanings) of the conditioned sentences and four negating them. As may be seen, propositional affirmation and negation were the overriding determiners of the amount of generalization: 59%, for instance, to "Wealth is uplifting" but only 37% to "Poverty is not degrading" and only 33% to "Poverty is uplifting," with the differences between the first and the last two sentences statistically significant as the 1% level. The findings were similar with the two other conditioned sentences and other variations of the generalization sentences.

TABLE 2

Mean Generalization of Salivation in Four College Students Conditioned to Sentences: "Poverty is degrading," "Roosevelt will be elected," and "Socialism is desirable"[a, b]

Generalization sentences			Logical formula	Percentage of generalization	Mean percentage
We$\longrightarrow$ Ul;	De$\longrightarrow$ Df;	Ca$\longrightarrow$ Ud	S'CP' $\checkmark$	59; 53; 63	58
We$+\!\!\rightarrow$ Dg;	De$+\!\!\rightarrow$ El;	Ca$+\!\!\rightarrow$ Ds	S'C'P $\checkmark$	49; 50; 58	52
Po$+\!\!\rightarrow$ Ul;	Ro$+\!\!\rightarrow$ Df;	So$+\!\!\rightarrow$ Ud	SC'P' $\checkmark$	44; 41; 51	45
We$\longrightarrow$ Dg;	De$\longrightarrow$ El;	Ca$\longrightarrow$ Ds	S'CP X	38; 31; 39	36
Po$+\!\!\rightarrow$ Dg;	Ro$+\!\!\rightarrow$ El;	So$+\!\!\rightarrow$ Ds	SC'P X	37; 28; 34	33
Po$\longrightarrow$ Ul;	Ro$\longrightarrow$ Df;	So$\longrightarrow$ Ud	SCP' X	33; 36; 30	33
We$+\!\!\rightarrow$ Ul;	De$+\!\!\rightarrow$ Df;	Ca$+\!\!\rightarrow$ Ud	S'C'P' X	19; 28; 27	25

[a] Each entry in the third column is a mean of 64 measurements, 16 for each of the four subjects in the experiment.

Abbreviations and symbols: We—wealth; Ul—uplifting; De—Dewey; Df—defeated; Ca—capitalism: Ud—undesirable; Dg—degrading; El—Elected; Ds—desirable; Po—poverty; Ro—Roosevelt; So—socialism; S—subject; C—copula; P—predicate; S', C', P'—reversed subjects, copulae, and predicates; $\rightarrow$, is or will be; $+\!\!\rightarrow$, is not or will not be; $\checkmark$, proposition affirmed; X, proposition negated.

[b] From G. Razran, Sentential and propositional generalization of salivary conditioning to verbal stimuli. *Science,* 1949, **109**, 447–448.

5. *Conditioned Semantics of Evaluations and Concepts Formation*

In Volkova's (1953) oft-quoted experiment, a 13-year-old Russian boy was conditioned to salivate at the spoken word *khorosho* [good, well] and to differentiate it from *plokho* [poorly, bad, badly] and then was tested, at intervals of 2 to 8 min, with three- to five-word sentences. Nine of the sentences were expected to win approval, and six, disapproval. Examples of the first kind of sentences were: "The Soviet army was victorious," "The pioneer helps his comrade," "The fisherman caught many fish." Examples of the second were: "The fascists destroyed many cities," "My friend is seriously ill," "The student offended his teacher." Clear-cut differences between the generalizations to the "approval" and "disapproval" sentences were disclosed: 14 to 24 drops of saliva in 30 sec to the first; 0 to 2 drops to the second. Acker and Edwards (1964) replicated in large measure Volkova's study with 24 subjects and conditioned vasoconstriction. The US was a 110-dB white noise, the CS the sounds of the word *good* for half the subjects and *bad* for the other half, and the generalization stimuli were words rated, correspondingly, on Osgood's seven-point semantic differential scale of "good–bad" before the conditioning. The results were unmistakable: The conditioning increased the mean vasoconstriction to the generalization words from .031 to .062 $\mu\lambda/10$ cm^3 with $p < .001$. Interestingly, the conditioning had no effect on the subjects' subsequent ratings of the words which may well indicate that the generalization was noncognitive.

Brotsky, experimenting with the GSR (US, a 100-dB white noise) in 200 college students divided into 25 subgroups, demonstrated semantic generalization from conditioned words *Oldsmobile, Plymouth, Pontiac, Mercury,* and *Ford* to the nonconditioned word *car* — from "concept instants" to a "concept name," to use Underwood and Richardson's (1956) designation. Her findings are most instructive for two reasons: (*a*) The CS–US relations were masked to the extent that a number of subjects could not verbalize them postexperimentally, (*b*) the findings were clearly not an outcome of the operation of the orienting reflex as Maltzman assumes. Brotsky's (1968) summary statement reads: "Although *S*s who produced large GSRs to the first US (high OR *S*s) produced large GSRs to other auditory stimuli, they showed neither stronger conditioning, and generalization, nor more adequate verbal reports than low OR *S*s [p. 244]."

Theory

The five categories of evidence were obviously selected for their unique theoretic import. But, unfortunately, although I initiated the study of the first four, and the fifth is in accord with my thinking, I left the evidence of the third and fourth in pilot states and left off experimental probing of the field entirely by 1952. And others, who continued, were, apparently, too distant from my theoretical approach to test my special findings. Only the semantic phase of my general CR claim that generalization is effected during subsequent generalization testing and not during original CR training — since modified by me with respect to nonsemantic learning (Razran, 1971, pp. 150–151) — has undergone considerable experimentation and been verified to a considerable extent. The core of the approach — to extend earlier indications — is that *meanings are more or less enduring* sui generis *neurocognitive configures and semantic conditioning is a noncognitive means of disclosing their structures — is a locator or tracer of their topography and morphology — but not an intrinsic principle of their cognitive modes of functioning.* [Note, however, that meanings, like percepts, may be modified by noncognitive simple conditioning (Staats & Staats, 1957; and others).]

More specifically, the approach (*a*) eschews common American views that the referential relation of meaning is an inferred mediational concept of linear R_G–S_G behavioral parametrics, and (*b*) posits that the referent of the relation is itself a percept or concept and the outcome is, accordingly, a higher-level neurocognition than is perception. Pavlov's (1932) view that "with the advent of the second-signal system a new principle of [learned] neural action is introduced [p. 34]" overlies — it is held — Beritoff's (1932) thesis that "supplementary neural centers are activated when higher animals learn to respond to a configure without responding to its components [p. 43]."

The behavioral phase of human symboling is also very special. First, its ultimate units, or symbols, are a particular superimposed tier of microeffector reactions that increase rapidly in early ontogeny and exceed many times the macroreactions of normal man's soma and viscera by early maturity. Second, there is the consideration that symbols come to outpace their perceptual referents and resultant meanings — specifically, that memorial symboling becomes more and more common than on-the-spot perceiving and, more generally, that as *afferent* perceptual and semantic neurocognition becomes more and more configured and abstract in quality, *efferent* symbols are able to match it only through increases in quantity. And, of course, the amalgam of microeffector action and neurocognition is *sui generis* — the crux of man's very special overtowering evolution.

Chomsky and Lenneberg

Putting it differently, behavioristic views that the genesis and essence of language are basically an outcome of simple conditioning may not need to be so negated that they are overridingly regarded as an unfolding of a species-specific generative grammar (Chomsky, 1957, 1959, 1965, 1966 [Allen & van Buren, 1971]; Lenneberg, 1967, 1968). The thesis that "the unlearned contains and models all that is learned" is a complement and not a contrary of "the learned modifies and models all that is unlearned" and older and less absolutistic concepts of "innate disposition" and "maturational readiness" seem more fitting than "species specificity." Nor is there reason to assume that innate programming is a more complex mechanism than learned neuronal integration, to ignore the common lore that the ratio of the learned to the innate is a growing positive function of evolution, and sidestep the evidence and logic of views that higher-level human (to an extent, also higher-animal) learning is largely configural in quale (cf. Brown & Fraser, 1964). More specifically, the impressive challenge of the Chomsky–Lenneberg "revolution" is counterweighed by a number of discordant considerations:

1. Language has been on this planet too short a time to have evolved an overriding *sui generis* innateness.

2. A modicum of it was recently taught to two chimpanzees suggesting that its putative innateness should not be severed from corresponding prehuman antecedents in Cartesian manner.

3. Recent laboratory experiments, from both East and West, disclose, contrary to earlier beliefs, that man's learning is quantitatively and qualitatively superior to that of other primates, right after birth. Bystroletova (1954; see Fig. 3) reported temporal classical conditioning in 12 human neonates after two to six days (evident in macaques only after several weeks or even months (see Voronin, 1948)). Siqueland and Lipsitt (1966; see Fig. 4) demonstrated clear-cut reversal of operant conditioning in 46 neonates less than 4 days old. And there is evidence of perceptual learning in infants several months of age (Lyakh, 1968, among others; see Fig. 5; Razran, 1971).

4. The pacemaker of language is the neurocognition of meaning which, even more than the neurocognition of perception, is primarily a learned system of afferently organized configures (structures, syntaxes) — a system that governs, but by no means abrogates, the operation of subsidiary efferent conditioning and that, one may well assume, is much more governing now than in primal anthropogeny.

5. Underlying innate determinants do not foreclose the heuristic and pragmatic import of the parameters of learning which, it may well be argued, are themselves evolutionary mechanisms in the sense that, through natural selection, they convert remote ontogenetic acquisitions into erstwhile phyletic bequests (Razran, 1973, in press).

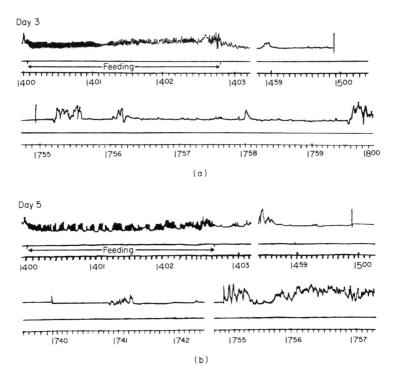

Day 3

Day 5

(a)

(b)

Fig. 3. Prefeeding, sucking, and head reactions of neonate K. on the third and fifth days of life: 4-hr feeding schedule. (a) Reactions on the third day. (b) Reactions on the fifth day. Upper line in (a) and (b): sucking and head reactions; marks in middle lines of upper segments of (a) and (b): — beginning and end of feeding. Lower line — time in 5-sec units. Note the clear-cut appearance of sucking and head reactions about 20 sec before the 18:00 (6:00 p.m.) feeding on the third day and increased and persistent manifestations of them about 5.4 min before the feeding on the fifth day. (From Bystroletova, 1954.)

Fig. 4. (a, b, c) Simple, differential, and reversal reinforcement conditioning and extinction in 46 human neonates less than 4 days old: (———) experimental group; (- - - -) control group. Head turning, elicited by ipsilateral touch of the subjects' cheeks, was the reinforced reaction and a dextrose solution the reinforcer. Only one cheek was stimulated in the groups of (a) and (c), and bottom panels; both cheeks alternatively in the group of (b). The number of experimental and control subjects in the group of (c) was 8. See page 80. (From Siqueland & Lipsitt, 1966.)

Fig. 5. Sample record of 2- to 4-month-old infants learning to produce vowels "a" and "oo" (Russian "y") through imitating experimenter's silent articulations. See page 80.

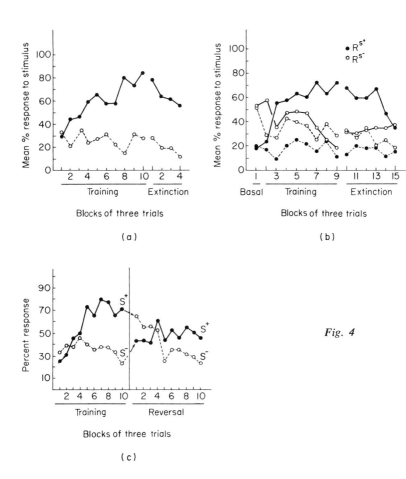

Mean % response to stimulus

Training   Extinction

Blocks of three trials

(a)

Mean % response to stimulus

● R$^{S^+}$
○ R$^{S^-}$

Basal   Training   Extinction

Blocks of three trials

(b)

Percent response

S$^+$
S$^-$

S$^+$
S$^-$

Training   Reversal

Blocks of three trials

(c)

Fig. 4

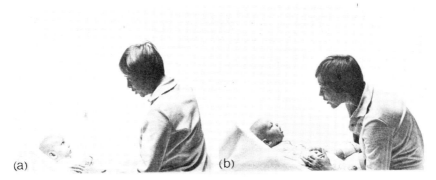

(a)   (b)

Fig. 5

80

Overall, like the Gestaltists and ethologists before them, Cartesian psycholinguists seem to suffer from an overkill of the thesis which they negate and a functional fixity toward the antithesis which they offer.

Anthropogeny

It is thus that I venture a third approach, or rather a lead to it, in which I will permit myself wide "inductive leaps." Such "leaps" are a "must" not only because of scanty definitive experimental data but also because, as an evolutionist, I would like to extrapolate the anthropogeny of language which, needless to say, is inadequately paralleled by its ontogeny and is itself no longer within experimental reach. Five putative anthropogenetic stages will be posited and briefly explicated.

1. The Beginning: Conditioned Communications

Language began when microeffector vocal (and some gestural) reactions became associatively linked to learned percepts and concepts. Prelinguistic man must certainly have had a large store of each category and their initial linkage was effected, I assume, through simple conditioning in the sense that the relation between the categories was unperceived and thus lacked the *sine qua non* of perceptual learning. Yet this unperceived conditioning was clearly the crucial springboard of the specificity of language — "efferentation" and consequent extraorganismic communication of the learned perceptual–conceptual realm of neurocognition, which only man evolved in his natural habitat and without which this learning is of no import to group interaction and "social heritage."

2. Semantic Neurocognition

Soon, however, the conditioned microeffector–percept linkage was perceived — first, no doubt, by the communicatee but then also by the communicant — and represented as such in the top echelons of the brain. And thereby came into being an overriding *sui generis* realm of referential and replicative semantic neurocognition which, unlike that of perception, is based not on the interaction of environment-evoked sensory-orienting reactions but on that of internalized percepts and concepts and readily reproducible stocks of symbolic microeffectors turned into vehicles of meaning and not just of communication. The evolutionary cycle of mind was thus, in the main, completed: from behavior to on-the-spot perceptual cognition in higher animals, and from that cognition plus symbolic behavior to symbolic cognition in man. Or — forgive my rhetoric — the domicile of man's mind became much more a time-bound biography than a space-bound contemporaneity. To quote a Sechenov statement of 80-year vintage: "Man juxtaposes not only his experience of childhood, adolescence and old age, not only what he saw, say, in America, and here, in Moscow, but also the life of today with that of antiquity . . . he becomes a part, so to speak, of the life of the universe without leaving the narrow limits of his terrestrial existence [1892, p. 201]." And let me stress that the symbol–referent relation of semantic neurocognition is not a signal but a configure akin to Selz's 1913 view that *"Sachverhältnis* [relational fact] is unified knowledge of a thing-in-relation to another and not either the thing by itself or the relation by itself."

3. Higher-Order Sememes

Semantic configures paralleling behavioral symbols have in time become integrated into higher semantic units, each subserved by a manifold of related symbols, in accordance with the natural trend of neurocognition to become more and more abstracted, which data of conditioned semantic generalization corroborate. Moreover, while one may plausibly assume that sememes, like percepts, are represented by specific patterns (or even loci) of brain action, there is a modicum of objective evidence that they, unlike percepts, are void of phenomenal imagery, in line with the meaning analyses of the Würzburg School, Binet (1903), Bühler (1907), and Woodworth (1906). In one of my experiments (Razran, 1949c), the generalization of the salivary conditioning of nine subjects along logical association categories were significantly increased by prior practice of concordant controlled word–word associations and significantly decreased when the practiced associations were discordant ($p < .01$ in both cases). Yet no imagery of the induced semantic relations (coordinate, supraordinate, subordinate) were reported by any subject in a postexperimental questionnaire — only "vague feelings" of "directed thought."

4. Sentence Formation and Correct Syntax

Sentences are outcomes of configural learning: neither bequeathed heritages (Chomsky, Lenneberg) nor formed through simple association of ideas (Paul, 1886) or simple S–R conditioning (Mowrer, 1954). Their formation was very slow in coming and correct syntax much slower. I would speculate that for tens of thousands of years the anthropogeny of language was pre-sentential naming, mostly of contentives. In like vein, I question the view that single words in early ontogeny are in essence non-differentiated sentences.[5] To my mind, a more plausible assumption is that *they often are composites of a word and nonsymbolic perceptual imagery* (and words evoke, of course, sentences that had been learned). And correct syntax is, I submit, learned through corrected interactions of individual grammatical sememes and constrains by formed sentences, the basic mechanism of which are presaged in the lower-level learning of perceptual organization and configural conditioning (Petrov, 1941, among others; see Fig. 6).

5. *Propositions and Verbal Evaluations and Concepts*

The generalization of propositions or total meanings of sentences (Razran), of "good–bad" evaluations (Volkova, and Acker and Edwards), and of "concept instances" to a "concept name" (Brotsky) may well disclose the highest rung of the semantic structure of words (phonemes), phrases, sentences and propositions which, in the main, are in line with evidence of *clustering and structures in verbal associations* (Bousefield, 1953; Deese, 1962, 1965; and others). And I am tempted to add that my specific data of total meaning or propositional generalization cohere with Wundt's 1900 thesis of subject–predicate *Gesamtvorstellung*.

My final word will note several wishes and suggestions for the future: (*a*) that linguists and experimental psychologists continue to interrelate with one another and neither abandon the concept of learned integration; (*b*) that true-blue noncognitive semantic conditioning be fructified and multiplied and that, irrespective of theoretic penchants, psychologists and linguists see its apt merit as an indirect means of disclosing and separating the deep structure of semantics from the surface one of phonology, particularly when it is used comparatively in ascending ontogeny, varying intellectual levels, disruptive pathology, and temporary effects of drugs and related physiological

---

[5] Lenneberg's (1967) statement that "there is overgeneralization" when "at the beginning word such as *daddy* covers a different and wider range of objects than later [p. 281]" is, he will admit, a *non sequitur*. How does "beginning overgeneralization" differ from "beginning nondifferentiation" in all learning, when, say, a puppy does not at first recognize specifically the sight and smell of his master?

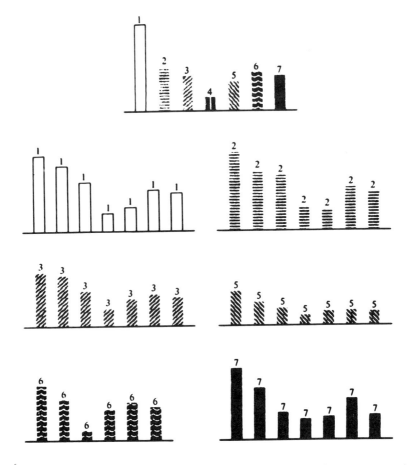

Fig. 6. Dynamic stereotypes in the salivary conditioning of a dog to one negative and six positive CSs. Column heights denote CR magnitudes. Top: results of 17 months of a trained sequential pattern to different CSs. Other panels show the pattern of magnitudes when only one CS was used throughout. 1, metronome of 150 beats/min; 2, a noise; 3, a crackling sound; 4, differentiated metronome of 75 beats; 5, light; 6, electric bell; 7, bubbling water. (From Petrov, 1941.)

and psychological agents and states; (c) that psychologists of verbal association do not stray too far from those of conditioning; (d) that neuropsychology seek the loci and patterns of enduring neurocognition and (e) that all sign on mind in evolution — first learning, then perc p.ion and imagery, and then language and meaning (thought). To quote a noted Soviet evolutionist: "The second-signal system did not drop from heaven [Orbeli, 1950, p. 15]."

References[6]

Acker, L. E., & Edwards, A. E. Transfer of vasoconstriction over a bipolar dimension. *Journal of Experimental Psychology,* 1964, **67,** 1–16.

Allen, J. P. B., and van Buren, P. *Chomsky: Selected readings,* London: Oxford Univ. Press, 1971.

Ayrapet'yants, E. Sh. *Higher nervous activity and the receptors of internal organs.* Moscow: Akademiya Nauk SSSR, 1952.

Beritoff, J. S. (Beritov, I. S.) *Individually acquired activity of the central nervous system.* Tbilisi: GIZ, 1932.

Binet, L. *L'étude expérimentale de l'intelligence.* Paris: Alcan, 1903.

Bousefield, W. A. The concurrence of clustering in the recall of randomly arranged associates. *Journal of General Psychology,* 1953, **49,** 229–240.

Brotsky S. J. Classical conditioning of the galvanic skin response to verbal concepts. *Journal of Experimental Psychology,* 1968, **76,** 244–263.

Brown, R., & Fraser, C. The acquisition of syntax. *Monographs of the Society for Research in Child Development,* 1964, **29**(No. 92), 43–78.

Bühler, K. Tatsachen und Probleme zu einer Psychologic der Denkenvorgange. I. Über Gedanken. *Archiv für die Gesamte Psychologie,* 1907, **9,** 297–365.

Bystroletova, G. N. Formation of conditioned reflexes to time intervals in neonates during periodic feeding. *Zhurnal Vysshey Nervnoy Deyatel'nosti imeni I. P. Pavlova,* 1954, **4,** 601–609.

Chistovich, L. A. The formation of galvanic skin reflexes to unaware auditory stimuli *Izvestiya Akademii Nauk SSSR, Seriya Biologicheskaya,* 1949, **5,** 570–583.

Chomsky, N. *Syntactic structures.* The Hague: Mouton, 1957.

Chomsky, N. A review of *Verbal Behavior* by B. F. Skinner. *Language,* 1959, **35,** 26–58.

Chomsky, N. *Aspects of the theory of syntax.* Cambridge, Massachusetts: M.I.T. Press, 1965.

Chomsky, N. *Topics in the theory of generative grammar.* The Hague: Mouton, 1966.

Cook, S. W., & Harris, R. E. The verbal conditioning of the galvanic skin response. *Journal of Experimental Psychology,* 1937, **21,** 202–210.

Cramer, P. Semantic generalization: IAR locus and instructions. *Journal of Experimental Psychology,* 1970, **83,** 266–273.

Dawson, M. E., & Grings, W. W. Comparison of classical and relational conditioning. *Journal of Experimental Psychology,* 1968, **76,** 227–231.

Dawson, M. E., & Satterfield, G. H. Can human GSR conditioning occur without relational learning. *Proceedings of the 77th Annual Convention of the American Psychological Association,* 1969, 69–70.

Deese, J. On the structure of associative meaning. *Psychological Review,* 1962, **69,** 161–165.

Deese, J. *The structure of association in language and thought.* Baltimore: The Johns Hopkins Press, 1965.

Dunlap, K. *An outline of psychology.* Baltimore: Johns Hopkins Press, 1914.

El'kin, D. G. The characteristics of conditioned reflexes to complex verbal stimuli. *Voprosy Psikhologii,* 1955, **1**(4), 79–89.

El'kin, D. G. Conditioned reflexes to complex verbal stimuli in school children. In

---

[6] All articles in Soviet Union publications are written in Russian unless otherwise noted. The titles are translated here.

B. G. Anan'yev, A. N. Leont'yev, A. R. Luria, N. A. Menchinskaya, S. L. Rubin-shteyn, A. A. Smirnov, M. V. Sokolov, & B. M. Teplov (Eds.), *Materials to the conference on psychology*. Moscow: Akademiya Pedagogicheskikh Nauk, 1957. Pp. 370–379.

Feather, B. W. Semantic generalization of classically conditioned responses. A review. *Psychological Bulletin*, 1965, **63**, 425–441.

Fedorov, A. Ya. Quoted in N. I. Krasnogorsky, *Studies of the higher nervous activities of man and animals*. Moscow: Medgiz, 1954. Pp. 478–480.

Fedoseyev, P. N. (Ed.). *Philosophical problems of higher nervous activity and psychology*. Moscow: Akademiya Nauk SSSR, 1963. P. 756.

Gershuni, G. V. Interaction of reflex reactions to external stimuli and sensations in the sense organs of man. *Fiziologichesky Zhurnal SSSR imeni I. M. Sechenova*, 1949, **35**, 541–560.

Gershuni, G. V. Characteristics of conditioned galvanic reflexes and alpha-rhythm blocking in subsensory and supersensory auditory stimulation in man. *Zhurnal Vysshey Nervnoy Deyatel'nosti imeni I. P. Pavlova*, 1955, **5**, 655–676.

Gibson, J. J. *The senses considered as perceptual systems*. Boston: Houghton Mifflin, 1966.

Hefferline, R. F., Keenan, B., & Hartford, R. A. Escape and avoidance conditioning in human subjects without their observation of the response. *Science*, 1959, **130**, 1338–1339.

Krushinsky, L. V. *Formation of animal behavior: Normal and abnormal*. Moscow: Moscow University, 1960. (English translation: New York: Consultants', 1962.)

Lange, N. Beitrage zur Theorie der sinnlichen Aufmerksamkeit und der aktiven Apperception. *Philosophische Studien*, 1888, **4**, 390–422.

Lange, N. *Psikhologiya*. St. Petersburg: Mir, 1914.

Lenneberg, E. H. *Biological foundations of language*. New York: Wiley, 1967.

Lenneberg, E. H. Language in the light of evolution. In T. A. Seboek (Ed.), *Animal communication: Techniques of study and results of research*. Bloomington: Indiana. Indiana University Press, 1968. Pp. 192–308.

Luria, A. R., & Vinogradova, O. S. An objective investigation of the dynamics of semantic system. *British Journal of Psychology*, 1959, **50**, 89–105.

Lyakh, G. S. Articulatory and auditory mimicry in the first months of life. *Zhurnal Vysshey Nervnoy Deyatel'nosti imeni I: P. Pavlova*, 1968, **18**, 831–835.

Makarov, P. O. *The neurodynamics of man*. Leningrad: Medgiz, 1959.

Maltzman, I. Theoretical conceptions of semantic conditioning and generalization. In T. R. Dixon & D. L. Horton (Eds.), *Verbal behavior and general behavior theory*. Englewood Cliffs, New Jersey: Prentice Hall, 1968. Pp. 291–399.

Maltzman, I. The orienting reflex and thinking as determiners of conditioning and generalization to words. In H. H. Kendler and J. J. Spence (Eds.). Essays in Neobehaviorism: A memorial volume to Kenneth W. Spence. New York: Appleton, 1971. Pp. 84–111.

Maltzman, I., Langdon, B., & Feeney, D. Semantic generalization without prior conditioning. *Journal of Experimental Psychology*, 1970, **83**, 73–75.

Max, L. W. An experimental study of the motor theory of consciousness. IV. Action current responses in the deaf during awakening, kinesthetic imagery and abstract thinking. *Journal of Comparative Psychology*, 1937, **24**, 301–344.

Mowrer, O. H. The psychologist looks at language. *American Psychologist*, 1954, **9**, 660–694.

Orbeli, L. A. The dialectical method in the physiology of the nervous system. *Fiziologichesky Zhurnal SSSR imeni I. M. Sechenova*, 1950, **36**, 5–18.

Paul, H. *Prinzipen der sprachgeschichte.* Halle: Niemeyer, 1886.

Pavlov, I. P. *A physiological attempt to understand the symptoms of hysteria.* Leningrad: Akademiya Nauk SSSR, 1932.

Pavlov, I. P. *Wednesdays: Protocols and stenograms of physiological colloquia.* Moscow-Leningrad, 1949. 3 vols.

Peastral, A. Studies in efficiency: semantic generalization in schizophrenia. Unpublished doctoral dissertation, Univ. of Pennsylvania, 1961.

Petrov, S. Dynamic stereotype type effects of individual stimuli in differential sequential positions. *Trudy Fiziologicheskikh Laboratorii I. P. Pavlova,* 1941, **10**, 332–336.

Razran, G. Conditioned responses in animals other than dogs. *Psychological Bulletin,* 1933, **30**, 261–324.

Razran, G. Conditioned responses: An experimental study and a theoretical analysis. *Archives of Psychology (New York)* 1935, **28** (Whole No. 190).

Razran, G. A simple technique for controlling subjective attitudes in salivary conditioning of adult human subjects. *Science,* 1939, **89**, 160–162. (a)

Razran, G. A quantitative study of meaning by a conditioned salivary technique (semantic conditioning). *Science,* 1939, **90**, 90–91. (b)

Razran, G. Sentential and propositional generalization of salivary conditioning to verbal stimuli. *Science,* 1949, **109**, 447–448. (a)

Razran, G. Semantic and phonetographic generalization of salivary to verbal stimuli. *Journal of Experimental Psychology,* 1949, **39**, 642–652. (b)

Razran, G. Some psychological factors in the generalization of salivary conditioning to verbal stimuli. *American Journal of Psychology,* 1949, **62**, 257–256. (c)

Razran, G. Attitudinal determinants of conditioning and generalization of conditioning. *Journal of Experimental Psychology,* 1949, **39**, 820–829. (d)

Razran, G. Stimulus generalization of conditioned responses. *Psychological Bulletin,* 1949, **46**, 337–365. (e)

Razran, G. Experimental semantics. *Transactions of the New York Academy of Sciences,* 1952, **14**, 171–177.

Razran, G. *Mind in evolution: An East-West synthesis of learned behavior and cognition.* Boston: Houghton Mifflin, 1971.

Razran, G. Autonomic substructure and cognitive superstructure in behavior theory and therapy. In M. Hammer, K. Salzinger, and S. Sutton (Eds.). *Towards a science of psychopathology. Contributions from the biological, behavioral, and social sciences. In honor of the seventieth birthday of Joseph Zubin.* New York: Wiley, 1972. Pp. 147–173.

Razran, G. Reply. *Animal Behaviour,* 1973. (In press.)

Riess, B. F. Genetic changes in semantic conditioning. *Journal of Experimental Psychology,* 1946, **36**, 143–152.

Sechenov, I. M. Object-thought and reality. In D. Anuchin (Ed.), *Pomoshch golodagushchim* [Help to the hungry]. Moscow: Russkiye Vedomosti, 1892. Pp. 193–209.

Selz, O. *Über die Gesetze des geordenter Denkverlauf.* Stuttgart: Spimann, 1913.

Shicko, G. A. *The second-signal system and its physiological mechanisms.* Leningrad: Meditsina, 1969.

Shvarts, L. A. The significance of words and their sound forms as conditioned stimuli. *Byulleten' Eksperimental'noy Biologii i Meditsiny,* 1948, **25**(4), 292–294.

Shvarts, L. A. Meanings of words and their sound forms as conditioned stimuli. *Byulleten' Eksperimental'noy Biologii i Meditsiny,* 1949, **27**(6), 412–415.

Shvarts, L. A. The problem of words as conditioned stimuli. *Byulleten' Eksperimental'noy Biologii i Meditsiny*, 1954, **38**(12), 15–18.

Shvarts, L. A. Conditioned reflexes to verbal stimuli. *Voprosy Psikhologii*, 1960, **6**(1), 86–98.

Siqueland, E. R., & Lipsitt, L. P. Conditioned head-turning in human newborns. *Journal of Experimental Child Psychology*, 1966, **3**, 356–376.

Sokolov, E. N. *Perception and the conditioned reflex.* Moscow: Moscow Univ., 1958.

Staats, C. K., & Staats, A. W. Meaning established by classical conditioning. *Journal of Experimental Psychology*, 1957, **54**, 74–80.

Tolman, E. Principles of purposive behavior. In S. Koch (Ed.), *Psychology: A study of a science.* Vol. 2. *General systematic formulations, learning, and special processes.* New York: McGraw-Hill, 1959. Pp. 92–157.

Underwood, B. J., & Richardson, J. Verbal concept learning as a function of instructions and dominance level. *Journal of Experimental Psychology*, 1956, **51**, 229–238.

Vinogradova, O. S., & Eysler, N. A. The manifestations of verbal connections in records of vascular reactions. *Voprosy Psikhologii*, 1959, **4**(2), 101–116.

Volkova, V. D. On certain characteristics of the formation of conditioned reflexes to speech stimuli. *Fiziologichesky Zhurnal SSR imeni I. M. Sechenova*, 1953, **39**, 540–548.

Volkova, V. D. Quoted in N. I. Krasnogorsky, *Studies of the higher nervous activity of man and animals.* Moscow: Medgiz, 1954. Pp. 478–480.

Voronin, L. G. Development of unconditioned and conditional reactions in newborn macaques. *Fiziologichesky Zhurnal SSSR, imeni I. M. Sechenova*, 1948, **34**, 333–338.

Warren, J. M. Oddity learning set in cats. *Journal of Comparative and Physiological Psychology*, 1960, **53**, 433–434.

Washburn, M. F. *Movement and mental imagery.* Boston: Houghton Mifflin, 1916.

Whitmarsh, G. A., & Bousefield, W. A. Use of free associational norms for the prediction of generalization of salivary conditioning to verbal stimuli. *Psychological Reports*, 1961, **8**, 91–95.

Woodworth, R. S. Imageless thought. *Journal of Philosophy, Psychology and Scientific Method*, 1906, **3**, 701–707.

Wundt, W. *Völkespsychologie.* Vol. 1, Pt. 2. *Die sprache.* Leipzig: Englemann, 1900.

LANGUAGE AND THE CEREBRAL HEMISPHERES: REACTION-TIME STUDIES AND THEIR IMPLICATIONS FOR MODELS OF CEREBRAL DOMINANCE

Morris Moscovitch

Erindale College, University of Toronto

Introduction

The problem of localization of function is one of the oldest in neurology and physiological psychology. The classical approach to the problem has been to study the effects that lesions of the nervous system have on behavior and thereby determine the psychological functions or behaviors which different structures of the nervous system subserve. Such an approach, it has been assumed, would ultimately reveal the functional organization of the nervous system of normal organisms.

The localizationist school of brain function gained its first true respectability with Broca's discovery that lesions of the left hemisphere cause aphasia. Therefore, it is fitting that the classical approach has perhaps made its most dramatic contributions in the study of aphasia, especially in developing behavioral tests for localizing brain damage associated with the different aphasias and related disorders (Geschwind, 1970; Luria, 1970). Success at describing the functional organization of the normal nervous system has been more elusive. This approach has several methodological and theoretical problems which have been discussed at length by others (Head, 1926; Goldstein, 1948; Luria, 1970, 1972), but I want to concentrate on only one aspect of these. Until very recently, most neurologists and physiological psychologists regarded the idea that the lesion or classical approach can be used to reveal the structural basis of normal behaviors as an article of faith, as an axiom, rather than as a hypothesis that should itself be tested. Though justifiable when no techniques were available to monitor the activity of different brain structures in normal humans, this attitude persists among many neurologists despite the fact that adequate behavioral and electrophysiological techniques have been developed to test brain functions in normal humans (Cohn, 1971; Kimura, 1967; McAdam & Whitaker, 1971; Morrell & Salomy, 1971; White, 1969; Wood, Goff, & Day, 1971).

By accepting the premises upon which the classical approach is based, rather than testing them whenever possible, one also tends to perpetuate problems which, in a sense, this approach created. Despite over 100 years of intensive research on aphasia, controversies similar to those that existed in Broca's time are still present. One such controversy concerns the extent to which psychological processes are represented or lateralized in the cerebral hemispheres. Currently, there are two neurologically derived models which claim to describe the degree of lateralization of verbal functions in the cerebral hemispheres of normal people. The first model states that verbal functions are localized exclusively in the left hemisphere. This model, which I will refer to as the *strict localization model,* is based primarily on data obtained from patients who have sustained lesions in their cerebral hemispheres. The second model states that verbal functions are represented in both hemispheres, though more strongly in the left. Since this model is based mainly on data obtained from patients whose corpus callosum had been surgically sectioned, I will refer to it as the *split-brain model.* Though I believe the classical approach to be invaluable, I will argue that one cannot infer the functional organization of the cerebral hemispheres of normal people from studies conducted exclusively on brain-damaged individuals. I hope to convince the reader that research into the behavior of normal individuals is both necessary for testing neuropsychological hypotheses suggested by studies of brain-damaged people, and useful in formulating new models about the functional organization of the cerebral hemispheres of both normal and brain-damaged individuals. Before I relate the results of some studies conducted on normal people, I will briefly review the literature from which the strict localization model and the split-brain model are derived.

Brief History of the Strict Localization Model

In 1861, Broca presented his famous case of a patient nicknamed "Tan" who showed a mild right hemiplegia and who was unable to speak. The lesion causing the aphasia was localized in the third frontal convolution in the left hemisphere. Other patients showing similar symptoms displayed similar lesion patterns at autopsy causing Broca (1865) to conclude that speech is localized in the left cerebral hemisphere. His conclusion was controversial in his day but has become less so with the passage of time. There are at least hundreds of reported cases in which circumscribed lesions in the dominant hemisphere have been shown to produce profound and lasting impairment of verbal functions despite the fact that by neurological signs the minor hemisphere is healthy and unimpaired. Even the anti-localizationist schools of Jackson, Head, and Goldstein were forced to concede that verbal functions are more easily and more profoundly disrupted by lesions in the left hemisphere than by lesions in the right. Research in this area has, in fact, extended Broca's findings to the point that now it is generally believed that not just speech, but many functions related to verbal behavior are localized in the left hemisphere. Thus, lesions of the left posterior temporal lobe impair a person's ability to comprehend verbal information, either written or spoken. Lesions of the mesial temporal lobe and hippocampus of the left hemisphere cause severe memory loss mainly for verbal material and lesions of the frontal lobe in the left hemisphere renders a patient unable to order verbal stimuli in time (Milner, 1967a, 1971). Thus, it seems as if much of the left hemisphere is organized to process verbal information and produce verbal behavior.

Except for some people who are left-handed or ambidextrous, or who have a history of left-handedness in their family, lesions of the minor hemisphere, leave verbal functions unimpaired (Luria, 1970; Zangwill, 1960). Although occasional reports stated that lesions of the minor hemisphere affect individuals' performance on complex verbal tasks such as sentence completion, the authors of these reports (Hebb, 1942; Eisenson, 1962; Weisenberg & McBride, 1935) thought that these lesions led to a general impairment in intelligence which would affect all skills rather than to a specific impairment which affected only verbal skills. This evidence led to a school of thought that believed that pure right-handed people without a family history of left-handedness had verbal functions represented exclusively in the left, dominant hemisphere. The right or minor hemisphere subserved no verbal functions. The ability of some patients to recover from dominant hemisphere aphasia was attributed to the recovery of function in the remaining healthy tissue in the dominant hemisphere rather than to the adoption of verbal functions by the minor hemisphere.

Recently, investigators have begun paying attention to the special role which the minor hemisphere plays. Just as the dominant hemisphere specialized in verbal behavior, so the minor hemisphere specializes in performing nonverbal functions. Minor hemisphere lesions selectively impair a person's performance on nonverbal tasks. Thus, lesions of the mesial temporal lobe and hippocampus of the right hemisphere impair a person's ability to learn to tap blocks in a given spatial sequence, or to remember music, nonsense figures, or faces; lesions of the frontal lobe impair his ability to order figural stimuli in time; and lesions of the parietal lobe impair his performance on visual–spatial tasks (see Milner, 1971, for review).

The prevailing notion is that each hemisphere specializes in certain skills. Verbal functions are localized exclusively in the dominant hemisphere whereas nonverbal functions are thought to be predominantly, but not exclusively, lateralized in the minor hemisphere. The fact that lesions of the minor hemisphere do not always produce profound impairments on nonverbal tasks may reflect the experimenter's inability to find tasks that preclude the use of verbal strategies rather than the degree of lateralization of nonverbal functions in the minor hemisphere.

Brief History of the Split-Brain Model

At the turn of the century, cases of left-hand dyspraxia and of alexia without agraphia were reported by Dejerine (1892) and Liepmann (1906). These authors believed the symptoms to have been caused by lesions of the corpus callosum, thereby disconnecting the speech areas of the left hemisphere from the right motor cortex in the case of left-hand dyspraxia and from the visual pathways on the right side in the case of alexia. These interpretations were, however, challenged by Akelaitis (1944) in a series of studies conducted on a group of 24 patients in whom the corpus callosum had been sectioned completely in 9 and partially in 15. He found no disturbance of verbal functions on either side of the body. The patients could write with both hands and read material presented exclusively to one or the other hemisphere. The defects these patients exhibited were so minimal that it prompted Lashley (1950) to state, only partially in jest, that the only function the corpus callosum might serve is to hold the two halves of the brain together.

In the middle 1950s, Sperry and his students embarked on a series of animal studies showing that the cerebral commissures relay information from one hemisphere to the other (for review, see Sperry, 1961). He later extended these studies to include human subjects whose cerebral commissures had been sectioned to prevent epileptic discharges from spreading from one hemisphere to the other. The results of the human studies agreed with the animal work and were clearly discrepant with Akelaitis' findings. It is now generally conceded that the discrepancy between Sperry's and Akelaitis' results may have been caused by some of the following factors:

(1) the completeness of the section, the Akelaitis' section sparing parts of the corpus callosum in many cases (Hurwitz, 1971); (2) the fact that the surgery in Akelaitis' patients was conducted in two stages, whereas Sperry's was conducted in only one; and (3) Akelaitis' testing technique may have been less sophisticated than the present techniques used by Sperry, Gazzaniga, and their students (see Goldstein & Joynt, 1969, for a follow-up study of one of Akelaitis' patients).

To illustrate how the split-brain studies bear on the problem of localization of function, a brief review of the modern split-brain literature will follow. The split-brain patients offered Sperry, Gazzaniga, Bogen, and their collaborators a perfect opportunity to test the performance of the minor hemisphere on verbal tasks in relative isolation from the dominant hemisphere. The testing procedure makes use of the fact that each visual half field and the pathways conducting fine stereognostic and somesthetic information from the fingers project directly to the contralateral hemisphere. In addition, control over fine finger movements is also exerted only by the contralateral hemisphere (for a schematic representation of these pathways, see Fig. 2, page 97). Thus, by requiring the minor hemisphere to indicate manually whether or not it comprehended information presented to it, it was possible to determine what verbal capacities the minor hemisphere possessed. A couple of examples will clarify this point. The word "nut," for example, was presented tachistoscopically to the left visual field, thereby restricting the input to the minor side (see Fig. 1). The subject was then required to retrieve from an array of objects hidden from sight the object that corresponded to the word that was flashed. The subject succeeded in choosing the correct object only if he used his minor hand, that is, the hand controlled by the minor hemisphere. As further proof that the minor hemisphere executed this task without the help of the dominant hemisphere, the subject was unable to identify vocally the object which he correctly retrieved with his minor hand, speech production being confined to the dominant hemisphere. To test for minor-hemisphere speech comprehension, the subject is required to retrieve spoken objects or carry out spoken commands with his left hand. Another way of testing speech comprehension and reading ability is to require the subject to match visually presented words to a spoken word or phrase. A series of words is tachistoscopically presented to the minor hemisphere and the subject must indicate with his left hand when the written word, corresponding the spoken word or phrase, appears.

In a series of such tests, most of them very carefully controlled to prevent cross-cuing between hemispheres (see especially Gazzaniga, 1970; Gazzaniga & Hillyard, 1971), Sperry, Bogen, Gazzaniga, and their students (Gazzaniga, 1970, 1972; Gazzaniga & Sperry, 1967; Sperry, 1968; Sperry,

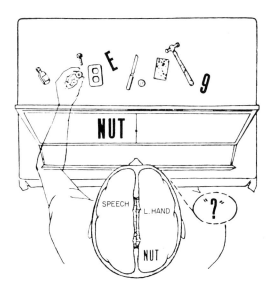

Fig. 1. Names of objects flashed to the left half-field can be read and understood, but not spoken. Subject can retrieve the named object by touch with the left
hand, but cannot afterward name the item nor retrieve it with the right hand. (From
Sperry, Gazzaniga, & Bogen, 1969.)

Gazzaniga, & Bogen, 1969) succeeded in demonstrating that the minor
hemisphere possessed considerable verbal skills, though its verbal abilities
were clearly inferior to those of the dominant hemisphere. The minor
hemisphere could not speak. Its comprehension of verbal material was
limited to spoken and written nouns, some phrases, and very simple sentences. It showed some understanding of verbs in that it could distinguish
whether an affirmative or negative sentence properly described an action
sequence. Furthermore, its understanding of spoken or written material
was not confined to a simple relationship between a noun and the object
the noun denotes, but rather the minor hemisphere had a reasonably
sophisticated verbal concept for each word. Thus, it knew that a "match"
is "used to light fires," that a "ruler" is a "measuring instrument" and that
a "glass" is a "liquid container." As a result of these studies, a model of
lateralization of function was proposed in which language functions were
represented in both hemispheres, though more strongly in the left (Gazzaniga, 1971).

Statement of the Problem

As even this brief presentation shows, the split-brain studies lead to
conclusions about the minor hemisphere's verbal abilities that are in marked

contrast to those derived from lesion studies. In numerous cases of left-hemisphere aphasia, lesions in the dominant hemisphere produce a profound inability to comprehend language despite the fact that these patients have reasonably healthy minor hemispheres. If the split-brain data are to be taken at face value, the aphasic patients should at least display whatever verbal capacity the minor hemisphere of split-brain patients possesses. Nonetheless, some patients with relatively small, circumscribed lesions in the dominant hemisphere can be word-blind or word-deaf, and often be unable to identify such simple words as "nose" or "eye" (Geschwind, 1965, 1970; Gazzaniga, 1972; Luria, 1970).

A number of suggestions have been proposed to reconcile the split-brain data and the lesion data. It may be that the epilepsy from which split-brain patients suffered caused a reorganization of their hemispheres so that language functions are bilaterally represented in the hemisphere of split-brains. In normal patients, language functions remain confined to the dominant side. To counter this argument, Sperry *et al.* (1969) and Gazzaniga (1972) have suggested that lesions in the dominant hemisphere may disrupt the behavior of the minor hemisphere or produce global debilitating symptoms such that the verbal competence of the minor hemisphere cannot be observed.

These arguments give no logical reason to accept one model over the other. Since both the strict localization model and the split-brain model claim to describe the lateralization of language function in normal people, it seemed an obvious step to conduct research on normal subjects and see if the results will select between the two models. The experiments conducted on normal people that will be reported shortly, viewed in the light of the split-brain and aphasia data, suggest a possible solution to the controversy. One of the causes of the controversy may stem from the failure to clearly specify the conditions under which the minor hemisphere's verbal competence becomes manifest in performance and those conditions under which its verbal competence is masked. A new model of lateralization of function will be proposed which takes into account the distinction between competence and performance. This model, which I will refer to as the *functional localization model,* states that the verbal competence of the minor hemisphere of normal and aphasic patients is equal to that of split-brain patients. However, so long as critical portions of the dominant hemisphere and cerebral commissures remain intact, the verbal competence of the minor hemisphere will be suppressed. Thus, the verbal behavior of normal and aphasic patients will usually reflect the verbal competence of the normal or malfunctioning dominant hemisphere, respectively. Sectioning the cerebral commissures or extirpating the entire dominant hemisphere will remove the suppressive or inhibitory effects of the dominant hemisphere and allow the minor hemisphere's underlying competence to express itself in behavior. I will elaborate on this model and discuss some of its psychological, clinical, and developmental implications after I present some data.

Experiments Conducted on Normal People

The idea to test neuropsychological models of brain dominance on normal people is not new. For about 20 years, investigators have been successfully using dichotic listening and tachistoscopic techniques to determine both the nature and the degree of laterality effects in normal people (see Kimura, 1967; White, 1969; McKeever & Huling, 1971; Studdert-Kennedy & Shankweiler, 1970). By and large, these experiments have shown that normal right-handed people detect verbal stimuli projected primarily along left-hemisphere pathways better than those projected along right hemisphere pathways, thereby confirming that the left hemisphere is dominant for verbal functions. Though both techniques are valuable as research tools, they provide information regarding only the relative superiority of one hemisphere over the other with respect to certain abilities. As such, they cannot be used to answer the question with which this paper is concerned, namely: Does the normal minor hemisphere exhibit any verbal behavior? This question requires that we know the absolute, not the relative, level of performance of the two hemispheres on verbal tasks. A reaction time (RT) technique first used by Poffenberger (1912) is better suited to answer this question.

The rationale behind the technique is quite simple. Figure 2 shows a simplified drawing of the brain accompanied by the appropriate visual and motor projections.[1] Each visual half-field projects directly to the contralateral hemisphere. According to this diagram, stimuli projected to the hemisphere emitting the response should produce shorter RTs than stimuli presented to the opposite visual field. The difference should equal the time it takes to transfer information from one hemisphere to the other. If the left hemisphere is responding, RTs to stimuli presented in the right visual field, RT_D, will be shorter than to stimuli presented in the left visual field, RT_M, by T msec. The reverse holds if the right hemisphere is responding. In computing RTs to simple stimuli, Poffenberger in 1912, and more recently Smith (1947), Bradshaw and Perriment (1970), Jeeves (1969),

---

[1] The diagram should be treated as a flow or stage diagram for information transmission rather than as an exact replication of the pathways and their synaptic relations.

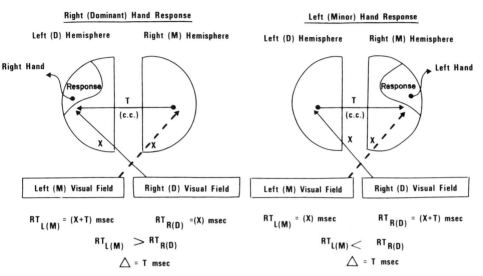

Fig. 2. Pathway along which a visual stimulus presented to either the right (dominant) or left (minor) visual field must travel before it evokes a manual response. T is the interhemispheric transmission time (msec); X is the transmission time from visual field to hemisphere.

and Berlucchi, Heron, Hyman, Rizzolatti, and Umilta (1971) have obtained results predicted by this simplified diagram — that is, RTs were shorter to stimuli presented to the visual field which projects directly to the hemisphere emitting the response.

It is easy to modify this technique for studies of hemispheric dominance. Instead of responding manually, the subject can respond vocally to stimuli presented visually. In the first experiment that Jack Catlin and I conducted (Moscovitch & Catlin, 1970), the subject had to identify vocally a letter that flashed in his left or right visual field. Since both the split-brain research and the lesion research agree that speech is localized exclusively in the dominant hemisphere, both would predict that RTs in this task would favor the dominant visual field (see Fig. 3). Thus, this experiment would serve as a good test of the RT technique. We did, in fact, obtain the predicted result (Fig. 4). Reaction times favored the dominant visual field by 10 msec (Wilcoxon sign-rank test, $p < .05$ in five of seven subjects). Filby and Gazzaniga (1969) and McKeever and Gill (1972) obtained similar results.

Validation of the RT technique permitted its use in assessing the verbal behavior of the normal minor hemisphere. The experimental paradigm

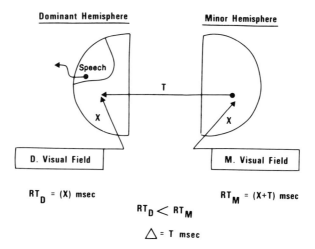

Fig. 3. Pathway along which a test letter presented to either the minor or dominant visual field must travel before it evokes a vocal response. For clarity, each visual field was drawn on the side closest to the hemisphere to which it projects, rather than on the contralateral side. T is the interhemispheric transmission time; X is the transmission time from visual field to hemisphere.

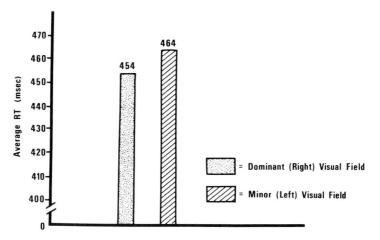

Fig. 4. Reaction times of vocal responses to test letters presented to the dominant (right) or minor (left) visual field in a letter identification task.

differed slightly from the first experiment. The subject wore earphones and faced a screen. A single letter (memory set) was presented binaurally via the earphones. Two seconds later a test or probe letter was presented to the visual field projecting directly to either the dominant or the minor hemisphere. The subject was then required to indicate with the fingers of his

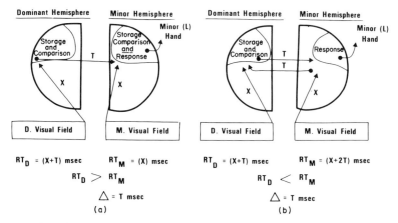

Fig. 5. Matching a visual test letter to a single auditory set letter. Pathway along which a test letter presented to either the dominant or minor visual field must travel before it evokes a minor-hand response. (a) According to the split-brain model. (b) According to the strict localization model. T is the interhemispheic transmission time (msec); X is the transmission time from visual field to hemisphere.

minor hand whether or not the test letter he saw was identical to the letter he had heard. Restricting the response to the minor hemisphere would hopefully create the optimal conditions under which the minor hemisphere could display its verbal skills. Furthermore, this paradigm closely resembles one used by Gazzaniga and Sperry (1967) to test the verbal competence of the minor hemisphere of split-brain patients.[2]

Figure 5 illustrates the hypotheses under consideration. If, as the split-brain model claims, the minor hemisphere can store a representation of the auditory set and compare it with the visual test letter, i.e., if it has the capacity to perform this simple verbal task, then RTs should favor the minor visual field. If, on the other hand, only the dominant hemisphere could perform these operations, RTs would favor the dominant and not the minor visual field, since all test letters would have to travel to the dominant hemisphere before a response occurred. Such results would support a strict localization model.

The results, which appear in Fig. 6, support the split-brain model. In all subjects tested, RTs favored the minor visual field by an average of 22 msec for "same" responses (t test for correlated samples, $df = 5$, $p < .005$). For "different" responses, RTs slightly, but insignificantly, favored the

---

[2] For more details about the design of the experiment see Moscovitch (1972a, b).

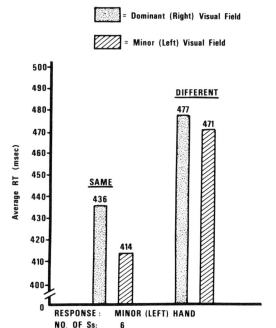

Fig. 6. Reaction times to test letters presented to the minor (left) or dominant (right) visual field in a letter matching task.

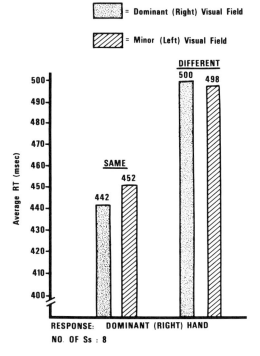

Fig. 7. Reaction times to test letters presented to the dominant (right) or minor (left) visual field in a letter matching task.

100

minor visual field (Moscovitch, 1972a).[3] To ensure that the task required some verbal skills, a control group of subjects responded with their dominant hand. If the tests were verbal, then RTs should favor the dominant visual field. Though the average RTs favored the dominant visual field by 10 msec (see Fig. 7), the effect was not significant.

These results cast doubt upon the notion that the letter matching task assessed any verbal skills. The assumption underlying this test was that the subject would name the visual test letter covertly and then compare this name with the auditory set letter. The subject, however, may have treated the letter matching task as a purely visual, rather than as a verbal task. The auditory set letter, for example, could evoke a visual representation of itself. The subject would then match the visual test letter against the visual image of the originally acoustic set letter. Many subjects spontaneously reported using this strategy. If this was the strategy that the subjects adopted, then, clearly, the letter matching experiment could not be used to assess the minor hemisphere's verbal skills.

To determine whether subjects used a verbal or visual strategy in the letter matching task, it was necessary to rely on evidence that is more reliable than the subjects' introspective report. A possible source of such information is the RT data for "different" responses to memory set and test letters that were either visually similar, such as (V–U, V–Y, X–Z) or acoustically similar (X–S, I–Y, V–Z). If subjects compared the letters along a visual dimension, they should find it more difficult to distinguish between visually or figurally similar pairs than acoustically similar pairs. The relative difficulty of performing this discrimination should be reflected in their RTs, such that "different" responses should take longer for visually similar, rather than acoustically similar, pairs. If, on the other hand, the subjects compared the letters along an acoustic–verbal dimension, the reverse would obtain with RTs for acoustically similar pairs being longer. After completing the regular matching task, they continued in the experiment for another day. The procedure used was identical to the matching task, except for each "different" trial, the test letter was either acoustically or visually similar to the set or sample letter. A total of 72 "different" trials consisting of an equal

---

[3] In all the experiments that I will report, RTs for "different" responses never yielded significant visual field effects. Consequently, I will base my conclusions mainly on data from "same" responses. The lack of significant effects for "different" responses is not peculiar to these experiments. Cohen (1972) found similar discrepancies as did Lee Brooks (1971, personal communication). I suspect Berlucchi *et al.* (1971) and Umilta, Frost, and Hyman (1972) also found "different" responses difficult to interpret since their subjects are required to respond only "same" and refrain from responding when the stimuli are different. For brief discussions of some possible reasons that can account for the discrepancy between "same" and "different" responses, see Moscovitch (1972a, b, footnote 3) as well as Egeth and Blecker (1971).

number of acoustically and visually confusable pairs, divided equally among visual fields, were presented. The results (see Fig. 8) show that RTs were longer for the visually similar pairs, regardless of the hand of response. The results suggest that the subjects used a visual strategy in the letter matching task, and are consistent with a great deal of evidence, both neurological and behavioral, that the minor hemisphere's processing abilities and memory capacity for visual or figural material is superior to that of the dominant (Milner, 1971). The results also indicate that the dominant hemisphere is not totally deficient in these abilities, since subjects responding with their right hand and favoring the dominant visual field also matched the items along a visual dimension.

Though these experiments attest to the sensitivity of the RT technique in assessing the visual capacities of the two hemispheres, the problem remained to find a task that would adequately test the verbal abilities of the minor hemisphere. One possible solution was to prevent the subjects from converting the auditorily presented set letter to a visual representation before the test letter appeared. To this end, the number of letters in the memory set was increased to six. The presumed difficulty in transferring six letters from a verbal to a visual representation in a period of 2 sec, increases the likelihood that the subject will match the test and set letters along a verbal modality.

A possible consequence of this change is that even if the minor hemisphere has the ability to process verbal information, the large auditory set

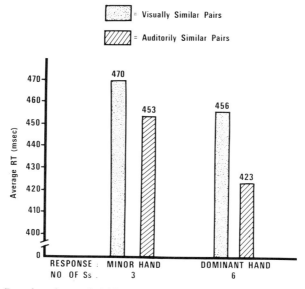

Fig. 8. Reaction times of "different" responses to visually similar and auditorily similar test-set pairs.

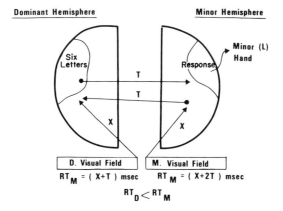

Fig. 9. Searching an auditorily presented set of six letters for the presence of a visually presented test letter. Pathway along which a test letter presented to either the dominant or minor visual field must travel before it evokes a minor-hand response. T is the interhemispheric transmission time (msec); X is the transmission time from visual field to hemisphere.

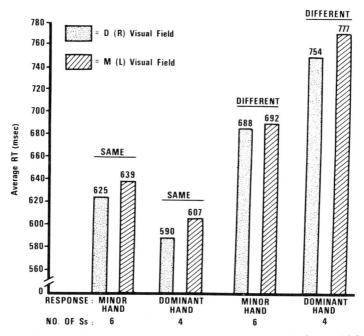

Fig. 10. Reaction times to test letters presented to the dominant (right) or minor (left) visual field in a memory scanning task.

TABLE 1

Mean Reaction Time for Subjects Scanning an Auditorily Presented Set of Either One or Six Letters for the Presence of a Visual Test Letter

| Subjects | Responding hand | Set size | Mean RT (msec) to letters presented in the dominant (DVF) and minor (MVF) visual fields | | | | | |
| | | | Same | | | Different | | |
			DVF	MVF	(D − M)	DVF	MVF	(D − M)
R.B. (m)	Minor (L)	1	382	340	+42	408	417	−9
	Minor (L)	6	458	481	−23	558	571	−13
R.G. (f)	Minor (L)	1	458	446	+12	448	425	+23
	Minor (L)	6	660	671	−11	638	650	−12
A.A. (m)	Minor (L)	1	421	369	+52	470	471	−1
	Minor (L)	6	739	742	−3	753	751	+2
M.G. (m)	Minor (L)	1	393	367	+25	442	460	−18
	Minor (L)	6	643	646	−3	845	866	−21
J.N. (f)	Minor (L)	1	495	457	+38	526	506	+20
	Minor (L)	6	768	812	−44	895	924	−26
E.E. (f)	Minor (L)	1	437	428	+9	513	535	−21
	Minor (L)	6	464	490	−26	644	645	+1

TABLE 2

Mean Reaction Time for Subjects Scanning an Auditorily Presented Set of Either One or Six Letters for the Presence of a Visual Test Letter

| Subjects | Responding hand | Set size | Mean RT (msec) to letters presented in the dominant (DVF) and minor (MVF) visual fields | | | | | |
| | | | Same | | | Different | | |
			DVF	MVF	(D − M)	DVF	MVF	(D − M)
C.G. (f)	Dominant (R)	1	574	552	+22	602	611	−9
	Dominant (R)	6	590	620	−30	634	670	−36
L.P. (m)	Dominant (R)	1	356	392	−36	429	434	−5
	Dominant (R)	6	592	595	−3	799	822	−23
H.L. (f)	Dominant (R)	1	441	471	−30	563	579	−16
	Dominant (R)	6	624	646	−22	854	845	+9
M.L. (m)	Dominant (R)	1	452	462	−10	490	460	+30
	Dominant (R)	6	535	569	−34	661	687	−26

may exceed the minor hemisphere's verbal memory capacity and must, therefore, be stored in the dominant hemisphere. If that is the case, all test letters would then have to travel to the dominant hemisphere for comparison with the memory set (see Fig. 9). The results of this experiment, presented in Fig. 10, confirm this hypothesis. Reaction times of "same" responses favored the test letters presented in the left visual field by 14 and 24 msec ($p < .01$) for a left- and right-hand response, respectively. The 14- and 24-msec differences were not significantly different from each other.

To replicate the results of this experiment within subjects, 10 subjects participated in both the one- and six-letter conditions. Six of these subjects responded with their left hand and four with their right. The pattern of results within subjects agreed with the group data almost perfectly (see Tables 1 and 2).

The results of the memory scanning experiment argue that the minor hemisphere has a much smaller capacity for verbal behavior than the dominant hemisphere. They do not, however, prove that the minor hemisphere lacks the ability to perform well on simple verbal tasks. As conjectured earlier, the six-letter memory set may have overloaded the minor hemisphere's verbal storage capacity. Given a verbal task that would not unduly strain its memory capacity, the minor hemisphere might perform quite adequately.

To test the possibility that the minor hemisphere can perform adequately on verbal tasks that are relatively memory free, a matching task was designed that was similar to the one used in the first experiment, but which required verbal or linguistic processing, thereby rendering useless any visual strategy which the minor hemisphere might employ. The first single-letter matching task showed that the minor hemisphere can retain at least one letter in its memory. In the present matching task, therefore, the subject again heard only a single letter and 2 sec later he saw a visual test letter in either his right or left visual field. The subject had to indicate with either his right or left hand whether the test letter had the same terminal phoneme as the set letter. Thus, if the set letter was B and the test letter was V or C, the subject indicated "yes"; if, however, the test letter was M or L he indicated "no" since M and L do not end in *e*. All the memory set letters, in fact, ended in *e*. On one-sixth of the trials, for which the appropriate response was "yes," the test letters were identical to the set letters. This condition replicated the original letter matching task. It was included to see if subjects told to match only for a common terminal phoneme would treat identical test-set pairs the same as they would end-alike pairs, which have only a terminal phoneme in common.

Aside from those trials in which test and set letters are identical, the subject cannot use a visual strategy to match the test-set pairs. He must compare the letters along an auditory–verbal or linguistic dimension if he is to determine that they share a common terminal phoneme. Finally, since the memory set contains only one letter, considerations about the minor hemisphere's capacity to store that letter should not enter into the interpretation of the results.

The results of the phoneme-matching experiment appear in Fig. 11. The overall RTs for identical pairs were significantly shorter than for end-alike pairs [$F(1, 42) = 68.50$; $p < .001$]. Figure 11 also shows these results broken down by visual field. There was a significant visual field by similarity interaction [$F(1, 42) = 4.11$; $p < .05$], with end-alike pairs significantly favoring the dominant visual field [$F(1, 15) = 7.06$; $p < .025$], and identical pairs insignificantly favoring the minor visual field. The overall difference in RT between the identical and end-alike pairs as well as the significant visual field by similarity interaction suggest that different cognitive processes are involved in producing a "yes" response for the identical and end-alike pairs. The minor hemisphere seems slightly, but not significantly, more competent than the dominant in making identity matches, whereas the dominant hemisphere is superior in determining whether or not the two letters have a terminal phoneme in common. These results support the earlier speculation that identity matches are mediated mainly by visual–spatial processes

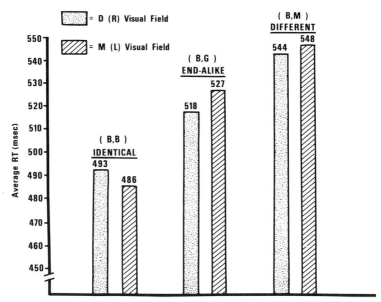

Fig. 11. Reaction times (averages over *S*s and response hand) to test letters presented to the dominant (right) or minor (left) visual field in a phoneme matching task.

whereas phoneme comparisons require an additional auditory–verbal or linguistic component.

Besides confirming the results of earlier investigations using tachisto-scopic and dichotic listening techniques, a closer analysis of the RT data will help determine whether or not the minor hemisphere displays *any* verbal skills. This information is critical in deciding whether the strict local-ization model or the split-brain model adequately describes the functional organization of the cerebral hemispheres of normal people.

Arguments against a Split-Brain (or Efficiency) Model

The results of the RT study have shown that the dominant hemisphere's performance on verbal tasks is superior to the minor hemisphere's. A number of interpretations can account for such results. According to the strict localization model, the minor hemisphere cannot process verbal information. If this is true, then all test letters in the phoneme matching task must travel to the dominant hemisphere because only the dominant hemi-sphere can process the stimulus information to determine whether the name of the test letter ended in the phoneme *e*. This hypothesis is illustrated in Fig. 12. As the diagram shows, RTs should favor the dominant visual field by identical amounts (*T* msec) no matter which hand the subject uses to respond. That is, if the strict localization hypothesis is correct, there should be no visual field by response-hand interaction.

Another interpretation can handle the results of the phoneme-recognition experiment equally well. Both hemispheres, for example, may independently process verbal information, but the dominant hemisphere does so more effi-ciently. Consequently, its response times would be faster than those of the minor hemisphere. This is essentially a modified version of the split-brain model. One prediction that such a model would make is that RT differences between dominant and minor visual field stimuli should be unequal for dominant and minor hand responses. Thus, as Fig. 13 shows, RT differences for a minor-hand response should be smaller than for a dominant-hand response. For a dominant-hand response, the time advantage gained by easy access to the response pathway is added to the verbal processing advantage which the dominant hemisphere already has ($Y + T$ msec), whereas for a minor-hand response, the response advantage favors the minor hemisphere and so must be subtracted from the dominant hemisphere processing advantage ($Y - T$ msec). In short, if the minor hemisphere dis-plays even limited verbal skills, as this modified split-brain or efficiency model states, then a visual field by response interaction should exist.

To test whether the efficiency hypothesis is correct, one has only to

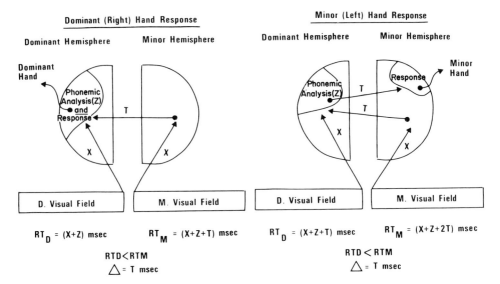

Fig. 12. Neural-cognitive diagram of the phoneme matching task according to the strict-localization model. *T* is the interhemispheric transmission time (msec); *X* is the transmission time from visual field to hemisphere (msec); *Z* is the processing time required for phonemic analysis (msec).

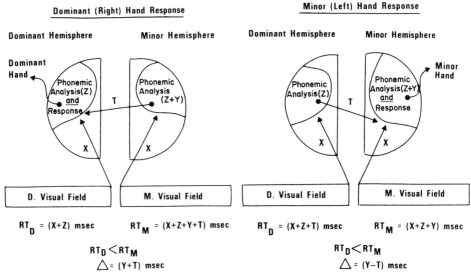

Fig. 13. Neural-cognitive diagram of the phoneme matching task according to the efficiency (modified split-brain) model. *T* is the interhemispheric transmission time (msec); *X* is the transmission time from visual field to hemisphere (msec); *Z* is the processing time for phonemic analysis in the dominant hemisphere; *Y* is the additional processing time required for phonemic analysis in the minor hemisphere.

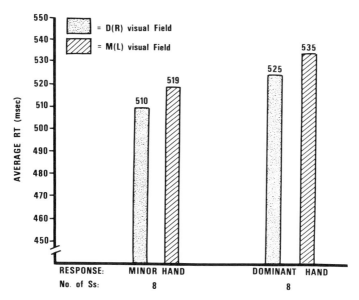

Fig. 14. Reaction times, broken down according to response hand, to test letters presented to the dominant (right) or minor (left) visual fields in the end-alike condition of a phoneme matching task.

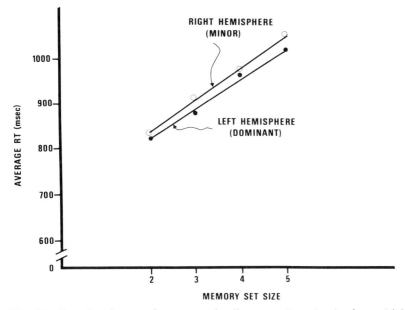

Fig. 15. Reaction time to picture test stimuli presented to the dominant (right) or minor (left) visual field in a picture-letter matching task. (From Klatzky & Atkinson, 1971.)

109

determine the effect of response hand on the size of the RT differences to test letters presented in the right or left visual field. In the phoneme match-ing task, overall RTs favored the dominant visual field by 10 msec. Break-ing this down by response hand we find, as Fig. 14 shows, that RTs favor the dominant visual field by 10 msec for a dominant-hand response, and by 9 ntsec for a minor-hand response. These differences are statistically insig-nificant from each other. The absence of a visual field by hand interaction argues in favor of a strict localization model of cerebral dominance for language, but does not necessarily eliminate an efficiency explanation. The minor hemisphere may be so inefficient at processing the phoneme matching task that a dominant hemisphere signal indicating it has completed the task will cross the corpus collosum and trigger a minor-hand response before a comparable signal arrives from the minor hemisphere. Even if this is true, it does not change the fact that for all practical purposes the strict localiza-tion model adequately describes the subject's behavior, since his behavior reflects only the competence of the dominant hemisphere.

The lack of interaction between responding hand and visual field is not unique to this study, but has been reported in every other study using RTs to test the verbal behavior of the two hemispheres. Geffen, Bradshaw, and Wallace (1971) have found that subjects identify digits more quickly when presented in the dominant visual field than in the minor visual field. Rizzo-latti, Umilta, and Berlucchi (1971) obtained similar results in a letter recognition task. A memory scanning study by Klatsky and Atkinson (1971) most elegantly demonstrates this point. They presented their sub-jects with a visual memory set of two to five letters followed by a picture flashed to either the right or left visual field. They then required their sub-jects to indicate whether or not the name of the object depicted in the picture began with the same letter as one of the letters in the memory set. Clearly, this task involves substantial verbal processing. Were the minor hemisphere merely less efficient than the dominant in executing this task, its performance relative to the dominant hemisphere should deteriorate as the number of items in the memory set increased. The difference in RTs to stimuli presented in the minor and dominant visual field should increase along with the size of the memory set. No such increases were observed. Their results (Fig. 15) show that the difference in RTs between test figures projected to the dominant and minor hemispheres remains constant over set size regardless of the hand used to respond. Finally, in a study combining a dichotic listening paradigm with a RT technique, Springer (1971) found that subjects detected spoken syllables by pressing a response button more quickly, as well as more correctly, when they heard the test syllable in their right ear than in their left. She, too, did not find any hand by ear interaction. In another study using monaural verbal presentation, Springer (1972) obtained similar results. The evidence from all these studies minimizes the importance of efficiency considerations and supports, instead, the strict localization model.

Arguments against the Sufficiency of an Expectancy or Attention Hypothesis

It is worthwhile at this point to mention one last interpretation that challenges the strict localization model. The case for a localization theory of normal brain function rests on the assumption that RT differences in these tasks measure interhemispheric crossing times. Kinsbourne (1970) offered an alternative hypothesis. Reaction time differences, he claimed, do not measure the time it takes to transfer information across interhemispheric paths, but rather reflect attentional asymmetries about a visual or auditory field. The hemisphere most actively involved in executing the task at hand directs the subjects' attention to that part of the visual or auditory field that has the strongest projection to that hemisphere. His model can be classed as an expectancy or attention model. His model requires that the subjects' attention be directed to the appropriate field before the stimulus is presented. Kinsbourne himself has said that if the subjects' expectancy about the nature of the task is reduced, then the appropriate hemisphere will not be primed and the subject will not attend to the corresponding visual field, thereby eliminating any laterality effect once the stimulus is presented. Although Kinsbourne has conducted a number of studies to support his hypothesis and, no doubt, such attention mechanisms contribute to some of the laterality effect, his model cannot account for the range of results obtained in the phoneme-recognition study. In that study, the subjects were presented with a mixed list of test-set pairs that were either identical or shared a common terminal phoneme. Before the test, the a priori probability of the appearance of an end-alike pair was six times greater than an identical pair. Since the attention model states that laterality effects are influenced by the circumstances prevailing prior to the presentation of the test stimulus, then the test stimulus in the identity or end-alike category should produce similar laterality effects or no laterality effects, that is, there should be no visual field by type of test-stimulus interaction. Figure 16 illustrates the results of the analysis, showing that a significant interaction occurred. RTs for end-alike pairs significantly favored the dominant visual field whereas RTs for identical pairs slightly but insignificantly, favored the minor visual field. These results go against the predictions made by the expectancy model. The fact that the laterality effect for identical pairs was small indicates that attention factors may have had some effect.

A more convincing demonstration of the same effect appeared in a recent

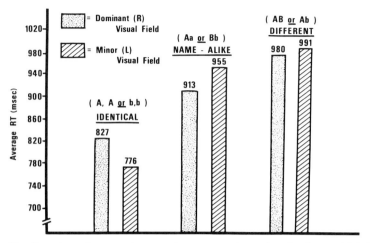

Fig. 16. Reaction times to letter pairs presented to the dominant (right) or minor (left) visual field in a name-matching task. (From Cohen, 1972.)

study by Cohen (1972). She used a modified Posner task (Posner & Mitchell, 1967) to test for laterality differences. Her subjects saw a pair of letters flash in their right or left visual fields and indicated whether or not the two letters forming the pair had the same name. Half of the letter-pairs had the same name and the other half did not. On the half that had the same name, half were in the identical case such as two lower case ays (aa) or two capital ays (AA), whereas the other half were in different cases, e.g., aA or Bb. In responding to identical pairs, her subjects' RTs favored the minor visual field (see Fig. 16). This would be in keeping with our data, since, for identical pairs, a correct response can be given by simply comparing the pair along visual–spatial or figural dimensions. For nonidentical pairs, a correct response requires the subject to compare the pair along a verbal or linguistic modality. Reaction times in the nonidentical name match favored the dominant visual field (Fig. 16). Since there was an equal a priori probability of occurrence of name-alike and identical pairs, Kinsbourne's attention model clearly cannot handle results such as these but, as explained earlier, a strict localization model can. Attentional biases, then, may magnify, but not cause, laterality effects.[4]

Summary of Reaction Time Research

Thus far the chapter has concentrated on showing the need as well as the value of conducting experiments on a normal population to test neuro-

[4] Similar arguments against Kinsbourne's attention or expectancy hypotheses appear in a recent paper by Geffen, Bradshaw, and Nettleton (1972).

logically derived hypotheses concerning the functional organization of the cerebral hemispheres of normal people. The conclusion drawn from these RT studies is that a model of cerebral organization based on the split-brain evidence cannot properly describe the functional organization of the cerebral hemispheres of normal people. The RT experiments have supported the classical localization model. These studies, however, have left some problems unsolved and have created others. The remainder of this chapter will discuss some of these problems, review two hypotheses concerning cerebral organization that offer solutions to these problems, and, finally, examine other clinical data to test the two hypotheses. The second part of this chapter will therefore, be somewhat more theoretical and speculative than the first.

The Model of Functional Localization

The primary problem concerns the controversy which inspired this series of studies — how can the split-brain data on the minor hemisphere's verbal abilities be reconciled with a strict localization model that denies the existence of verbal abilities in the minor hemisphere?

One possible solution to the problem mentioned earlier is that the minor hemisphere of split-brain patients is abnormal and does not reflect the true capacities of the normal minor hemisphere. This hypothesis will be referred to as the neural reorganization hypothesis. There is reason to believe that the split-brain patients had a history of cerebral malfunction dating to childhood (see Hurwitz, 1971, for review of the cases). It is known that damage to the dominant hemisphere, before differentiation into verbal and nonverbal hemispheres is complete, causes the minor hemisphere to assume verbal functions (Basser, 1962; Gardner, Karnosh, McClure, & Gardner, 1955; Krynauw, 1950; Landsdell, 1969). It is, therefore, conceivable that the representation of language functions, which under circumstances of normal early development would be restricted to the dominant hemisphere, would be distributed to some extent in both hemispheres in split-brain patients. The neural-reorganization hypothesis is, furthermore, consistent with the evidence on lateralization of function in normal and brain-damaged individuals. What is disturbing about this hypothesis is that it relegates the split-brain phenomena to a curiosity which should not be taken seriously in formulating models of normal cerebral organization. Such an attitude would be justified if all the evidence supported the neural reorganization hypothesis. There are, however, reports in the neurological literature of cases of minor hemisphere language which cannot be said to have originated as a result of early damage to the dominant hemisphere.

Before I present this evidence, I wish to propose an alternative model to account for the observed differences in the minor hemisphere's language abilities. The model states that, within limits, the verbal competence of the minor hemisphere is the same in all right-handed people, including split-brains. The extent to which the minor hemisphere's performance on verbal tasks reflects its limited underlying competence, however, depends on the degree to which the dominant hemisphere can control the verbal behavior of the minor hemisphere via the midline commissures and other pathways.

This is a more dynamic model and, as such, may be properly called a model of *functional,* as opposed to strict, *localization.* Similar suggestions were made by Liepmann (1906) and Orton (1937). More recently, Geschwind (1969) suggested that verbal functions are present in the minor hemisphere, but that retrieval of verbal information is effected only from one side. Inhibition of access to minor hemisphere information may be caused by the dominant hemisphere or by processes occurring within the minor hemisphere (Geschwind, personal communication). He further postulates that a period of time is necessary to overcome this inhibition which may explain why language functions in hemispherectomized patients improve with time. Its ability to resolve the problems mentioned will now be examined.

First, it can explain why the minor hemisphere of normal people does not exhibit any ability to process verbal information. Though the minor hemisphere may have the competence to perform adequately on tasks requiring verbal skills, its competence will be masked by the control the dominant hemisphere can exert via interhemispheric and other pathways. Second, this hypothesis can account for the minor hemisphere's improved performance on verbal tasks once the commissural fibers are cut. The split-brain operation which sections the corpus callosum and anterior commissures removes major pathways via which the dominant hemisphere can influence the activity of the minor side. Freed from the control of the dominant hemisphere, the minor hemisphere's verbal competence becomes manifest. Thus, the verbal behavior exhibited by the minor hemisphere of split-brain patients can be thought of as a release phenomenon in the Jacksonian sense. Finally, the functional localization model can account for the classical aphasic syndromes caused by lesions confined to the dominant hemisphere. Aside from the traditional language areas, such as Broca's and Wernicke's, recent evidence has shown that many other structures in the dominant hemisphere serve some verbal function. The mesial temporal lobe and hippocampus consolidate verbal information in long-term memory, the frontal lobes help order verbal stimuli in time (Milner, 1971), and the superior precentral gyrus influences speech production (Penfield & Roberts, 1959). Lesions in the dominant hemisphere capable of producing aphasia, still leave much of the dominant hemisphere intact and able to exert a substantial influence over the verbal behavior of the minor hemisphere. So long as some critical amount of neural tissue remains in the dominant hemisphere, the minor hemisphere will not escape from the dominant hemisphere's control. Consequently, the verbal performance of patients with lesions to the dominant hemisphere will usually reflect only the verbal competence of a malfunctioning dominant hemisphere, which, in many instances, will be poorer than the verbal behavior which a healthy minor hemisphere might execute were it not under dominant hemisphere control. This applies especially to cases of word blindness (alexia without agraphia) or word deafness, which are usually associated with relatively mild lesions restricted to the dominant hemisphere (see Gazzaniga, 1972, p. 316, for a recent study of word-deaf patients). Though it has limited verbal capacities, the minor hemisphere of split-brain patients is neither word blind nor word deaf.

The data presented so far are consistent with both the release of function hypothesis on which the functional localization model is based, and the neural reorganization hypothesis. Additional clinical evidence, however, can help choose between these two alternatives. According to the functional localization model, patients whose entire dominant hemisphere has been removed in adulthood because of damage presumably sustained in adulthood should display verbal behaviors comparable to the verbal behavior of the minor hemisphere of split-brains. The neural reorganization hypothesis, however, predicts that unless the damage occurred in childhood, language functions should remain confined to the dominant hemisphere, thus leaving dominant hemispherectomized patients totally aphasic. There are six cases on record in which dominant hemispherectomies were performed in adulthood (Crockett & Estridge, 1951; French, Johnson, Brown, & von Bergen, 1955; Hillier, 1954; Zollinger, 1935).[5] The psychological data from all but one of these patients (Smith, 1966; Smith & Burkland, 1966) are scanty. Nevertheless, the available data clearly favor the functional localization model. Though poor, speech was present in all five patients who regained consciousness. Furthermore, language comprehension was surprisingly good, all patients being able to obey at least simple commands. At least three of the patients (Hillier, 1954; Smith, 1966; French *et al.*, 1955) recovered language functions to the extent that they could understand all that was said to them and could communicate in propositional sentences, despite the fact that all three were severely aphasic before the operation. Unless we are willing to assume that in some patients malignant

[5] One of these cases (Hillier, 1954) was marginal since the patient was 14 at the time of operation and another case. Case 4 of Crockett and Estridge (1951) never fully regained consciousness after the operation.

tumors began to grow in childhood and were detected only in late middle age, the evidence from hemispherectomized patients is clearly more compatible with the functional localization model than with the neural reorganization hypothesis and the strict localization model which it supports.

The data from hemispherectomized patients are interesting because they further reveal the nature of the minor hemisphere's language functions and the type of control exerted over them by the dominant hemisphere. The verbal behavior of those patients who are not grossly debilitated by the operation even surpasses the verbal behavior of the minor hemisphere of split-brains. Most hemispherectomized patients could speak, though imperfectly, whereas aside from Butler and Norsell's (1968) study, all the evidence suggests that the minor hemisphere of split-brain patients is mute (Gazzaniga, 1970; Gazzaniga & Hillyard, 1971; Sperry, 1968). The hemispherectomized patients' comprehension also seems superior to the split-brains' minor hemisphere. All this implies that the dominant hemisphere can influence the behavior of the minor hemisphere across pathways other than the corpus collosum and anterior commissures. A surprising corollary of this statement is that the minor hemisphere's true capacities do not become wholly manifest until the entire dominant hemisphere is removed. Even then, however, its verbal abilities are inferior to those of the dominant hemisphere. Those patients, however, whose minor hemispheres have been entirely excised and who are left with only a dominant hemisphere, show no detectable verbal impairment.[6] If anything, their speech is more unrestrained than normal, suggesting that the minor hemisphere keeps the dominant one in check.

Functional hemispherectomies are almost as effective as true hemispherectomies in releasing the minor hemisphere's verbal behavior. Patients whose dominant hemisphere is temporarily anesthetized by sodium amytal usually cannot speak (Wada & Rasmussen, 1960). The minor hemisphere, however, can comprehend language, as is evidenced by the patients' ability to obey written and spoken commands (Wada & Rasmussen, 1960; Rossi & Rosadini, 1967; Milner, 1967b; Kinsbourne, 1971).

It is obvious from studies on both split-brain and hemispherectomized (functional and actual) patients that the minor hemisphere is far more competent at comprehending speech than producing it and that its skill regarding both of these functions varies from individual to individual. It is possible that the degree of minor hemisphere language competence with regard to both speech and comprehension will determine how easily the minor hemisphere can escape the control of the dominant. Many have acknowledged

---

[6] There is, however, a clearly visible impairment of visual perception and orientation (Austin & Grant, 1955).

that a principle similar to this one accounts for the relatively mild and short-lasting aphasias in left-handers as well as in right-handers with a family history of left-handedness (Luria, 1970). The same principle, however, may apply to pure right-handers. Kinsbourne (1971) reports three cases of right handers in whom damage to the dominant hemisphere produced expressive aphasia. By anesthetizing the hemispheres with sodium amytal, he found that the hemisphere producing the aphasic speech was the minor hemisphere and not the dominant one. The speech capacity of the minor hemisphere may have been sufficiently great in these patients to have been released after only some, and not all, of the dominant hemisphere had been destroyed. Kinsbourne's studies, furthermore, should encourage a reexamination of the notion that aphasic symptoms reflect only the poor performance of a damaged dominant hemisphere. In some circumstances, symptoms of receptive, as well as expressive aphasia, may reflect the limited verbal capacity of only the minor hemisphere or the distorted verbal performance of a damaged dominant hemisphere, as well as the performance of the minor hemisphere.

The data reviewed in this section argue against a neural reorganization hypothesis which maintains that verbal functions are localized exclusively in the dominant hemisphere unless early pathology of the dominant hemisphere induces the lateralization of these functions on the minor side as well.[7] The arguments presented suggest that verbal functions, though represented in both hemispheres, are *functionally* localized in the dominant side in normal and aphasic patients. Thus, a model of functional localization must replace the old strict localization model. Central to the functional localization model is the release of function hypothesis which states that removing the dominant hemisphere's influence releases the minor hemisphere's verbal behavior as is the case in split-brain and hemispherectomized patients.

Implications of the Functional Localization Model

Development of Lateralization

The substitution of the concept of functional localization for a strict localization model does not imply that both hemispheres are equipotential for all behaviors. Verbal abilities are functionally localized in the dominant hemisphere because its competence for these behaviors is greater than the

---

[7] The neural reorganization hypothesis may be salvaged by assuming that the development of tumours or seizures late in life can also cause structural–functional reorganization.

minor hemisphere's. Furthermore, anatomical asymmetries in the hemispheres have been found in adults (Geschwind & Levitsky, 1968) and infants
(Wada, 1969), suggesting that the predispositions for both hemispheres to
develop language functions may already be different at birth. Nor does the
concept of functional localization deny the applicability of a neural reorganization hypothesis to explain data dealing with pathology of the
dominant hemisphere in childhood. It merely asserts that such a hypothesis
will not account for all the available data on lateralization of function. The
release of function hypothesis on which the concept of functional localization is based does, in fact, consider that such neural reorganizations, rather
than being aberrant phenomena, are the outcome of normal processes. It is
known from behavioral (Bryden, 1970) as well as neurological evidence
(Basser, 1962) that verbal abilities are not fully lateralized before the
child is between 5 and 10 years old. It is conceivable that over this time the
dominant hemisphere acquires the ability to suppress the verbal behavior of
the minor hemisphere. The verbal competence that the minor hemisphere
possessed in childhood by and large remains, though some functions may
deteriorate through disuse and others may be lost through differentiation.
Pathology of the dominant hemisphere in childhood, however, will diminish
the degree of control that the dominant hemisphere can exert over the
minor one, thereby leaving the minor hemisphere relatievly free to develop
and practice its verbal skills. This view also predicts that not only damage
to the dominant hemisphere, but damage to or absence of interhemispheric
pathways via which the dominant hemisphere exerts its influence, should
also produce similar effects on the minor hemisphere's verbal performance.
Saul and Sperry (Sperry, 1970) in a series of investigations of a right-
handed patient with callosal agenesis have shown that both hemispheres
speak and comprehend language. Reports of more elaborate tests determining whether language functions are represented equally in both hemispheres have not yet appeared.

Therapy for Aphasia

If the functional localization model is correct, it follows that a possible
therapeutic approach for the rehabilitation of aphasic patients would be to
exploit the latent verbal abilities of the minor hemisphere. Gazzaniga
(1972) and his students have already embarked on a program of teaching
severely aphasic patients the picture–symbol language developed by
Premack (1971) for use on language learning in chimpanzees. By presumably using their healthy minor hemisphere, these patients easily learn to
comprehend and manipulate these artificial language symbols. Though this

program is in its infancy, it is conceivable that the aphasic patients will be able to communicate sophisticated thoughts by using these new symbolic devices.

Another approach is more radical, hazardous, and highly speculative, but may enable the patient to regain his use of natural language. The functional localization model suggests that some aphasic symptoms might be alleviated by freeing the verbal capacities of the minor hemisphere from the control of a debilitated, malfunctioning dominant hemisphere. By anesthetizing the dominant hemisphere with sodium amytal, a procedure that is itself not without hazards, one can determine the residual verbal capacities of the minor side. If they are extensive, sectioning the cerebral commissures may release the verbal behaviors of the minor hemisphere, thereby making verbal skills, which were previously inaccessible, once more available to the patient. Though the effects of commissurotomy seem to be extremely mild and almost undetectable except with sophisticated testing techniques, the surgical approach just suggested should be undertaken reluctantly, if at all, and then only after a great deal of evidence has been accumulated to justify such a radical procedure.

Mechanism of Dominant Hemispheric Control

What is the mechanism whereby the dominant hemisphere exerts its control over the verbal behavior of the minor hemisphere? The predictions that follow from the functional localization model do not necessarily depend on the manner in which the minor hemisphere's verbal abilities are controlled. Nonetheless, knowledge of these mechanisms will certainly contribute to a theory of cerebral lateralization as well as to clinical practice. A number of hypotheses are reported in the literature. The dominant hemisphere may inhibit the corresponding verbal behavior on the minor side (Butler & Norsell, 1968; Orton, 1937); it may interfere with the minor hemisphere's verbal processes (Milner, 1970, p. 258); it may cause all verbal information to bypass the minor hemisphere (Moscovitch, 1972a); or it may compete with the minor hemisphere for control over motor and perceptual pathways (Levy, Trevarthen, & Sperry, 1972). The experimental evidence does not yet favor one mechanism over the other.

Efficiency of Functional Localization

Why are verbal abilities only *functionally* localized in the dominant hemisphere? What useful purpose could the minor hemisphere's latent verbal skills serve? One possibility is that the minor hemisphere's verbal skills might be used to decode verbal information transferred to it from the dominant hemisphere. A more likely possibility is that the minor hemisphere serves no verbal function in adulthood. Whatever verbal competence it possesses is vestigial, a remnant of the extensive verbal skills it possessed and probably used in childhood before the dominant hemisphere assumed control. The minor hemisphere's verbal competence in childhood could serve as a fail-safe mechanism in case the dominant hemisphere were damaged. Language would then develop normally on the minor side.

Why must the minor hemisphere's verbal abilities be suppressed in the first place? If both hemispheres actually had equal verbal capacities, they would process verbal information in parallel with each other and in large measure duplicate the work done. If it existed, such an arrangement would still leave only one common response pathway over which speech could be emitted. The hemispheres would thus be forced to compete with each other for access to that motor pathway. Since the sequence of the delicate motor movements responsible for speech require fast precision timing (differences of only 20 msec in onset of one movement in the sequence may produce a different phoneme), the greater chance of interference produced by the competing hemispheres may distort speech output. The four cases reported by Jones (1966) in which stammering in patients with bilateral speech representation was relieved by eliminating the speech mechanisms on one side are extreme examples of the debilitating effects of having both hemispheres control speech. This may also explain why speech production is functionally more localized than comprehension.[8]

Finally, the lateralization of language functions to the dominant hemisphere may leave the minor hemisphere free to specialize in functions that do not require linguistic ability, such as processing visual, spatial, and nonverbal acoustic information (Levy, 1969). Neurological evidence, in fact, shows the minor hemisphere to be superior in those abilities in adulthood. Individuals in whom language is poorly lateralized, such as left-handers, as well as right-handed individuals who developed right hemisphere speech as a result of early birth injury, on the average do more poorly than pure right handers on tests measuring visual–spatial skills (Levy, 1969; Nebes, 1971; Miller, 1971; Landsdell, 1969), but normally on tests measuring verbal

---

[8] Significantly, a similar scheme has evolved for probably similar reasons in another species with an elaborate vocal communication system. Nottebohm (1970) discovered that in chaffinches, control over the distinctive elements of song production, such as trills, is lateralized to the left side. In addition, he showed that neutral control over the song pattern is not lateralized at birth but develops over "childhood." If the right-side nerves innervating the syrinx are severed before a male comes into full song, the left side nerves assume their function.

abilities. Saul and Sperry found a similar pattern of deficit in a patient with callosal agenesis in which language functions were bilateralized (Sperry, 1970). Thus, if language functions are not restricted to one hemisphere, they seem to interfere with the development of nonverbal capacities in the other hemisphere. This suggests that the lateralization of language functions are a prerequisite for the lateralization of nonlinguistic functions. Research on the development of laterality in children should show whether the functional lateralization of verbal capacities must precede the functional lateralization of nonverbal capacities.

Communication between the Hemispheres

If, for all intents and purposes, the minor hemisphere is functionally unable to process verbal information, how can the verbal thoughts of the dominant hemisphere be communicated to it? It is unlikely that in normal people, as in split-brain patients, the thoughts of one hemisphere are kept hidden from the other. There is evidence that an intimate relationship exists between visual memory processes (in which the minor hemisphere specializes) and verbal memory processes (in which the dominant hemisphere specializes) (Bower, 1970; Jones, 1971; Patten, 1972). Information must therefore pass between the two hemispheres. To accomplish this, the two hemispheres must have a "language" or code in common. The RT data hint that both hemispheres can process and store visual information, although the dominant hemisphere is inferior to the minor one. The same may be true for somesthetic, stereognostic, and nosmic functions. Verbal information may be translated to one of the modalities which the two hemispheres have in common and then transferred to the minor hemisphere. Information passing from the minor to the dominant hemisphere will also be conveyed in these modalities. Another possibility is that the minor hemisphere's latent verbal functions may be used only for interhemispheric communication. Subsequent conversion of the verbal information to a modality which the minor hemisphere handles more easily could occur in the minor and not the dominant hemisphere. A final intriguing possibility is that complex linguistic utterances or visual experiences may be decoded into something quite neutral, a thought, which preserves the relations or meaning conveyed by the utterance or experience without necessarily preserving the particular form from which this thought was abstracted. These "thoughts" would be transferred from one hemisphere to the other where they would be re-expressed in the hemisphere's preferred modality. This suggestion is meant to convey in loose cognitive language that information may be relayed across interhemispheric paths in an unknown, modality unspecific, neural code. Which of these codes are involved in transmitting interhemispheric information is an area of investigation that is just beginning. There is an obvious advantage to conduct research into the properties of the inter-hemispheric code on a normal population. After all, they have healthy brains with intact commissures along which information can be relayed. Such a program of research will perhaps eventually discover how two hemi-spheres, specializing in different functions and speaking different "languages," are nevertheless able to communicate with each other and produce a unity in consciousness.

Acknowledgments

The experiments reported in this paper were part of a doctoral thesis submitted to the Psychology Department of the University of Pennsylvania in 1972. The many discussions that I had with Paul Rozin, my advisor, were invaluable in helping me design, conduct, interpret, and finally report these experiments. I am also grateful to Dr. Norman Geschwind, Dr. Henry Gleitman, Dr. Jacob Nachmias, Dr. Harris Savin, and Dr. Saul Sternberg for their helpful comments and criticisms. Finally, I would like to thank Dr. Tom Alloway and Dr. Bill Milgram and especially Danny Klein for the many suggestions they made after reading earlier versions of this manuscript.

References

Akelaitis, A. J. Studies of gnosis, praxis, and language following section of corpus callosum and anterior commissure. *Journal of Neurosurgery,* 1944, **1**, 94–102.

Austin, G. M., & Grant, F. C. Physiologic observations following total hemispher-ectomy in man. *Surgery,* 1955, **38**, 239–258.

Basser, L. S. Hemisphegia of early onset and the faculty of speech with special reference to the effects of hemispherectomy. *Brain,* 1962, **85**, 427–460.

Berlucchi, G., Heron, W., Hyman, R., Rizzolatti, G., & Umilta, C. Simple reaction times of ipsilateral and contralateral hand to lateralized visual stimuli. *Brain,* 1971, **94**, 419–430.

Bower, G. H. Analysis of a mnemonic device. *American Scientist,* 1970, **58**, 496–510.

Bradshaw, J. L., & Perriment, A. D. Laterality effects and choice reaction time in a unimanual two-finger task. *Perception and Psychophysics,* 1970, **7**, 185–188.

Broca, P. Perte de la parole. Ramollissement chronique et destruction partielle du lobe antérieur gauche du cerveau. *Bulletin de la Société d'Anthropologie,* 1861, +II.

Broca, P. Sur la faculté du language articule. *Bulletin de la Société d'Anthropologie,* 1865, **4**, 493–494.

Bryden, M. P. Laterality effects in dichotic listening: relations with handedness and reading ability in children. *Neuropsychologia,* 1970, **8**, 443–450.

Butler, S. R., & Norsell, V. Vocalization possibly initiated by the minor hemisphere. *Nature,* 1968, **220**, 793–794.

Cohen, G. Hemispheric differences in a letter classification task. *Perception and Psychophysics,* 1972, **11**, 137–142.

Cohn, R. Differential cerebral processing of noise and verbal stimuli. *Science,* 1971, **72**, 599–601.

Crockett, H. G., & Estridge, N. M. Cerebral hemispherectomy: A clinical, surgical, and pathologic study of four cases. *Bulletin of the Los Angeles Neurological Society,* 1951, **16**, 71–87.

Dejerine, J. (1892). Cited in Benson, D. F., & Geschwind, N. The Alexias. In P. J. Vinken, & G. W. Bruyn (Eds.). *Handbook of Clinical Neurology,* Vol. 4. Amsterdam: North-Holland Publ., 1969. Pp. 112–140.

Egeth, H., & Blecker, D. Differential effects of familiarity on judgements of sameness and difference. *Perception and Psychophysics,* 1971, **9**, 321–326.

Eisenson, J. Language and intellectual modifications associated with right cerebral damage. *Language and Speech,* 1962, **5**, 49–53.

Filby, R. A., & Gazzaniga, M. S. Splitting the normal brain with reaction time. *Psychonomic Science,* 1969, **17**, 335–336.

French, L. A., Johnson, D. R., Brown, I. A., & von Bergen, F. B. Cerebral hemispherectomy for control of intractable convulsive seizures. *Journal of Neurosurgery,* 1955, **12**, 154–164.

Gardner, W. J., Karnosh, L. J., McClure, C. C., & Gardner, A. K. Residual function following hemispherectomy for tumour and for infantile hemiplegia. *Brain,* 1955, **78**, 487–502.

Gazzaniga, M. S. *The bisected brain.* New York: Appleton, 1970.

Gazzaniga, M. S. Conference report of the Fifteenth International Symposium of Neuropsychology, Cambridge, 1970; *Neuropsychologia,* 1971, **9**, 479–480.

Gazzaniga, M. S. One brain – Two minds? *American Scientist,* 1972, **60**, 311–317.

Gazzaniga, M. S., & Hillyard, S. A. Language and speech capacity of the right hemisphere. *Neuropsychologia,* 1971, **87**, 415–422.

Gazzaniga, M. S., & Sperry, R. W. Language after section of the cerebral commissures. *Brain,* 1967, **90**, 131–148.

Geffen, G., Bradshaw, J. L., & Wallace, G. Interhemispheric effects on reaction time to verbal and non-verbal stimuli. *Journal of Experimental Psychology,* 1971, **87**, 415–422.

Geffen, G., Bradshaw, J. L., & Nettleton, N. C. Hemispheric asymmetry: Verbal and spatial encoding of visual stimuli. *Journal of Experimental Psychology,* 1972, **95**, 25–31.

Geschwind, N. Disconnexion syndromes in animals and man. *Brain,* 1965, Part I (237–294), Part II (585–644).

Geschwind, N. Anatomical understanding of the aphasias. In A. L. Benton (Ed.), *Contributions to clinical neuropsychology.* Chicago: Aldine, 1969.

Geschwind, N. The organization of language and the brain. *Science,* 1970, **170**, 940–944.

Geschwind, N., & Levitsky, W. Human brain: Left–right asymmetries in temporal speech region. *Science,* 1968, **161**, 186–187.

Goldstein, K. *Language and language disturbances.* New York: Grune & Stratton, 1948.

Goldstein, M. N., & Joynt, R. J. Long-term follow-up of a callosal-sectioned patient. *Archives of Neurology,* 1969, **20**, 96–102.

Head, H. *Aphasia and kindred disorders of speech.* Cambridge, England: Cambridge Univ. Press, 1926.

Hebb, D. O. The effects of early and late brain injury upon test scores and the nature of normal adult intelligence. *Proceedings of the American Philosophical Society,* 1942, **85**, 275–292.

Hillier, W. Total left cerebral hemispherectomy for malignant glioma. *Neurology,* 1954, **4**, 718–721.

Hurwitz, L. J. Evidence for restitution of function and development of new function in cases of brain bi-section. *Cortex,* 1971, **7**, 401–409.

Jeeves, M. A. A comparison of interhemispheric transmission times in acallosals and normals. *Psychonomic Science,* 1969, **16**, 245–246.

Jones, M. K. Imagery as a mnemonic aid after left temporal lobectomy. Unpublished master's thesis. McGill University, 1971.

Jones, R. K. Observations on stammering after localized cerebral injury. *Journal of Neurology, Neurosurgery, and Psychiatry,* 1966, **29**, 192–195.

Kimura, D. Functional asymmetry of the brain in dichotic listening. *Cortex,* 1967, **3**, 163–178.

Kinsbourne, M. The cerebral basis of lateral asymmetries in attention. *Acta Psychologica,* 1970, **33**, 193–201.

Kinsbourne, M. The minor cerebral hemisphere as a source of aphasic speech. *Archives of Neurology,* 1971, **25**, 302–306.

Klatzky, R. L., & Atkinson, R. C. Specialization of the cerebral hemispheres in scanning for information in short-term memory. *Perception and Psychophysics,* 1971, **10**, 335–338.

Krynauw, R. S. Infantile hemiplegia treated by removing one cerebral hemisphere. *Journal of Neurology, Neurosurgery, and Psychiatry,* 1950, **13**, 243–267.

Landsdell, H. Verbal and non-verbal factors in right-hemisphere speech: relations to early neurological history. *Journal of Comparative and Physiological Psychology,* 1969, **69**, 734–738.

Lashely, K. S. In search the engram. *Society of experimental biology symposium No. 4: Animal behaviour.* Cambridge, England: Cambridge Univ. Press, 1950. Pp. 478–505.

Levy, J. Possible basis for the evolution of lateral specialization in the human brain. *Nature,* 1969, **224**, 614–615.

Levy, J., Trevarthen, C., & Sperry, R. W. Perception of bilateral chinuvic figures following hemispheric deconnexion. *Brain,* 1972, **95**, 61–78.

Liepmann, H. (1906). Cited in Geschwind, N., 1965.

Luria, A. R. *Traumatic aphasia.* The Hague: Mouton, 1970.

Luria, A. R. Aphasia reconsidered. *Cortex,* 1972, **8**, 34–40.

McAdam, D. W., & Whitaker, H. A. Language production: electroencephalographic localization in the normal human brain. *Science,* 1971, **172**, 499–503.

McKeever, W. F., & Gill, K. M. Interhemispheric transfer time for visual stimulus information varies as a function of the retinal locus of stimulation. *Psychonomic Science,* 1972, **26**, 308–310.

McKeever, W. F., & Huling, M. P. Lateral dominate and tachistoscopic word recognition performance obtained with simultaneous bilateral input. *Neuropsychologia,* 1971, **9**, 15–20.

Miller, E. Handedness and the pattern of human ability. *British Journal of Psychology,* 1971, **62**, 111–112.

Milner, B. Brain mechanisms suggested by studies of temporal lobes. In C. H. Millikan & F. L. Darley (Eds.), *Brain mechanisms underlying speech and language* New York: Grune & Stratton, 1967. (a)

Milner, B. Discussion on cerebral dominance in man. In C. H. Millikan, & F. L. Darley (Eds.), *Brain mechanisms underlying speech and language.* New York: Grune & Stratton, 1967. (b)

Milner, B. Interhemispheric differences and psychological processes. *British Medical Bulletin,* 1971, **27**, 272–277.

Milner, P. M. *Physiological psychology.* New York: Holt, 1970. P. 258.

Morrell, L. K., & Salomy, J. G. Hemispheric asymmetry of electrocortical responses to speech stimuli. *Science,* 1971, **174**, 164–166.

Moscovitch, M. Reaction time studies assessing the verbal behaviour of the minor hemisphere in normal right-handed, adult humans *or* what does someone in his right mind know? Unpublished doctoral dissertation, University of Pennsylvania, 1972. (a)

Moscovitch, M. A choice reaction time study assessing the verbal behaviour of the minor hemisphere in normal, adult humans. *Journal of Comparative and Physiological Psychology,* 1972, **80**, 66–74. (b)

Moscovitch, M., & Catlin, J. Interhemispheric transmission of information: measurement in normal man. *Psychonomic Science,* 1970, **18**, 211–213.

Nebes, R. D. Handedness and the perception of port-while relationships. *Cortex,* 1971, **7**, 350–356.

Nottebohm, F. Ontogeny of bird song. *Science,* 1970, **167**, 950–956.

Orton, S. *Reading, writing, and speech problems in children.* London: Chapman & Hall, 1937.

Patten, B. M. The ancient art of memory. *Archives of Neurology,* 1972, **26**, 25–31.

Penfield, W., & Roberts, L. *Speech and brain mechanisms.* Princeton, New Jersey: Princeton Univ. Press, 1959.

Poffenberger, A. T. Reaction time to retinal stimulation with special reference to the time lost in conduction through nerve centres. *Archives of Psychology,* 1912, **13**, 1–73.

Posner, M. I., & Mitchell, R. F. Chronometric analysis of classification. *Psychological Review,* 1967, **74**, 392–409.

Premack, D. Language in chimpanzee? *Science,* 1971, **172**, 808–822.

Rizzolatti, G., Umilta, C., & Berlucchi, G. Opposite superiorities of the right and left cerebral hemispheres in discriminative reaction time to physiognomical and alphabetical material. *Brain,* 1971, **94**, 431–442.

Rossi, G. F., & Rosadini, G. Experimental analysis of cerebral dominance in man. In C. H. Millikan & F. L. Darley (Eds.), *Brain mechanisms underlying speech and language.* New York: Grune & Stratton, 1967.

Smith, A. Speech and other functions after left (dominant) hemispherectomy. *Journal of Neurology, Neurosurgery and Psychiatry,* 1966, **29**, 467–471.

Smith, A., & Burklund, C. W. Dominant hemispherectomy: Preliminary report on neuropsychological sequelae. *Science,* 1966, **153**, 1280–1282.

Smith, K. Y. Bilateral integrative action of the cerebral cortex in man in verbal association and sensory motor coordination. *Journal of Experimental Psychology,* 1947, **37**, 367–376.

Sperry, R. W. Cerebral organization and behavior. *Science,* 1961, **133**, 1749–1757.

Sperry, R. W. Hemispheric deconnection and unity in conscious awareness. *American Psychologist,* 1968, **23**, 723–733.

Sperry, R. W. Cerebral dominance in perception. In F. A. Young & D. B. Lindsley (Eds.), *Early experience in visual information processing in perceptual and reading disorders.* Washington, D.C.: National Academy of Sciences, 1970. Pp. 167–178.

Sperry, R. W., Gazzaniga, M. S., & Bogen, J. E. Interhemispheric relationships: The neocortical commissures; syndromes of hemispheric disconnection. In P. J. Vinken & G. W. Bruyn (Eds.), *Handbook of clinical neurology.* Vol. 4. Amsterdam: North-Holland Publ., 1969.

Springer, S. Ear asymmetry in a dichotic detection task. *Perception and Psychophysics,* 1971, **10**, 239–241.

Springer, S. The effect of contralateral noise on the perception of speech: A reaction time analysis. Paper presented to the Western Psychological Association, Portland, 1972.

Studdert-Kennedy, M., & Shankweiler, D. Hemispheric specialization for speech perception. *Journal of the Acoustical Society of America,* 1970, **48**, 579–594.

Umilta, C., Frost, N., & Hyman, R. Interhemispheric effects on choice reaction times to one-, two and three-letter displays. *Journal of Experimental Psychology,* 1972, **93**, 198–204.

Wada, J. Paper presented at 9th International Congress of Neurology, New York, 1969 (see Geschwind, N. (1970)).

Wada, J., & Rasmussen, T. Intracorotid injection of sodium amytal for the lateralization of cerebral dominance: Experimental and clinical observations. *Journal of Neurosurgery,* 1960, **17**, 266–282.

Weisenberg, T., & McBride, K. E. *Aphasia: A clinical and psychological study.* New York: Commonwealth Fund, 1935.

White, M. J. Laterality differences in perception: A review. *Psychological Bulletin,* 1969, **72**, 387–405.

Wood, C. C., Goff, W. R., & Day, R. S. Auditory evoked potentials during speech perception. *Science,* 1971, **173**, 1248–1251.

Zangwill, O. L. *Cerebral dominance and its relations to psychological function.* Edinburgh: Oliver & Boyd, 1960.

Zollinger, R. Removal of left cerebral hemisphere: Report of a case. *Archives of Neurology and Psychiatry,* 1935, **34**, 1055–1062.

MOTHER–INFANT DYAD:
THE CRADLE OF MEANING

Michael Lewis and Roy Freedle

Educational Testing Service

> *Language is a recent acquisition. Physiologically, the localized speech center is uniquely human. Biological evidence suggests that when new organs arise, they operate through previously extant ones, modulating and moderating them rather than abolishing them . . . Sperry . . . reports evidence suggesting that the rule is true of speech as well. Human information processing in this view may be taken as basically perceptual, with words and language operating upon the basic perceptual system.*
>
> — REITMAN (1965, p. 250)

To understand much of what is to follow, it is necessary to experience the data base out of which much of our thinking grew. Such a data base would require that you view, as well as hear, what transpires between a mother and her very young infant. The following transcription cannot do it justice — absent are the nuances, the color and subtlety of what makes up this dyadic relationship. Be that as it may, what follows is a sample description of the interaction of a mother with her 12-week-old infant. The interaction occurs over a 50-sec period of time. The infant was awake sitting in an infant seat in the kitchen while the mother was cleaning up the breakfast dishes.

127

9:30:10

F is sitting in her seat holding a rubber toy which is tied to the side of the chair. Mother has her back to *F* as she reaches for dish. *F* squeaks rubber toy making noise. As a "consequence" *F* kicks her feet and squeals with apparent delight. Mother turns toward *F* smiling. *F* looks at mother and vocalizes. Mother walks toward *F* smiling and vocalizing. *F* quiets, eyes fixed on mother. Mother touches *F*'s face. *F* vocalizes and moves her hands toward mother. Mother sits in front of *F* and vocalizes to her. (Talking about the toy which mother now holds.) *F* watches mother and listens. Mother pauses, *F* vocalizes. Mother touches *F* and vocalizes to her. *F* vocalizes.

9:31:00

The observer of this interaction cannot help but be struck by the communication network that the mother and her infant have established. Examination in detail of this type of interaction reveals a behavior matrix made up of both maternal and infant behaviors. Each member of this dyad is an active participant, each affects the determinants of the other's behavior. Moreover, the structure of the dyadic relationship reveals the kinds of chaining and pausing processes that one would expect to obtain from a two-way communication system (Jaffe & Feldstein, 1970). Take chaining as a first example. Here we refer to chaining as simply the number of actor changes; thus, "mother touches, infant vocalizes, mother vocalizes" consists of a three-chain structure. Observation of mother–infant interactions indicate that by 12 weeks as many as six-chain structures exist, these initiated by the infant as well as the mother. In a recent study by Lusk and Lewis (1972), it was shown that the length of these chains increases within the first year of life although the initiator of these chains does not seem to be developmentally related. It would seem that the patterns or sequential complexity of responses that the infant can sustain in interaction with the caretaker increases as the infant matures.

Our conception of a general communication system would be one that constrains behavior and therefore gives meaning. By meaning, we mean the differentiation or partitioning of the infant's world (be it spatial, temporal, internal, or external). We shall show that this differentiation can occur by situation and general behavior, as well as more specific sequences of vocalization states.

The interaction of the infant and its mother reflects what we believe to be a rather finely tuned and potentially meaning-laden system wherein each allows the other to act. Nowhere is this more readily seen than in the vocalization interaction of these two dyadic members. If we forget that the infant at 12 weeks of age is totally without any formal language system, observation of his vocal interactions strikes one as having a "conversational" quality. Mother vocalizes, infant listens; infant vocalizes, mother listens — the chain of vocalizations varying in length. The resulting phenomenon might very well be said to resemble that of two adult language-users carrying out a conversation.

Lieberman (1967) reports that infants of about 3 months appear to be able to respond differentially to friendly as contrasted with hostile voices. Other differentiations that infants appear capable of making are between exaggerated (baby talk) and normal intonation (Lieberman, 1967) and between inflection and noninflection (Kagan & Lewis, 1965). Other evidence (also cited by Lieberman, 1967) regarding the primitive behaviors from which language may later evolve concerns the cries of infants which he believes "provide the basis for the linguistic function of intonation in adult speech." While Lieberman argues for an innately determined basis of crying behavior, the work of Bell and Ainsworth (1971) suggests that infant crying and caretaker response are subject to learning principles. Their work reveals that, contrary to simple response-learning theory, reinforcement of crying behavior in the first quarter year (responding by holding the infant, etc.) does not produce subsequently more crying at 1 year, but, in fact, more subsequent communicative behavior. The authors state, and we must concur, that crying, even in the first quarter year of life, is a communicative behavior, reinforcement of which leads subsequently to other noncrying communicative behaviors. Infant crying then is part of the general communicative network of the infant and his world.

From a phonetic viewpoint, others have hypothesized infant language capacities. Even at this very early age it is possible to identify regularities such as the "innate breath group" which will later be adapted to serve a linguistic function — segmentation of the speech signal into sentences (Lieberman, 1967). Moreover, the recent work of several investigators indicates that phonetic properties of the language — the consonants /b/ and /p/ — are differentiated at very early ages (see Eimas, Siqueland, Jusczyk, & Vigorito, 1971). Whether from a phonetic or semantic viewpoint, Lieberman's finding of speech frequency differences in infants as a function of who is talking to them is rather interesting. Infants will attempt to mimic the fundamental frequency of the person talking to them, whereas in a free-play situation, the child's fundamental frequency is different, usually higher.

The corpus of observations on infant linguistic behavior, although limited, compels us to consider that at a very early age it may be possible to detect precursors of a system which may be, or may evolve into, a more formal language system. While the details may be in some doubt, there exists from birth a communication network between the infant and his mother.[1] *It is our general hypothesis that the anlage of language is developed of and from aspects of this communication system.* The major focus of this chapter, therefore, will be on the communication and semantic aspects found in infant–mother interaction.

For us, the function of language is to communicate. Like Lévi-Strauss (1966) we believe that language is a symbolic system which cannot exist apart from social interaction. Conversely, social interaction is a symbolic system. Man alone is by nature helpless and needs others, making social commerce axiomatic. In view of the fact that the function of language is to communicate, it would appear that meaning becomes the central factor to be considered when one wishes to explore the development of language. If it is semantics[2] that needs study, the problem becomes increasingly difficult: how to talk about meaning in an organism without formal language properties. The problem is not new, and in its general form deals with the interrelationship of language, thought, and mind. If the primary way to get at meaning is through language, is it possible to study meaning in a nonverbal organism? This problem has been dealt with for deaf children (see Furth, 1966) and for nonhuman primates (for example, Gardner & Gardner, 1969; Goodall, 1971). However, little attempt has been made to deal with this problem in infants prior to single word utterances.[3]

We intend to study semantics without language for we are interested in the earliest forms and/or precursors of meaning. We hope to demonstrate that at least by 3 months one can already discern some regularities in vocalization behaviors which occur nonrandomly and are distributed differentially as a function of situational context. A close analysis of these regularities suggests that they reflect perceptual–cognitive structures which are, or become, the earliest forms of such semantic notions as "location of," "object or subject of," "presence versus absence of," etc.[4]

Meaning may initially rely upon the perceptual isolation and recognition of featural or relational differences in the external world, such as noticing

---

[1] We use the term mother although we recognize that anyone may serve as a caregiver and constitute a member of the dyad.

[2] We use meaning and semantics synonymously.

[3] In some sense one might consider the study of genetic epistemology in the first two years as an attempt to deal with this. However, Piaget has committed himself to consider only very special aspects of meaning — cognitive as opposed to affective — and has, for the most part, linked most higher forms of cognitive activity with language.

[4] Although we have not mentioned the syntactical aspects of the communication network, we do not wish to imply that it is not present. For example, "object of" can be defined as a syntactical as well as semantic notion. See Fillmore (1968) and Kernan (1970) for a discussion of the newer emphasis of semantics in contrast with the primarily syntactic models of language and/or language development.

the direction of approach versus withdrawal, who does what to whom, which is a subject–object distinction, etc. One can deduce that the organism probably perceives such differences by noting a significant shift in its behavioral patterns which occur in situations which distinguish, for example, whether the infant is or is not the object of the mother's vocalizations. Also, if behavioral patterns shift as a function of mere changes in location such that the particular location favors a different spontaneous emission of behaviors, then one might claim that this forms a necessary, but perhaps not sufficient basis for the development of the semantic notion of location, or for the more specific problem of mapping function to location. Similarly, a change in behavior when a stranger approaches an infant versus withdraws from the infant can be interpreted as a potential precursor of the semantic notion of direction.

Thus, it seems more than reasonable to explore semantics in the communication network of the very young infant. After all, it would be even more implausible to maintain that the infant magically leaps to semantic conceptions only after he begins to struggle with single word utterances. No one could maintain that during the first year the infant is without knowledge (Piaget, 1952; Vygotsky, 1962). Thus, we felt it reasonable to assume that some form of semantic as well as phonetic and intonational substrates of language are developing continually from the moment of birth.

Method

To obtain data on the mother–infant interaction, it was necessary to observe each dyad over a relatively long period in a naturalistic setting. Each infant seen was 3 months old (± 1 week). The sample of infants seen was deliberately chosen in order to obtain as heterogeneous a group as possible. For this reason, boys and girls of two racial groups (black and white) as well as from the entire socioeconomic spectrum (using the Hollingshead five-point scale; Hollingshead, 1957) were included. There were infants of black professionals as well as infants of poor working class white families. In all, over 80 dyads have been seen; however, the data analysis is laborious and the number of dyads varies as a function of the analysis.

Each infant was seen in its home. Contact with the mothers was made in a variety of ways: contact through the mothers' initiative, selection of the mother–infant by looking through birth announcements in the newspapers, and through church groups in lower socioeconomic areas. Two observers were trained and used in this study, one for the black community and one for the white. The observer reliability was moderately high, at least for overall frequency of infant behaviors (ρ's ranged from .50s to .80s). The vocal behavior reported in this chapter has a much higher reliability, typically in the .80s.

The mothers were instructed that the observer was interested in studying the infant's behavior. The observer sat next to, but out of sight of the infant. It was stressed that it was the infant who was to be observed — not the mother. Moreover, the mother was to try to forget the presence of the observer and not engage her in conversation. When conversation was attempted, the observer reminded the mother that she was to ignore her. Prior to observation, the observer spent time with the mother attempting to put her at ease.

While every attempt was made to make the observation session as natural as possible, the presence of the observer was bound to have an effect. This problem has been discussed before (see Lewis & Goldberg, 1969); because of the ethical consideration of observation without the mother's knowledge and approval, this was the only procedure available.

The observation data were collected using a checklist sheet. Each sheet represents 60 sec, divided into six 10-sec columns. Infant behaviors are listed in the upper portion of the sheet, while adult behaviors are in the lower portion. When a behavior not listed on the sheet occurred, the observer wrote it in. For the most part, the behavior categories are self-explanatory and include vocalization, feed, smile, extra movement, fret/cry, quiet play and noise/nonvocalization. The "extra movement" category consisted of all gross physical movements such as limb movement or rolling of the body. "Quiet play" consisted of the child watching a toy move, playing with his fingers; and noise/nonvocalization was similar to extra movement, except that noise accompanied the behavior (by kicking feet against the crib). It is clear that these behaviors are not totally exclusive, reflecting a further difficulty in studies of this sort. Although the behaviors have some overlap, the observers were, in general, able to differentiate between them. Maternal behaviors listed included touch, hold, vocalization, look at, smile/laugh, play, feed, change clothes, rock, vocalization to others, reading or watching TV. Mother's touch and holding categories were used to distinguish between a discrete touch versus a physical support. If during a "hold" the mother also discretely touched the child, both categories would be scored. Finally, the categories of reading/TV and vocalizing to others were used to indicate that the mother was involved in activities *not* directed toward the child.

For each 10-sec interval, the observer checked off the occurrence of both infant and mother behaviors, also recording when possible which behaviors preceded which.

Also recorded by minute was a general description of the physical situation that the infant–mother were engaged in at that time; for example, "infant–mother in kitchen, infant in infant seat on table."

If the infant closed his eyes for longer than 30 consecutive seconds, observation stopped. In order to obtain two full hours of eyes-open data, a minimum of 2 hr of observation and on some occasions as much as 3 or 4 hr were necessary. In fact, for one-third of the sample, two visits to the home were required.

Methods of Data Analysis

Various levels of interactive analysis are possible with these types of data. In several recent papers (Lewis, 1972; Lusk & Lewis, 1972) some of the more obvious were presented. In the present paper we shall deal with three methods of data analysis.

The simplest is the *frequency distribution,* that is, how much vocalization, quiet play, smiling, etc., the infant exhibited in the two hours of observation. The same data analysis is possible for the mother's behavior.

Simultaneous Behavior within 10-Sec Unit. This measure is the number of 10-sec units for which there are both child and mother behaviors, keeping in mind the specific nature of the interaction. Since it is often difficult to determine exactly which one of the pair initiates a behavior sequence and time duration of the sequence, a more conservative approach is to restrict the analysis to a 10-sec time unit, recognizing that it is an arbitrarily selected unit of time.

Directional Interactive Analyses. Under this analysis, four categories of interactive behavior are possible for each specific behavior. For example, consider the infant's vocalization. One question to be asked is whether the vocalization was a response to a maternal behavior or was an initiator of a maternal behavior, these being scored as two separate categories. This was accomplished by making use of the scoring of a "1" or a "2," "1" indicating initiating. Two additional categories were necessary for interactions with less clarity of direction. For example, the child vocalizes and it was observed that the mother had been vocalizing to the infant for 30 sec prior to and 10 sec after the child's vocalization. Does the mother's vocalization constitute an initiation, and her vocalization subsequent to the child's, a response? It is not at all clear since the infant did not vocalize immediately. In this case, this type of interaction was scored separately. Finally, a fourth category was necessary for interactive behavior whose direction could not be assessed. Thus, for each infant behavior, each maternal behavior had four possible direction components. While we have illustrated this for vocalization data, it applies equally well for all behavioral categories.

There are, of course, many more measures of interaction for which individual measures may be obtained. For example, one can look at length of interaction; for another, density of response. In considering these types of data analysis, one must consider that we are discussing the possibility that each of these varies as a function of the context or situation in which they take place, as well as the idiosyncratic nature of the infant–mother interaction.

Results

Consistent with our theme, the results section will deal with three aspects of the problem of infant vocalization in order to demonstrate the non-random, selective and interactive quality of the infant's vocalization: (1) the general communication network, or the matrix of maternal and infant behaviors; (2) a model of sequential interaction between the infant and maternal vocalizations; and, finally, (3) an examination of the influence of situation on the infant and mother's vocalization.

General Communication Matrix

At first consideration, the vocalization matrix between two adult members of a dyad would appear to be the vocalizations of each member – a vocalization of A elicits a vocalization by B. Examination reveals, however, that this is only part of the vocalization matrix. The matrix consists of more than the words and sentences of A and B. A's sentence may elicit a frown from B which in turn elicits a new sentence by A.

Likewise, the caretaker–infant communication matrix is made up of more than the vocalizations of each member. In order to understand the function and meaning of vocalization (by either party) it will first be necessary to place these vocalizations within the communication matrix in which they appear and for which they are uttered.

The first analysis consists of the frequency of maternal and infant vocalizations which occurred within the two hours of observation. The data for over 40 infant–mother pairs reveal considerable individual differences. For example, the number of 10-sec periods in which there was an infant vocalization ranged from 28 to 438 10-sec periods! On the average, vocalizations occurred for approximately 25% of the observation time. Frequency of maternal vocalization also showed individual differences ranging from 101 to 493 10-sec periods. Maternal vocalization was relatively frequent during the two hours of observation — approximately 38% of the time. The frequency of maternal to infant vocalizations was significantly related so that high frequency vocalization of one was associated with high frequency of the other ($r = .43$, $p < .05$). Interestingly, while sex of the infant is not reflected in the mean frequency differences, the sex of the infant does affect the maternal output. Mothers of girls vocalize significantly more to their infants than do mothers of boys (mean 291.3 versus 227.1; $t = 2.04$, $p < .05$).

Still another individual difference has to do with the socioeconomic level of the family. The families were divided into social class according to Hollingshead's scale — a scale utilizing occupation and educational level. The frequency data for the mothers failed to indicate any social class effect; however, the frequency of the infants' utterances was clearly related to class. There was almost a perfect ordering, with the lower class infant vocalizing more. While these analyses are not meant to inform us as to the relationship of the utterance to the communication network, they do indicate that there are vast and significant (concerning their social consequences) individual differences in the output of vocalization for both a mother and her 12-week-old infant.

These individual differences will be discussed again; however, it is important to consider the frequency of output data from the beginning. In order to observe the general communication matrix in which the utterances are embedded, it is necessary to consider the matrix of when who does what to whom. In Table 1, such a matrix is constructed in which infant vocalization is related to the variety of maternal behaviors while maternal vocalization is related to the variety of infant behaviors. The data represent the mean number of 10-sec intervals in which a particular set of behaviors occurred. There could be a maximum of 720 such intervals. Look first at the infant vocalization data (top half of Table 1), both in terms of the infant vocalizations eliciting a maternal behavior (left half) and the infant vocalizations as a consequence of maternal behaviors (right half). In both cases the vocalization–vocalization pairing is strongest. In the case of infant initiated vocalization–mother responds, the next three strongest maternal responses are smile, look at, and touch. The three strongest maternal elicitors of an infant vocalization are play with, look and smile. Thus, next to maternal vocalization, maternal looking at and smiling to are the two constantly strongest responses associated with infant vocalizations.

Next, observe maternal vocalization (bottom half of Table 1) and those infant behaviors associated with it. Again, the vocalization–vocalization

TABLE 1

A Portion of the General Communication Matrix of Infant and Maternal
Behaviors as They Relate to the Vocalizations of Each

	Mean number of 10-sec intervals when infant initiates vocalization; mother responds with:			Mean number of 10-sec intervals when infant vocalizes in response to mother initiated:		
	Total	Male	Female	Total	Male	Female
Touch	1.08	1.50	0.55	5.16	4.07	6.55
Hold	0.80	1.29	0.18	5.60	3.64	8.09
Vocalize	34.24	32.07	37.00	23.20	18.43	29.27
Look	2.36	2.86	1.73	6.40	4.79	8.45
Smile	2.76	2.86	2.64	5.88	4.64	7.45
Play with	0.48	0.57	0.36	7.88	5.71	10.64
Change	0.12	0.21	0.00	0.72	0.93	0.45
Feed	0.32	0.57	0.00	0.80	0.57	1.09
Rock	0.12	0.21	0.00	0.04	0.07	0.00
Vocalize to others	1.00	1.29	0.64	0.12	0.00	0.27
Read/TV	0.12	0.14	0.09	0.20	0.29	0.09

	Mean number of 10-sec intervals where mother initiates vocalization; infant responds with:			Mean number of 10-sec intervals when mother vocalizes in response to infant initiated:		
	Total	Male	Female	Total	Male	Female
Vocalize	23.20	18.43	29.27	34.24	32.07	37.00
Movement	2.40	2.57	2.18	10.88	11.50	10.09
Fret/cry	2.16	1.93	2.45	18.68	16.86	21.00
Play	1.40	1.71	1.00	2.32	3.00	1.45
Smile	11.24	9.79	13.09	2.40	2.86	1.82

pairing is strongest. In the case of maternal initiated vocalization–infant response (left side), the infant smile is next strongest. For infant initiated behavior–maternal vocalization, infant distress (either movement or fret/cry) is the likeliest (after infant vocalization) to elicit a maternal utterance (right side). While there is a parallel between maternal response and infant vocalization, regardless of the direction of the infant vocalization, the same does not hold for the maternal utterance and infant response.

Individual differences in response pattern can also be observed. Table 1 presents the data broken down by sex of infant. Of particular interest is that infant initiated vocalization is responded to more often by the mother if the infant is a male. *This is true for every behavior except maternal utterance.* However, an infant vocalization in response to a maternal behavior is more likely for a female than a male. Thus, while *total* input vocalization data show no sex differences, infant vocalization in response to maternal behavior shows clear sex differences. Individual infant behavior related to a maternal vocalization is again less clear. Only fret/cry is consistent and indicates that maternal vocalization is more associated with female than male fret/cry.

The infant–maternal vocalization data would seem to parallel that of two adults. Vocalization–vocalization pairing is the most common interaction; however, smiling, looking at and fret/cry (this is uniquely an infant behavior and may be a negative affect component) are all instrumental in both eliciting and reinforcing a member's vocalization. Finally, even within this matrix of behavior, individual differences (as a function of the sex of the infant) in the patterning of vocalization behavior emerge.

A Model of Vocalization Interaction

The communication matrix makes clear that a vocalization can be the response of or the elicitor of behaviors other than a vocalization. A look or smile can serve as an elicitor or response to a vocalization, this for either the infant or mother. Any model used to study the interactive quality of the vocalization between members of a dyad will need to consider this. As one might imagine, the inclusion of all behaviors in any interactive model results in an extremely complex picture. Thus, as an initial step and for the sake of clarity, consider only utterances, or the lack thereof, in an interactive model. Moreover, in order to utilize all of the vocalization data, simultaneous occurrence, rather than only directional vocalization data, will be considered. While this is an oversimplification of the true state of affairs, the data previously presented suggest that vocalization–vocalization relationships by far are the most prevalent.

One way of studying the sequential quality of the infant–mother vocalizations is to construct a matrix of transitional probabilities (see Freedle & Lewis, 1971). To do this it will be necessary to assume each 10-sec period as a discrete trial or category. The use of these periods is arbitrary and was determined on the basis of ease of recording as well as obtaining a small time unit. Thus, there is no reason to believe that the sequence of infant and maternal behaviors bear any special relationship to this time demarkation. Nevertheless, this time unit will be used recognizing that it may be too long a duration and hence may obscure some of the detail in the interaction of the infant and his mother.

Since the data were collected for 2 full hours, a total of 720 successive 10-sec periods exist for each dyad. The vocalization data can be categorized into six states: neither mother nor infant vocalize (0); infant vocalizes alone (1); mother vocalizes alone to infant (2); mother vocalizes alone to some other person (2i); mother and infant both vocalize(3); and mother vocalizes to another person and the infant vocalizes (3i).

Given these states of infant, mother and infant–mother interaction and the 10-sec time unit, we will use the transitional matrix values as a measuring instrument in order to ascertain individual as well as state differences in infant vocalizations.

The transitional or conditional probabilities can be estimated as follows: consider the following succession of states obtained from coding the successive 10-sec periods for a particular mother–infant pair: 3, 0, 1, 3, 1, 2, ... Set up a matrix with six rows and six columns labeled 0, 1, 2i, 2, 3i, and 3, reading from the top down for the rows and similarly labeled reading from left to right across the columns. Using the above sequence, notice that the first pair of states is 3, 0. Enter a tally in the rows labeled '3' and the column marked '0'. The second and third states form the next pair of states which is 0, 1. Enter another tally in the row labeled '0' and the column labeled '1.' The next pair of states is 1, 3, so enter a tally in row '1' and column '3' and so on until all successive pairs of states have been tallied. When this is done, sum up the tallies for each row and divide the frequency in each row cell by the sum for that row. These proportions that result in each row are then used as the estimates for the conditional probabilities of the transition matrix. For the data under consideration here, there were 719 tallied entries for each mother–infant pair studied.

Table 2 presents the transitional probabilities by sex for each of the vocalization states. From this table, it is possible to examine how the vocalization state on trial $n + 1$ is influenced by the state that occurred on trial n. Using this scheme, it is possible to investigate a series of interesting and important questions. For example, one might inquire as to the relationship of maternal vocalization (state '2') on trial n on infant vocalization (state '1') on trial $n + 1$, or the relationship of state '1' on trial n to state '1' on trial $n + 1$. The general form of the questions center around the probabilities of occurrence of vocalization states in the future as a function of a past state.

In general, the largest conditional probabilities in each row is along the diagonal of the matrix. This indicates that a vocalization state tends to persist over time — that is, these dyads will tend to have long runs of the same state. There are interesting and meaningful other patterns — for example, individual differences in an infant's ability to discriminate toward whom the mother is directing her vocalization. We observe that girl infants detect the difference between their mother's talking to them (where they are the object of the mother's directed speech — state '2') and when their mother is talking to someone other than themselves (where someone else

TABLE 2
*Conditional Probabilities of Vocalization
States by Sex of Infant*
$(N = 44)$

| | States | | Trial $n + 1$ | | | | | | States involving infant vocalizations |
			0	1	2	2i	3	3i	$1 + 3 + 3i$
Trial n	0	M	.654	.095	.138	.062	.041	.009	.145
		F	.625	.101	.167	.057	.046	.005	.152
	1	M	.352	.446	.073	.025	.087	.017	.550
		F	.412	.408	.075	.015	.077	.014	.499
	2	M	.280	.024	.492	.070	.125	.009	.158
		F	.233	.029	.551	.059	.124	.004	.157
	2i	M	.194	.027	.087	.587	.028	.076	.131
		F	.201	.013	.113	.608	.021	.044	.078
	3	M	.172	.089	.303	.045	.364	.027	.480
		F	.149	.071	.340	.025	.400	.015	.486
	3i	M	.131	.077	.060	.270	.075	.387	.539
		F	.183	.094	.089	.251	.120	.262	.476

is the object of the mother's speech — state '$2i$'). This fact can be demonstrated by examining the rows of the transitional probability matrix labeled '2' and '$2i$.' If we sum the probability that the infant will vocalize in the next time sequence (sum in each row the column entries '1,' '3,' and '$3i$' in which the infant vocalizes), we find that female infants show a significant tendency to vocalize more when the mother vocalizes to them than when she vocalizes to another (sign test, $p < .001$). The same analysis comparing '3' with '$3i$' indicates that female infants can discriminate the object of the mother's vocalizations (sign test, $p < .07$). These analyses for male infants fail to indicate any ability to differentiate their vocalizations as a function of whether they were or were not the object of their mother's vocalizations ($p < .50$ in both tests). These differences indicate that females may be showing more "advanced" language development even at 12 weeks.

Before turning to SES differences in these conditional probabilities, it is interesting to note that the probabilities of the infant vocalizing in a future time sequence is equally well accounted for by the amount of vocalization the infant exhibited previously (state '1') as well as the amount of directed infant–mother interaction (state '3'). Environmental input — at least maternal vocalization (states '2' or '$2i$') — is relatively weak in accounting for or influencing subsequent infant vocalization. In fact, it does not appear to be different from state '0' which represents no vocal behavior at all!

TABLE 3
*Conditional Probabilities of Vocalization States
by Social Class Level of Family*[a,b]

| | | States | Trial $n + 1$ | | | | | | States involving infant vocalization |
			0	1	2	2i	3	3i	1 + 3 + 3i
	0	SES I	.634	.076	.171	.084	.030	.001	.107
		II	.711	.089	.137	.030	.030	.003	.122
		III	.591	.103	.160	.069	.065	.013	.181
		IV	.671	.098	.136	.047	.045	.006	.149
		V	.619	.149	.135	.028	.062	.007	.218
	1	SES I	.467	.459	.100	.035	.056	.025	.540
		II	.650	.573	.089	.028	.065	.000	.638
		III	.331	.438	.063	.012	.144	.014	.596
		IV	.414	.341	.099	.035	.092	.019	.452
		V	.337	.489	.065	.015	.079	.016	.584
	2	SES I	.300	.031	.515	.078	.070	.006	.107
		II	.295	.032	.526	.053	.093	.001	.126
		III	.189	.031	.548	.053	.170	.009	.210
		IV	.192	.028	.587	.062	.127	.003	.158
Trial n		V	.250	.055	.458	.056	.173	.009	.237
	2i	SES I	.212	.017	.102	.630	.011	.027	.055
		II	.216	.015	.084	.628	.030	.027	.072
		III	.217	.023	.094	.522	.053	.091	.167
		IV	.164	.023	.080	.623	.025	.084	.132
		V	.136	.033	.128	.530	.028	.114	.175
	3	SES I	.251	.098	.356	.050	.234	.014	.346
		II	.174	.048	.426	.043	.300	.009	.357
		III	.120	.082	.297	.028	.450	.023	.555
		IV	.188	.067	.371	.032	.319	.023	.409
		V	.172	.099	.329	.039	.500	.031	.630
	3i	SES I	.218	.113	.097	.290	.089	.194	.396
		II	.286	.048	.143	.333	.048	.143	.239
		III	.129	.075	.080	.279	.104	.333	.512
		IV	.118	.078	.029	.373	.049	.353	.480
		V	.219	.143	.095	.314	.181	.429	.753

[a] SES I is the "highest" social class as determined by the Hollingshead scale (based on occupation and education levels).

[b] This table is constructed from more than 31,000 10-sec intervals.

Table 3 presents the transitional probabilities as a function of SES. Several rather interesting findings emerge. While in general the most powerful influence on the vocalization state of trial $n + 1$ is the same vocalization state on trial n, important SES differences appear. First, consider state '1' (infant's vocalization alone) as accounting for the infant's vocalization in a subsequent time. All SES levels have about the same conditional probabilities (.54, .64, .60, .45, .58 for SES I–V, respectively). When one considers state '3' (the mother–infant vocalization), one finds clear SES differences with *lower* SES infant vocalizations being *more* affected by past mother–infant interaction (conditional probabilities of .34, .36, .55, .41, .63 for SES I–V, respectively). Thus, there is no difference in the subsequent probability of a lower SES infant (V) vocalizing considering states 1 or 3 (.58 versus .63). However, there is a difference in the subsequent probability of a higher SES infant (I) vocalizing considering states 1 and 3 (.54 versus .34). This finding is partially explained by observing the effect of environmental impact – maternal vocalization – on the infant's subsequent vocalization. In general, state '2' has little effect on the probability of the infant vocalizing (probabilities of .11 to .24). What is interesting is that there is again an SES level effect with maternal impact having a *greater* effect for the lower SES levels (conditional probabilities of .11, .12, .21, .16, .24 for SES I–V, respectively). Exactly the meaning of this SES difference is not clear. However, the data suggest that the mother's vocalization (either alone as in state '2' or in conjunction with the infant as in state '3') does not facilitate the higher SES infants' vocalization. This may be a function of the fact that the mothers' vocalizations cause these infants to listen rather than vocalize. Previous work with middle class infants using human voices suggests that mother's voice does have the effect of inhibiting infants' vocalizations (Kagan & Lewis, 1965). This interpretation is further supported by observation of some specific subcycles in the conditional probability matrix. Consider the 3:3 cell and 3:2 cell in the matrix. In the 3:3 cell, the lower SES infants have a higher probability of continuing to vocalize as their mothers vocalize than the higher SES infants, whereas in the 3:2 cell it is the higher SES infants who appear to stop vocalizing once their mothers and they were vocalizing. This can be seen even more clearly in the 2:2 and 2:3 subcycles of the matrix. In the 2:2 cell, we find the higher SES infants (I) more likely to remain silent while their mothers are vocalizing than the lower (V) SES infants, while it is the lower SES infants who are more likely to start vocalizing when their mothers are vocalizing than the higher SES infants (cell 2:3).

Differentiation differences as a function of SES are also evident and reveal a pattern which tends to dovetail with these other differences. In the comparison of the differentiation between mother vocalizing to the infant

(infant as object — state '2') or mother vocalizing to someone else (infant not as object — state '2i'), there is an SES difference such that higher SES infants show greater differentiation. The percent of infants showing greater vocalization to 2 as compared to 2i is .82, .62, .73, .50, .60 for classes I–V, respectively. Interestingly this SES effect can be accounted for more by the female infants (1.00, 1.00, 1.00, 0.33, 0.50 for classes I–V, respectively). Observation of the other differentiation states, 3 and 3i, fail to indicate that higher SES infants show greater differences than lower SES infants. Thus, it is only when they are listening rather than talking that higher SES infants show this differentiation effect as compared to lower SES infants. Here again is support for the relationship between vocalization differentiation and listening. We have suggested from several of the other vocalization analyses that there may be important individual differences in subsequent differential vocalization as a function of previous listening behavior (as in states 2 and 2i). When the infants are themselves vocalizing, these individual differences cease.

What are we to make of this sequential analysis? This analysis indicates a highly complex and sophisticated communication relationship in the vocalization of the 12-week-old infant and its mother. Individual differences both in terms of SES and sex of the infant indicate that this communication network is highly specific and is already affected by factors known to make their appearance at a much later time — a time when formal linguistic properties of vocalization are present!

Situational Features of Vocalization

One of the assumptions underlying the theme of this discussion is that linguistic competency grows out of the communication matrix and that, moreover, the study of language development must emphasize the issue of function rather than structure. We also believe that context is the prime carrier variable for shared meaning.

Given this assumption, it would follow naturally that a study of the context of the communication matrix of the mother and her infant should be undertaken. To do this is not easy and what we will present is a first attempt at its exploration. Context is such an encompassing concept and so unexplored that a short description is all that is presently possible. In the following discussion, we shall only refer to the vocalization data of mother and infant, restricting our analyses to frequency of occurrence data. None of the sequential interaction data presented earlier is yet available for observation by situation. However, even at this level of analysis it soon becomes clear that the context of the vocalization of either mother or infant exerts an effect on the communication network.

Initially, it appeared reasonable to assume that context might be defined by the space in which the infant and mother were located. For adults, physical space usually carries with it a high degree of contextual meaning. Thus, a kitchen has associated with it food, eating, drinking, certain somatic sensations and the like, whereas the bedroom as a space is associated with sleeping, quiet play, etc. With this in mind, we first attempted to observe the infant–mother communication matrix as a function of physical space. Recall that the observer marked the location and general category of activity for each of the 120 min of observation and we utilized this in order to study context.

Much to our surprise we discovered that the physical space or location by function of a 12-week-old infant was not yet differentiated by his caretaker. The child typically was not fed in the kitchen, played with in the living room or family room, washed in the bathroom and put to sleep in the bedroom. Each of the activities most usually associated with a room in the house was performed by and large in any room. Physical space, such as a room, then, could not be used as a clear indicator of context.[5]

In order to study context, another approach was considered. For this analysis, we observed in what enclosure or where in a room a child was situated; for example, eight specific categories seemed to account for almost all of the observed time: infant seat, playpen, mother's lap, crib or bed, couch or sofa, floor, diaper changing table or bathtub, and jumper or swing. An "other" category was added to include the few remaining cases.

The data across sex and SES level are presented in Table 4. First, it was necessary to determine the distribution of time the infants spent in these situations. The data of Table 4 indicate that, across all infants, mother's lap was the most common situation in which the awake infant was observed. Crib/bed and infant seat were the next most frequent situations, while jumper, floor and playpen were the least frequent. Both sexes show this same relative distribution of situation frequencies; in fact, the rank order correlation between sex is .95. Of interest, however, are a few differences which were observed. Girl infants tended to spend more time in the infant seat (Mann-Whitney U test, $p < .10$), crib/bed ($p < .10$), couch/sofa and changing table, while boys spend more time in the playpen, mother's lap ($p < .05$), floor, and jumper. Interestingly, the sex differences in

[5] Interestingly enough, further observation of infants' activities in their homes does reveal that by 12 months of age the physical space was well differentiated, with rooms associated with specific functions.

TABLE 4
Mean Number of 10-Sec Intervals Spent in Each Situation

	Infant seat	Play-pen	Mother's lap	Crib/bed	Couch/sofa	Floor	Table/tub	Jumper	Other
Total	100.9	29.2	288.4	118.2	46.2	28.0	62.5	26.7	19.9
Male	80.2	33.0	329.5	91.6	42.0	35.1	52.9	29.7	24.0
Female	121.6	25.4	247.4	144.8	50.5	21.0	72.1	23.7	15.8
SES I	111.8	18.8	231.8	204.8	51.0	19.5	54.8	12.0	15.8
SES II	108.5	11.5	222.5	163.1	44.2	48.0	60.7	19.1	41.5
SES III	88.2	64.8	308.4	75.6	30.6	38.8	68.4	27.6	15.0
SES IV	112.8	0	286.8	68.4	51.6	32.4	52.8	99.6	14.4
SES V	90.6	36.0	387.0	67.2	57.6	0	69.6	9.6	0

TABLE 5
Relative Frequency of Occurrence of Infant and Maternal Vocalizations as a Function of Amount of Time Spent in Each Situation

	Infant seat	Play-pen	Mother's lap	Crib	Sofa	Floor	Table/tub	Jumper	Other
Infant vocalization									
Total	.233	.303	.171	.214	.200	.285	.216	.228	.211
Male	.308	.261	.183	.186	.170	.292	.225	.200	.228
Female	.179	.400	.150	.210	.227	.278	.207	.277	.137
SES I	.113	.345	.107	.204	.280	.350	.153	.130	.130
SES II	.222	.175	.097	.166	.133	.203	.153	.155	.240
SES III	.160	.460	.208	.280	.214	.345	.174	.420	.145
SES IV	.297	–	.168	.155	.320	.160	.200	.213	.180
SES V	.337	.050	.244	.262	.126	–	.464	.230	–
Maternal vocalization									
Total	.338	.257	.404	.325	.474	.518	.475	.365	.337
Male	.332	.265	.313	.385	.481	.562	.447	.393	.298
Female	.350	.243	.441	.272	.468	.466	.503	.310	.387
SES I	.244	.100	.342	.270	.480	.430	.456	.495	.240
SES II	.395	.300	.400	.318	.553	.600	.425	.170	.285
SES III	.376	.297	.423	.408	.562	.455	.630	.400	.535
SES IV	.312	–	.460	.625	.320	.553	.496	.130	.350
SES V	.407	.180	.398	.216	.205	–	.340	.515	–

situation vary along what seems to be a restrictive versus nonrestrictive activity dimension with girl infants generally being placed in situations which allow for *less* vigorous, muscular activity, while for boys the reverse is true.

SES differences in total time spent in a particular situation are also apparent (see Table 4). While there is relatively high agreement across situations as a function of SES (Friedman analysis of variance; $\chi^2r = 32.3$, df 8, $p < .001$), general differences emerge. Mother's lap is the most frequent situation for all SES levels, while crib/bed is next highest for the higher SES levels and infant seat for the lower SES. The playpen and jumper were the *lowest* situational frequencies for the highest SES levels, while only floor emerged as the lowest situation in any consistent way across the lower SES levels. In terms of mean data, the only striking differences between SES class I and V are in time spent in crib/bed ($I > V, p < .10$), floor ($I > V, p < .001$), and mother's lap ($V > I, p < .05$).

The frequency of location data, then, indicate that although there are consistencies in terms of where the infant is located by the mother, individual differences as a function of sex and SES level exist. Of concern to our discussion, however, is not the situational differences per se, but whether it is possible to observe vocalization differences as a function of these situations. Recall that it is our hypothesis that these situations help form the bases for acquiring meaning and, if true, should be extremely important in the acquisition of subsequent language skills.

Keep in mind that an analysis of the content of mother's verbal utterances in each situation would be the most ideal form of data collection, but as a first approximation we must be satisfied with the frequency of vocalization data independent of content.

Table 5 presents the relative frequency of vocalization for infant and mother with respect to the total amount of time the infant spent in that situation. Thus, although infants spend more time on their mother's lap than in any other situation, the data of Table 5 indicate that infants vocalize most often per unit time in their playpens, next most often on the floor and infant seat, while they vocalize least on their mother's lap and in their cribs or on their changing tables/bath tubs.

While there was high agreement between the sexes in terms of the amount of time in these situations, there is no relationship ($\rho = .08$) between girls' and boys' percentages of vocalizations across these situations. Hence, we cannot attribute the observed differences to different number of exposures to these situations. For boys, the infant seat and floor yield the most relative vocalization while for girls it is the playpen and floor. The least vocalization for boys is the crib and sofa, while for girls it is the mother's lap and infant seat (discounting the "other" category). Exactly why this sex difference exists is not clear. However, observation of the mother's relative vocalization data might reveal the reason. One might assume that mother's vocalization would be associated with (1) infant vocalizations, (2) infant quieting and no vocalization, or (3) unrelated. The data of Table 5 indicate that mother's relative vocalization over all infants was greatest for floor, changing table/bathtub and sofa and least for playpen, crib, and jumper. Interestingly, while there was no relationship across situation for girls' and boys' relative vocalizations, mothers' vocalization across situation was consistent across sex ($\rho = .67$, $p < .01$). The correlation of infant to mother's relative vocalization indicates that over all infants there is no relationship ($\rho = -.15$) although there is a slight indication that mother's vocalization is associated with lack of infant vocalization. The correlation for each of the sexes indicates a ρ of $-.30$ for boy–mother vocalizations and $-.27$ for girl–mother vocalizations as a function of situation.

The data for sex differences suggest, then, that the infant's relative vocalization across situation is sex specific and independent of the maternal vocalization. Vocalizations occur most frequently when the infant is relatively free of physical restraint as when it is in a playpen or on the floor, and vocalizations occur least when the child is on the mother's lap. The data suggest that one dimension of these situations or the underlying semantics of location may be the acquisition of constraint versus nonconstraint.

SES differences, both for the infants and their mothers, also appear in Table 5. Observation of the infant data indicate that there are SES differences in relative vocalization as a function of situation. Comparison between SES levels I and V indicates a negative rank order correlation of $-.54$ ($p < .10$) such that situations in which high SES infants vocalize, low SES infants do not. Situations which are restrictive, such as mother's lap, infant seat, changing table/tub, were associated with relatively *more* vocalization for the lower SES infants and relatively *less* vocalization for the higher SES infants (by Mann-Whitney U tests, $p < .002$, $.001$, and $.05$, respectively). Also, floor, playpen and sofa — nonrestrictive situations — were associated with more vocalization for the higher SES and less vocalization for the lower SES infants.

These social class differences in infant behavior seem only partially related to maternal vocalization. Thus, while infant vocalizations were inversely related as a function of SES, there was a positive rank order correlation between SES level I and V mothers' vocalization associated with these situations ($\rho = .40$). The relationship between infant–mother vocalization as a function of SES and situation is somewhat more complicated. For SES level I, there is no relationship between infant–mother relative frequency of vocalization as a function of situation ($\rho = -.05$) whereas there is a positive relationship for level V infant–mother vocalization ($\rho = .54$, $p < .10$).

The situational analysis has only utilized frequency of vocalization data. However, we are currently investigating the directional relationship between mother and infant as a function of situation. Like the frequency data, differences as a function of situation appear. Preliminary examination of 4 infants' conditional vocalization states by situation suggest to us that some situations influence the likelihood of discriminating state '2' from '2*i*,' whereas others fail to do so. But what about the situational differences we have reported? These differences parallel much of what we have reported earlier. For example, the data on using the floor as a situational setting indicate decreased use of this situation as SES level decreases. Thus, the lowest SES level mother *never* puts her infant on the floor. Why might this be true? Could it be that the floor for the poor is a dangerous place for their infants: cold, uncarpeted, and rat infested? This, of course, is generally not the case for the middle class. Thus, situations produce differences quite early as a function of social class.

One particularly interesting individual difference in situations has direct parallel with the earlier analyses. From some of the interaction data, we found that lower SES infants were more responsive to their mother's vocalization (by vocalizing more when their mothers vocalized). In this situational analysis, these infants also show (1) greater correlation with mother's vocalization over the various situations and (2) vocalize in those situations where they are relatively restricted. We suspect that relatively restricted situations are associated with being nearer to or unable to get away from the mother.

Situational determinants of vocalization have only been hinted at by these data. The kind of data necessary for determining precise effects is not yet available. Remarkably, the data do show that there are infant vocalization differences as a function of situation, and that these are not invariably influenced by maternal vocalization, this by 12 weeks of age!

Discussion

When we started this investigation, we suspected that our theme and the data collected would probably lead to more unanswered questions and confusion than light. In some sense this was deliberate in that we wished to initiate an unorthodox approach to developmental issues regarding language. Recall that our general theme was that there exists from birth a communication network between the infant and its mother and that the anlage of language is developed of and from aspects of this communication system. Given this general belief, a myriad of problems befell us. For example, how should we define the communication network between these two members? What are the relevant behavioral dimensions? In terms of specific linguistic issues, we were confronted by trying to study the emergence of meaning in the absence of formal language, itself a most complex issue. Some clues to direct us in this theoretical struggle were already available. In particular Bloom (1970) believes that some utterances probably have multiple meaning and that context may be critical in order to disambiguate the utterance.

Recently, Fillmore (1968), among others, has placed emphasis on a semantic analysis of language in contrast with the primarily syntactical approach, and in doing so has suggested to us such semantic notions as location of, direction, object of, etc., as being useful concepts in analyzing language development. These types of semantic notions can more readily be brought to bear in specifying what underlying concepts may be operating within the general communication network which we have tried to elaborate. Thus, it seemed possible to find ways to measure the communication system of the infant and its mother and to isolate some sequences in given contexts which might be considered as semantic dimensions.

Before returning to this, it is important to restate some of the more general findings about the communication network between infant and mother. The data make clear that the general communication network made up of the infant and its mother is more than just the vocalizations of each. Thus, a mother's smile may follow or a mother's look may precede an infant's vocalization. Likewise, an infant's smile may follow or an infant's cry may precede a mother's vocalization. The network is a complex web wherein the repertoire of each member actively interacts with the other. Vocalizations (infant and mother), therefore, may not be the only relevant data in understanding the unfolding process of meaning and language acquisition. This should not be surprising in that developmental processes are by their nature elaborate transformational processes wherein a particular behavior may not have an identical behavioral precursor.

If this is so, it is important to consider that the communication network we have described is in some sense limited in that it includes only the infant–mother and not the infant–world. In this context, Bruner's (1968) speculations are extremely interesting. Bruner proposes a similarity between manipulative hand skills and some formal language skills — specifically the notion of subject and predicate — and suggests that in infant action in the world of objects, one may find direct precursors of some of the formal aspects of language. In addition, Bruner casts doubt upon the use of babbling, at least using only its phonetic aspects as an adequate base for searching for language prerequisites. To this we must concur; rather than study the phonetic aspects of babbling as critical, it is in the communicative aspect of babbling in interaction with other infant behaviors and the mother's behaviors that precursors may be found.

But something still was gained from narrowing our attention to just vocalization: In particular, we argued that some of the sequential properties of the infant–mother vocalization states carried important information about the discrimination of who was the object of the mother's vocalizations. The transitional matrix contained useful information which demonstrated that by 12 weeks of age some infants (especially females) are better able to differentiate whether or not they are the objects of their mothers' vocalizations. Thus, the possible precursor of "object" (something acted upon regardless of whether it is a speech act or any other) is already imbedded in the early communication system. The sequential analysis also has been valuable in demonstrating the wide and varied patterns of infant–mother vocalization generating interaction data that bear directly on issues of vocalization chaining. Finally, not to be excluded, is the value of prediction of subsequent infant vocalization by use of this model. A complex conditional probability matrix would undoubtedly go a long way in telling us what are the important measures of a communication system which can predict subsequent vocalization measures.

The inclusion of "location of" as an important semantic notion at 12 weeks cannot be argued without qualifications. Location must be considered in the specific context of the infant in his physical space (for example, constrained space versus nonconstrained space). From any number of theoretical positions it seems arguable that one aspect of differential meaning is derived from the infant in his various physical spaces. We have found that situations alter the pattern of infant vocalizations at 12 weeks: thus, it appears that these infants are sensitive to situational differences. Whether they conceptualize this difference in any more formal way is impossible for one to assess without controlled studies.

Location, context and meaning are intimately related. This can be exemplified by a rather interesting experience. B is a 13-month-old female infant who is sitting in a high chair in the kitchen. She is holding an apple and is told on several occasions to either, "Bite the apple" or "Throw the apple." B in this situation always bites the apple and never throws it; however, when placed on the floor of a playroom and given the same two sets of instructions, she always throws the apple but never bites it. We would argue that in some sense the meaning of the particular command is determined by the context in which it is uttered.[6] Observation of the infant and its mother

---

[6] We cannot rule out the possibility that the child would have engaged in these activities, regardless of whether anything was said to her. Even so, specific behaviors have become associated with specific settings.

makes clear that physical place, nature of activity and specific language dimensions covary; in the kitchen one eats and talks about food, hot–cold, in–out, messy–clean, etc.

Location, in terms of specific situations, has been described and it is interesting to note the vast difference in location and the spontaneous vocalization activity associated with them. It may not be too far off the track to hypothesize that the infant who is allowed to freely roam (one placed on the floor or playpen as opposed to infant seat, etc.) may be better able to develop such semantic notions of direction. Thus, in some very specific and, unfortunately, undefined way, situations can carry a vast array of semantic information: how this "information" eventually alters the formal language system is still unspecified.

The communication network, even of the 12-week-old infant and its mother, is a nonrandom, sequential and situationally determined system suggesting a wide variety of activities which, on their face, are reminiscent of the more formal linguistic properties — especially the semantic ones — found at later ages. Individual differences in these activities are considerable and we should like now to turn to some of them before concluding with some information relating these early individual differences to more formal linguistic properties of these same children at 2 years of age.

Individual differences in infants' vocalizations by 12 weeks of age, whether in terms of the general communication matrix, sequential analysis or situation, are considerable. There is approximately 20 times as much difference in vocalization output from the most to the least vocal infant, and these differences are not lessened even when the infants are compared in similar situations. In the present paper, we have chosen to talk about individual differences along two dimensions, the sex of the infant and the socioeconomic background of the family. Note that our intention is not to demonstrate differences as a function of these variables, but rather, to utilize them in order to unravel the process producing differences in vocalization and its consequences. For example, knowing that there are differences in amount of time spent on the floor as a function of SES allows us to disregard the SES differences and concentrate on the effect of time on the floor on vocalization differences.

Sex differences were observable at all levels of analysis. While infant girls overall did not vocalize more than boys, the general communication matrix data make clear that girls vocalize more in response to a maternal behavior than boys. Moreover, boys show less differentiation than girls in terms of their vocalization, as a consequence of whether or not they were the object of their mother's vocalization. These data suggest that the girl infant appears, by 12 weeks, to be more advanced in her vocalization use (communication skill) than boys. Since there is some evidence that girls are precocious in their language development, these early differences appear consistent with this theme. They do raise the question as to the source of these differences. Because of the age of these subjects, the question of biological factors becomes suspect. While these certainly cannot be excluded, it is important to note that maternal behavior differences, as a function of the infant's sex, also appear by this time. In fact, Moss (1967) has shown maternal behavioral differences as early as 3 weeks and subsequent research will probably indicate that maternal behavior differences as a function of the infant's sex exist from the first contact with the child. For these 12-week-olds, mothers of girls talk more to them than to boys. Moreover, and most striking, while mothers of boys are more generally responsive to a boy's vocalizations than mothers of girls, this holds for all maternal behaviors except vocalization where the reverse is true. Thus, the specific vocalization–vocalization act occurs more for girl than boy infants. Situational differences also make clear the differential environmental factors and make attempts at theoretical untangling of the biological and learning determinants untenable.

The socioeconomic background of the infant was also effective in demonstrating individual differences and again raises the specter of biological advantage vis-à-vis early vocalization and subsequent language skills. Again, it must be remembered that while these infant differences are observed at a very young age, it is also possible to observe maternal differences. With this in mind, it is possible to "explain" individual differences as a function of the influence of the mother behaviors rather than as a function of genetic differences. While we cannot determine the source, the data suggest that the higher SES infants are more "advanced" in their vocalizations, at least in terms of being able to differentiate between being or not being the object of the mother's vocalization. What, perhaps, is even more interesting is the relationship of lower SES children's vocalization with that of their mothers. The data from the sequential as well as situational analyses suggest that lower class infants' vocalization is sustained by their mothers' vocalization and also that lower SES mothers' vocalizations are more effective in eliciting a vocalization from their children, that is, the vocalizations of higher SES mothers seem to inhibit the vocalizations of their infants; the reverse seems to be the case for lower SES groups. The cause for this is unclear; however, data on social class differences in vocalization *response* to their infants' vocalizations suggest that higher SES mothers are more likely to respond with a vocalization than lower SES mothers (Lewis & Wilson, 1972). This differential vocalization response pattern may be affecting the listening–vocalization pattern of the infant. It is apparent that the different SES groups are learning different things — some quiet as a consequence of maternal vocalization while others increase their vocalization.

Up to this point in our investigation, we have presented a wide variety of data bearing on the communication network of the infant and its mother and have been able to show wide individual differences. It has been our intention to argue that these parameters of behavior (within the communication network) and individual differences revealed by them are relevant to subsequent formal linguistic skills. Up until this point, our comments have been speculative; however, because we have been following these children we can report, albeit preliminarily, the relationship between communicative behavior at 12 weeks and formal linguistic skills at two years. The data for the first three children to complete the study are available.

The linguistic data collected at two years can be divided into three aspects: (1) collection of spontaneous utterances; (2) a language comprehension task; (3) a "standard" test of language. The collection of spontaneous utterances took place in a naturalistic free play situation (see Goldberg & Lewis, 1969) in which the child and its mother played together in a room filled with toys. Data were collected on tape, transcribed, and the following measures of linguistic development were obtained: mean utterance length; number of semantic distinctions, such as location, subject–verb, verb–object, direction, etc.; maximum semantic complexity within the most complex utterance of each child; and, finally, sequential analysis of the mother–child predications. The language comprehension task involved obtaining the child's knowledge of specific linguistic aspects, these being prepositions (locations, direction), subject–verb–object relationships, and adjective contrasts. The final task was a standard language test — the Peabody Picture Vocabulary Test — where both a comprehension and production score were obtained.

Interestingly, at age two these various language measures tend to order the available three subjects in the same manner. At two years of age, Pam showed the most linguistic development followed by John and Pat. We might add that each of these children are from the highest SES level and that their mothers' vocabulary scores from the WAIS were about the same. Now we shall turn to the 12-week communication network data and see what measures collected at this early age are related to subsequent linguistic skill at age two. In each of the three areas of study at 12 weeks (general communication matrix, sequential analysis, and situations) we find these three subjects are similarly ordered as at two years. For example, the total amount of infant vocalization and quiet play, as well as the total amount of maternal play at 12 weeks occur maximally for Pam and minimally for Pat. Much more startling is the sequential data; Pam, John, and Pat, in that order, show greater differentiation between mother's vocalization directed or not directed toward them.

The data must be viewed as preliminary; however, the results do suggest that the communication network at 12 weeks of age is a rich area of study and may well be developmentally linked with the more formal linguistic skills which emerge in the second and third years of life. We recognize the teasing quality of our speculations, but present them because we are encouraged that the data regularities at 12 weeks which we have uncovered thus far may prove to be a more fruitful foundation for tracing out developmental links between a variety of early behaviors and later linguistic ability than current theorizing about language development might suggest.

Acknowledgments

This research was supported in part by a grant from the Spencer Foundation.

References

Bell, S., & Ainsworth, M. D. S. Infant crying and maternal responsiveness: Reinforcement reassessed. Unpublished manuscript, 1971.

Bloom, L. *Language development: Form and function in emerging grammars.* Cambridge: M.I.T. Press, 1970.

Bruner, J. S. *Processes of cognitive growth: Infancy.* Volume III. Heinz Werner Lecture Series, Clark University Press, 1968.

Eimas, P. D., Siqueland, E. R., Jusczyk, P., & Vigorito, J. Speech perception in infants. *Science,* 1971, **171**, 303–306.

Fillmore, C. J. The case for case. In E. Bach & R. T. Harms (Eds.), *Universals in linguistic theory.* New York: Holt, 1968. Pp. 1–88.

Freedle, R. O., & Lewis, M. Application of Markov processes to the concept of state. Research Bulletin 71–34. Princeton, N. J.: Educational Testing Service, 1971.

Furth, H. G. *Thinking without language: Psychological implications of deafness.* New York: Free Press, 1966.

Gardner, R. A., & Gardner, B. T. Teaching sign language to a chimpanzee. *Science,* 1969, **165**, 664–672.

Goldberg, S., & Lewis, M. Play behavior in the year-old infant: Early sex differences. *Child Development,* 1969, **40**, 21–31.

Goodall, J. *In the shadow of man.* Boston: Houghton, 1971.

Hollingshead, A. B. Two-factor index of social position. New Haven, Connecticut: Author, 1957.

Jaffe, J., & Feldstein, S. *Rhythms of dialogue.* New York: Academic Press, Inc., 1970.

Kagan, J., & Lewis, M. Studies of attention in the human infant. *Merrill-Palmer Quarterly,* 1965, **11**, 95–127.

Kernan, K. T. Semantic relationships and the child's acquisition of language. *Anthropological Linguistics,* 1970, **12**(5), 171–187.

Lévi-Strauss, C. *The savage mind.* Chicago: University of Chicago Press, 1966.

Lewis, M. State as an infant-environment interaction: An analysis of mother–infant behavior as a function of sex. Paper presented at the Merrill-Palmer Conference on Research and Teaching of Infant Development, Detroit, Michigan, February 1971. *Merrill-Palmer Quarterly,* 1972, **18**, 95–121.

Lewis, M., & Goldberg, S. Perceptual-cognitive development in infancy: A generalized expectancy model as a function of the mother-infant interaction. *Merrill-Palmer Quarterly,* 1969, **15**(1), 81–100.

Lewis, M., & Wilson, C. D. Infant development in lower class American families. Paper presented at Society for Research in Child Development meetings, Symposium on Cross-Cultural Studies of Mother–Infant Interaction: Description and Consequence. Minneapolis, April 1971. *Human Development,* 1972, **15**, 112–127.

Lieberman, P. *Intonation, perception, and language.* Cambridge: M.I.T. Press, 1967.

Lusk, D., & Lewis, M. Mother–infant interaction and infant development among the Wolof of Senegal. *Human Development,* 1972, **15**(1), 58–69.

Moss, H. A. Sex, age, and state as determinants of mother-infant interaction. *Merrill-Palmer Quarterly,* 1967, **13**, 19–35.

Piaget, J. *The origins of behavior.* New York: Norton Simons, 1952.

Reitman, W. R. *Cognition and thought: An information processing approach.* New York: Wiley, 1965.

Vygotsky, L. S. *Thought and language.* Cambridge, Massachusetts: M.I.T. Press, 1962.

COMMUNICATION BY THE TOTAL EXPERIMENTAL SITUATION: WHY IT IS IMPORTANT, HOW IT IS EVALUATED, AND ITS SIGNIFICANCE FOR THE ECOLOGICAL VALIDITY OF FINDINGS

Martin T. Orne

Institute of the Pennsylvania Hospital
and
University of Pennsylvania

It is often assumed that knowledge of a message permits a meaningful analysis of communication. Not only may a message fail to adequately reflect the sender's intent, but its interpretation will depend upon the context and the perceptions of the receiver. This paper will attempt an analysis of communication in the psychological experiment. This is of interest for two reasons: first, as a substantive example of a situation in which the communication as intended and perceived by the investigator may be quite different from the communication as perceived by the subject and, second, since much of our knowledge about psychology in general and communication in particular derives from experimental data, distortions in our understanding of such data become especially meaningful.

The experimental setting is generally conceptualized as a standard situation which permits systematic study of the subject's response to the independent variables under controlled conditions. It is customary in reports of empirical research to provide the detailed instructions given to the subject because of an implicit assumption that knowledge of these instructions — the message — will clarify the nature of the communication for the reader. It is further assumed that the subject's response under the conditions of the experiment will be representative of the individual's response in other circumstances. This chapter will suggest that the manner in which the experimental situation is generally conceptualized may be largely responsible for errors in communication and consequently for errors in interpretation, and, further, that it is essential for the investigator to understand how a particular experimental situation is perceived by the subject in order to draw sensible inference from the subject's responses. Some of the means for accomplishing this goal will be discussed as well as the implications of an alternative conception of the psychological experiment for the interpretation of research findings in general and especially for an understanding of attempted replications.

The Consequences of Being in an Experiment: The Psychological Experiment as a Unique Form of Social Interaction

When a subject is asked to participate in an experiment and agrees to do so, his perception of the situation and consequently his response to instructions, tend to be altered drastically. This can easily be documented with a simple demonstration.

You take a group of casual acquaintances and ask them, "Will you do me a favor?" On receiving an affirmative response, you say, "Do five pushups." Typically, the individual will reply, "Why?" "Are you crazy?" "What's the point?" and so on. A matched group of casual acquaintances is then taken and again asked to do you a favor. On receiving an affirmative reply, you ask, "Are you willing to participate in a psychological experiment?" When another affirmative reply is given, you again present the instruction, "Do five pushups." The typical question now becomes, "Where?"

A slightly different version of the same experiment was done by a student[1] who took some whole fried .grasshoppers and asked casual acquaintances if they would eat them, eliciting a large number or refusals. Then he went to another group and asked if they would help him with a psychological experiment. On receiving affirmative responses, he took out a stopwatch and placed a platter of fried grasshoppers in front of the subjects and said, "I want to see how many of these you can eat in thirty seconds. Start!" Practically all of the subjects began to gobble the fried grasshoppers as rapidly as possible.

Apparently unambiguous communications tend to alter their meaning radically when they occur in the context of an experimental situation. This was particularly well illustrated by a series of substantive experiments on the question of whether hypnotized subjects can be compelled to carry out antisocial or self-destructive actions. First Rowland (1939) and then Young

---

[1] The informal study was carried out by George J. Smiltens.

(1952) had independently shown that deeply hypnotized subjects could be compelled to pick up a poisonous snake with their bare hands, to remove a penny from fuming nitric acid with their bare fingers, and, finally, to throw a beaker of concentrated nitric acid at a research assistant — actions that are clearly both self-destructive and antisocial. The face validity of this experiment was heightened by the report that the same subjects who were compelled to carry out such actions during hypnosis, when asked in the wake state whether they would be willing to carry them out, recoiled with horror. In a further replication of these studies, Orne and Evans (1965) used not only deeply hypnotized subjects but in addition included a special type of quasi-control group (to be discussed more fully later) consisting of nonhypnotized individuals instructed to simulate hypnosis. In line with the previous findings, we also observed that five out of six deeply hypnotized experimental subjects could indeed be compelled to carry out these actions. Of greater importance, however, was our observation that six out of six *non*hypnotized subjects asked to pretend to be hypnotized also performed the identical dangerous and antisocial acts. This led us to try the same procedure with random subject volunteers, and we noted that, depending upon the amount and type of social pressure involved, these behaviors could be elicited as easily from naïve volunteers as from simulators or real hypnotized subjects. These were startling observations for us because we realized, as do most people, that no one in his right mind would perform such acts unless he had substantial grounds for so doing.

Only by analyzing the nature of the communication in context did it become clear that it was entirely different to ask a subject whether he *would* be willing to remove a penny from fuming nitric acid with his bare fingers from demanding that he do so with a *clear expectation of compliance*. The appropriate response to the question of whether the subject would be willing to carry out this obviously dangerous action is a resounding "No!" However, once the investigator communicates that he expects the subject actually to carry out the behavior, he inevitably also communicates that the behavior is, in fact, harmless, regardless of appearances. As careful postexperimental discussions with our subjects substantiated, the demand to carry out actions apparently dangerous to the self or others communicated that it must be safe to comply. Even though appearances might have indicated otherwise, their common sense helped them to realize that we could not and would not have a subject hurt in our experiments nor, for that matter, were research assistants sufficiently expendable to allow someone really to hurt them; subjects therefore assumed, correctly of course, that appropriate safeguards had been taken and complied with the demand. The implicit communication, then, to all subjects was one of expectation and safety.

Certainly the meaning of the behavior as well as its implications were almost entirely determined by the context of "experiment." Instances such as these demonstrate the difficulties of interpreting the true meaning of both the instructions and the subjects' behavior without a full appreciation of the context, even when one is dealing with dramatic events which seem to have face validity. Interestingly enough, none of our colleagues on the faculty could be persuaded to carry out any of these tasks. They, however, had not agreed to participate in any experiment.[2] Their interpretation of the requested actions was very much like that of the previous investigators as well as readers of scientific articles — but significantly different from that of the subjects who actually participated in the experiment. Perception is not only in the eye of the beholder, it is also in the *position* of the beholder — whether observer or actor in the situation.

This difference between how an experiment may be perceived by the investigator versus how it may be perceived by the subject was again dramatically illustrated when we attempted to find an experimental task that subjects would rapidly discontinue, not because it was painful or excessively fatiguing, but rather because it was utterly meaningless and trivial (Orne, 1962). A serial additions task which most subjects found onerous to begin with was deliberately made progressively less meaningful. First, the subject was merely asked to carry out the task by the experimenter who took away the subject's watch and said he would be back "eventually. . . ." The next step was to provide an instruction card which told subjects to tear up the page they had just completed, throw it away, and then continue to go on working as rapidly and accurately as possible. When subjects continued to work for long periods even under these circumstances, the one-way screen used for monitoring was eliminated and the experiment was restructured so that it was clear the instructions would not change throughout the duration of the session.

Considerable care was taken to establish both the accuracy and rate of work under these circumstances in a manner that subjects were, in fact, unable to detect. Nonetheless, subjects continued to work both accurately and rapidly though apparently alone and unmonitored. Postexperimental discussion revealed, however, that subjects uniformly assumed — correctly, of course — that they were actually monitored throughout their performance. Furthermore, while we tried our best to make the task meaningless, it was not interpreted as such by any of our subjects who generously assumed that we must have had good and sufficient reasons for asking them to engage in

---

[2] In an entirely different setting, Silverman (1968) has shown that a persuasive communication presented in an experimental context increases acquiescence significantly more than it does in a nonexperimental context.

such ridiculous behavior. Simply because the experimenter contrived the task to appear meaningless did not prevent the subject from inferring sensible purpose and responding accordingly.

Subjects were paid an hourly rate and it could be argued that this fact accounted for our difficulties in designing a meaningless experimental task which subjects would discontinue despite its legitimization by the experimental context itself. Anyone doubting the uniqueness of the experimental context or overly impressed with the effectiveness of small amounts of money as reinforcers may wish to try an analogous experiment in real life with his secretary. Simply ask her to type a perfect letter and, on completing it, have her proofread it and, having done so, tear it up. Then instruct her to repeat the procedure. Two, or possibly three, such trials should provide an opening for a new secretary — despite the fact that secretaries are paid considerably more than experimental subjects, and their work is by the hour, not by the page. The crucial difference here is that the experimental subject, lacking appropriate means for determining why he is asked to perform certain actions, tends to assume that there is an important and legitimate purpose in the requests being made of him, whereas, in most non-experimental situations, the individual is better equipped to evaluate the appropriateness of the request.

The validity of conclusions drawn from any experiment will depend upon the degree to which the experiment as it is conceived by the investigator corresponds to the way it is perceived by the subject. Unfortunately, the assumption of a one-to-one congruence is rarely met. An experience told to me by a well-known sleep researcher serves as a particularly graphic illustration. One of the investigators in his laboratory noticed that a subject had considerable difficulty in falling asleep. After about an hour, he inquired of the subject whether anything was bothering him. He was told no, everything was fine. After another hour had passed, he again inquired, but was told by the subject who still failed to fall asleep that he was quite all right. This continued until the early hours of the morning when the investigator finally entered the subject's room and insisted that something must be bothering him since he still was not asleep. At this point, the subject asked, somewhat incredulously, whether he meant that the mouse in his bed was not really part of the experiment!

In each of the examples cited, the appropriate interpretation of the experimental situation was not possible until the investigator had understood the experiment from the subject's point of view. It seems self-evident that the experiment as it is experienced by the subject, rather than how it is conceived by the experimenter, will determine how the subject behaves.

Though these instances have tended to emphasize cooperativeness on the part of the subject in the context of an experimental interaction, it would be quite inappropriate to assume that subjects are necessarily compliant or willing to tolerate discomfort or indignity if such is perceived as unnecessary to the experimental purpose. In other words, subjects will tolerate pain, discomfort, or boredom so long as they can feel it is essential for the experiment in question (Orne & Watson, 1957). They become quite annoyed and angry if they feel that their discomfort is the consequence of carelessness or ineptness on the part of the experimenter. For example, in some studies we have found it necessary to take repeated blood samples, requiring several venipunctures. Subjects tolerate this mildly uncomfortable procedure with remarkably good humor. However, in a study which required only a single venipuncture, subjects would become visibly annoyed if the assistant failed to hit the vein on his first attempt and found it necessary to repeat the procedure two or three times in order to obtain a blood sample. In this instance, it was obvious to the subject that the repeated discomfort was not necessary for the purpose of the experiment and was rather the fault of the experimenter or the staff he chose.

Again, this example illustrates how it is the subject's perception of the meaning of a procedure which determines his response, or, in other words, what meaning the total experimental context communicates to him. While the psychological experiment tends to shape the subject's perception and makes it likely that he attributes meaning and purpose to whatever tasks are required of him, this is true so long as the subject can assume that the requests are legitimate and necessary for the purpose of the research. When he is in a position to recognize that this is not the case, the subject will respond as would an individual in a nonexperimental setting. Thus, for example, asking a subject to sit for 30 min while an experimental drug takes effect rarely causes annoyance, whereas waiting the same amount of time for an experimenter who is unaccountably "delayed" is quite a different matter.

The Motivation of the Experimental Subject

Human subjects do not just appear in an experiment; rather they must be motivated or coerced to participate. How they respond to the experimental situation and their attitude toward the total enterprise will, to a considerable extent, be determined by their motives for participation.

A good deal of research has been carried out using coerced volunteers as subjects. It is a common practice to require students in introductory psychology courses to participate in several experiments as subjects, ostensibly as part of their education. Though some of these students would have freely chosen to participate, subject populations of coerced volunteers are liable to respond differently from true volunteers. On the one hand, there is the effect of being forced to participate and, on the other, there is the absence of self-selection. The relationship between the "coerced" volunteer and the "true" volunteer is a complex one still requiring further research.

Subjects volunteering to participate in psychological experiments do so for a wide variety of reasons. They may be solicited by a friend, they may be curious and hope to learn something about psychology or about themselves, they may choose this manner of seeking help for personal problems, they may, if paid, see this as an easy way to make a few dollars, and so on. Despite the different idiosyncratic motives which may be involved, there are certain general characteristics of volunteer subjects that hold for most individuals. As I pointed out some ten years ago (Orne, 1962), over and above idiosyncratic motives,

> College students tend to share (with the experimenter) the hope and expectation that the study in which they are participating will in some material way contribute to science and perhaps ultimately to human welfare in general. . . . Both subject and experimenter share the belief that whatever the experimental task is, it is important. . . . If we assume that much of the motivation of the subject to comply with any and all experimental instructions derives from an identification with the goals of science in general and the success of the experiment in particular, it follows that the subject has a stake in the outcome of the study in which he is participating. For the volunteer subject to feel that he has made a useful contribution, it is necessary for him to assume that the experimenter is competent and that he himself is a "good subject." . . . We might well expect then that as far as the subject is able, he will behave in an experimental context in a manner designed to play the role of a "good subject" or, in other words, *to validate the experimental hypothesis.* Viewed in this way, the student volunteer is *not* merely a passive responder in an experimental situation but rather he has a very real stake in the successful outcome of the experiment. . . . The subject's performance in an experiment might almost be conceptualized as problem-solving behavior; that is, at some level he sees it as his task to ascertain the true purpose of the experiment and respond in a manner which will support the hypotheses being tested. Viewed in this light, the totality of cues which convey an experimental hypothesis to the subject become significant determinants of subjects' behavior. We have labeled the sum total of such cues as the *"demand characteristics of the experimental situation"* [pp.778–779].

A number of observations appear to support such an analysis of the subject's motivation. These observations include the remarkable willingness of subjects to comply with experimental instructions, their interest in learning more about an experiment in which they participated some time ago even though their own performance may not individually be identified as such, their willingness to return for follow-up experiments even at considerable cost of time and effort, the uniformly negative response subjects yield when they are led to believe that their data were not properly recorded due to equipment failure, their tendency not only to accept but also to exaggerate the importance of any research in which they were a participant, and so on.

While such an analysis of the experimental situation tends to hold under most circumstances, the subject's stake in the outcome will be maximized if he is a true volunteer,[3] if he has been scheduled to participate in the study well in advance, if it has taken some effort of his own to take part in the experiment, if the amount of monetary reward has been relatively small, and if he has been treated in a professional fashion by an experimenter who appears truly interested in and concerned about the experiment itself. Finally, there appears to be a relationship between the amount of discomfort involved in participating in an experiment and the importance a subject attaches to it. Discomfort, provided it is perceived as an essential and unavoidable aspect of an experiment tends to make him even more convinced about the importance of the experiment [an observation which could also have been predicted from Festinger's (1957) theory]. Experiments which expose the subject to stress are rarely, if ever, seen as negative experiences regardless of the transient discomfort or pain elicited by the procedure, so long as the subject sees his own response as appropriate and is able to see the situation as a mastery experience.

Conversely, of course, subjects participating in a study may well feel

[3] Our analysis of the experimental situation was based primarily on experiences with true volunteer subjects, since this is the population involved in the bulk of our research. In the absence of further data, caution is advisable in generalizing these observations to samples of coerced volunteers, though their similarity to true volunteers is likely to be greater than generally recognized. In considering differences between true and coerced volunteers, it is essential that the manner in which subjects are treated be held constant. Thus, there is a tendency for coerced volunteers, because of their ready availability, to be treated in a more offhand fashion and to be taken for granted in a manner that may be offensive to many subjects. When a human subject is treated as an object, this will have consequences for his behavior independent of the motivation which brings him to the research. Therefore, care must be taken in interpreting differences between settings as necessarily being a function of coerced volunteers. It seems likely that independent effects due to how subjects are treated as opposed to how they are solicited could be demonstrated.

annoyed and used. The more the above mentioned factors are absent, especially if the individuals with whom the subject has contact seem to view the experiment as trivial and if the experimenter himself seems bored, the more likely the subjects are to feel put upon and angry. Thus, if the setting is one where subjects come to feel like objects (which is almost assured if the experimenter himself conveys the feeling that the study is trivial), their responses may well be negativistic. Under such circumstances, any discomfort associated with the experiment will become highly aversive. Even in the absence of any discomfort, the subject's annoyance may be reflected in his experimental behavior which has led to Masling's (1966) observation about a "screw you" effect in psychological research. In our laboratory, we have failed to observe such a phenomenon, but we believe this to be a function of how subjects come to us and the manner in which they are treated. No doubt such a phenomenon could readily and predictably be produced by an appropriate – or more correctly termed, inappropriate – experimental setting.

One other characteristic of the experimental subject deserves special mention. Most subjects have a real concern about their own performance and also wish to be good subjects in the sense of behaving appropriately, the right way, the way normal individuals behave, and so on. As Rosenberg (1969) aptly points out, subjects see psychologists as individuals able to judge the competence, the intelligence, as well as the emotional adjustment of others, and they therefore value the experimenter's opinion of them. Rosenberg argues that "evaluation apprehension" is a powerful determinant of subjects' behavior. There can be no doubt of the importance of such a variable, and subjects will, of course, strive to look good, both in their own eyes and in the view of the investigator. To the extent that a subject sees one or another behavior as being interpreted by the experimenter as more healthy or more correct, such a perception will affect his response in the situation (Orne, 1969, 1970).

Recently, there has been some effort to specify precisely what are the most important motivational factors shared by experimental subjects. Rather than seeking to find one set of motives regnant in all experimental contexts, it would seem more appropriate to recognize that in some settings one or another of these factors will become operative; it would also seem appropriate to recognize that the nature of the subject population,[4] how subjects are solicited, and how they are treated, will enhance one or another of these factors. Moreover, it would seem most important to recognize that what-

[4] Subjects' preexisting attitudes toward psychology will also vary, and these may have profound effects on their behavior in experiments (see Adair & Fenton, 1971).

ever the matrix of motivations underlying the subject's perception, he will inevitably take some position vis-à-vis the experimental situation. This position will tend to shape his perception of what is communicated by the experimental situation and may consequently have profound effects upon his behavior. It seems inappropriate to conceptualize these motivational variables as simply another set of stimuli which impinge upon the subject, as this would tend to ignore the subject's active participation in the unique form of social interaction which is called the psychological experiment.[5]

Cues That Determine the Subject's Perception of the Experimental Instructions

In order to understand the experimental procedure from the subject's point of view, it is necessary first to keep in mind that subjects are aware that they are not supposed to know too much about an experiment and have reason to distrust what they are told about the procedure. They listen to instructions, they respond to instructions, but they also recognize that the experimenter may have to be less than totally truthful. Subjects are usually quite comfortable in accepting the possibility that they may be deceived in an experiment since they recognize that such deception may be necessary for the purposes of research. Their understanding in this regard is perhaps more comprehensive than that of some of our colleagues who have argued that all deception is inherently degrading and repugnant.

Regardless of whether subjects are willing to tolerate being deceived, or are in fact told the truth, it would be foolhardy to assume that they accept what they are told uncritically and at face value. Subjects tend to treat experimental instructions in a fashion closely analogous to the way most people treat the used car salesman's assertion that "this particular 1962 Dodge has been driven only 2000 miles a year by a little old lady who used it only to go to church on Sunday."

It is for this reason that it is necessary to recognize that the subject's participation in the psychological experiment begins when he first hears about the experiment and contemplates whether he will or will not participate. A number of studies of cognitive dissonance (see Brehm & Cohen, 1962) have shown that the manner in which a decision to participate is arrived at may in and of itself have profound effects on how the subject subsequently behaves. Of even greater importance, however, may be the information which is made available to the subject when he is solicited.

[5] See Rosnow and Aiken (in press) for an interesting alternative way of conceptualizing the mediation of demand characteristics.

Solicitation Cues

In order to have subjects participate in an experiment, they must somehow be solicited. Investigators do this by an announcement in class, on the bulletin board, by means of an ad, or by word of mouth. The experiment must somehow be described, and that description itself may profoundly affect who volunteers and how he responds. For example, hypnotizability among subjects who respond to an ad seeking "participants for a psychological experiment" is significantly lower than among subjects who respond to an ad seeking "subjects to participate in hypnosis experiments." (Hilgard, 1965; Shor & E. Orne, 1963).

Not infrequently, one finds a member of a fraternity volunteering, and, after he has participated, a large number of members from the same fraternity promptly volunteer. It would be naive to assume that the experience of participation for what might be considered the scout is the same as that of his fellow members. The latter have been reassured by statements such as "It is really nothing," or "It is a lot of fun," or "It is an easy way to make a few dollars," or "Don't worry about the electric shock they talk about—they never really give it to you," or "It is really a put-on," and so on. Not only are they less anxious, but also they are more informed — not necessarily correctly informed, but more informed.

Perhaps the most troublesome aspect of the kind of cues under discussion here is the fact that the cues are generally made available to subjects without the awareness of the experimenter. Indeed, most experiments are implicitly based on the premise that subjects arrive at the experimental room pristine and unaware of any aspects of the procedure. Yet inevitably a great deal of information has already been made available to the subjects. In order to run a psychological experiment, it is necessary first to schedule the subjects. Most frequently this is arranged by asking them to call, or by a sign-up list and later contacting them about an appointment time. Often the scheduling is arranged by a secretary or a research assistant, rarely by the experimenter himself unless he happens to be a graduate student. It is simply not possible to arrange an appointment time with a subject without providing a good deal of information about the experiment in which he is expected to participate. The amount and kind of information made available during this transaction inevitably will help shape the subject's response. Unfortunately, since the investigator is not generally present, he rarely if ever knows about what is actually communicated.

The importance of assessing solicitation cues became forcibly clear to us some years back in the process of evaluating the sensory deprivation phenomenon.[6] We noticed that the first studies used 2 weeks of sensory deprivation and reported that various signs of breakdown could be observed after approximately 10 days. Following these, other studies involving only 1 week of deprivation were run, and evidence of severe disturbance was noted after about 5 days. Subsequent studies which involved 3 days of isolation showed similar effects after 2 days. Twenty-four-hour studies led to the observation of deleterious effects after only 16 hr. Finally, investigators using 8 hours of deprivation observed psychic disturbances after only 6 hr. The effect might best be described as a "two-thirds of the way through the experiment" breakdown, yet the investigators reported that their subjects were not told how long the period of total isolation would be.

As we tried to set up such an experiment, it soon became obvious that it was absolutely impossible to schedule a subject without indicating to him at least approximately how long the experiment would take. While subjects might well be willing to volunteer for an experiment of undetermined length, a subject being scheduled for a Tuesday experiment would say, "Well, if the experiment isn't over on Wednesday, I can't participate because I have an important exam." The helpful research assistant, faced with the task of persuading subjects to take part, will respond, "Oh, don't worry about it. Of course you will be finished." Indeed, this information was usually volunteered only indirectly; for example, subjects might be told, "You will be paid $2 an hour and the experiment pays $20." As we became more alert to this source of information, we became aware that one could not meaningfully demand of a scheduling assistant that appointments be arranged "without giving the subject any information." While the investigator may insist on being told that this was actually accomplished, in fact, it rarely can be.

Largely through the efforts of Emily Orne, our laboratory has gradually evolved scheduling procedures which do provide reasonable control over the precise information given. Unfortunately, it requires a great deal of effort and continuing attention to detail. Thus, at any given time, several experiments may be going on within the laboratory. We are careful not only to monitor the precise nature of the initial solicitation, but also to control the information that is provided to the subject by telephone. To do this, advertisements for each experiment ask the potential subject to call a specific individual at a specific telephone number. We use several noninterchangeable telephone lines, and a particular research assistant is assigned to answer calls from a particular line. Which ad the subject has read is identified both by the telephone number on which his call is received, and by the individual for whom he asks, as well as by how he describes the study. The designated

---

[6] Orne, M. T., & Scheibe, K. E. The effects of sensory deprivation: A critical review, unpublished manuscript, 1962.

individual is the only one permitted to handle subject calls for a given study.

In advance of the experiment, a detailed list of the information which the research assistant is to make available to the subject is worked out, and, while scheduling, the assistant not only arranges the time, but also provides the specified information about the study in a casual conversation. This includes such aspects as what electrodes must be attached, whether shock may be involved, and so on. Furthermore, every effort is made to work out the kinds of questions the subject might ask, and they are gone over with the research assistant in advance, together with a set of answers designed to keep constant the amount of total information that is made available to each individual. Any additional questions which a particular subject then asks, as well as the answers given to them, must be noted. Thus, the process of handling all possible questions is continually monitored. A checksheet is provided for the research assistant where she notes each point as it is discussed in an apparently spontaneous, but actually carefully preprogrammed fashion.

Despite all of these precautions, we do not, of course, have complete control over the material communicated. The procedures do make certain that subjects have a reasonably stable amount of information and prevent the inadvertent communication of information which is likely to have a profound effect on subjects' experimental behavior.[7]

The significance of the information provided by the scheduling assistant is also apparent in an entirely different context. The information given informally by the research assistant is likely to be viewed by the subject as even more telling than that provided by the experimenter. Subjects see the scheduling assistant's task as merely arranging an appointment time, and therefore information which is casually and apparently inadvertently given has a very high degree of credibility. Subjects tend to perceive the scheduling assistant as uninvolved and thus unbiased; comments from such a communication source become especially trustworthy.

An additional source of information usually overlooked is the interaction with the technician, whose job is too often viewed as one of merely attaching electrodes or setting up the subject with complex equipment. It is almost impossible for an individual to attach electrodes and interact with a subject

---

[7] If a subject asks such pointed or unique questions that the scheduling assistant is forced to provide additional information or rework old information in a new manner, a special telephone contact form is prepared for the experimenter so that a decision can be made in advance of the experimental session as to whether the subject's run should be disqualified. Because the subject volunteered in good faith, he is still run, however, and from his point of view his data are meaningful to the laboratory.

for perhaps half an hour without responding to questions about the study. Because the technician is seen as a disinterested person who must be aware of what is going on, but who has little stake in concealing it, his casual remarks may carry a great deal of weight. This is somewhat analogous to the everyday phenomenon encountered in a doctor's office where a casual gratuitous comment by the nurse or technician tends to be accepted as gospel — often in preference to what the physician says — because the patient is afraid that the doctor may be trying to conceal his real illness from him.

Cues Arising from the Experimental Procedure Itself

The most important single source of cues available to the subject about the purpose of an experiment is provided by the experimental procedure itself. This reflects the well-known adage that actions speak louder than words, especially in a context where there is reason to distrust words. Thus, the experimental protocol inevitably must communicate something about the purpose of an experiment. Attitude research has had to come to terms with the fact that if a subject is given a test, presented with an intervening treatment, and then retested, the procedure clearly communicates that the investigator expects some kind of change, regardless of what the subject is told about the procedure. A variety of complex and sophisticated controls have been developed to evaluate pretest sensitization (see Lana, 1969; Solomon, 1949).

Despite its obvious importance as a source of communication, investigators have tended to overlook the significance of the experimental procedure in most fields of psychology. To take another example from work in hypnosis, Hull (1933) recognized the importance of order effects, and for this reason, in evaluating the effect of hypnosis on physical performance, he used the standard ABBA–BAAB procedure. In a number of studies, highly significant differences could be observed. Note that the logic of such a design is one where the performance of all subjects is averaged in order to statistically eliminate practice effects. In several studies, we have found very striking differences between these two orders which cannot be ascribed to practice (Evans & Orne, 1965). Subjects who are run in hypnosis first apparently perform much better in hypnosis than in the wake state, whereas a very small improvement can be achieved in subjects who are run in the wake state first. Subjects in the former case recognize from the design — not from anything they are told — that it is the intent of the investigator to compare the hypnotic performance with the waking performance and apparently at some level suppress their waking performance. On the other hand, subjects who are run in the wake state first yield a waking performance of the same order of magnitude as the hypnotic performance of other groups, with very little if any increment in the subsequent hypnotic performance.

It should be noted that the modification in experimental procedure not only alters simple order effects, but also changes the ease with which subjects can recognize and respond to the intent of the investigator. Zamansky, Scharf, and Brightbill (1964) documented the importance of the subjects' awareness of whether or not they would subsequently be tested in hypnosis. Thus, if subjects knew in the first waking performance that they would subsequently be tested in hypnosis, they yielded a significantly higher threshold, or worse performance, than subjects of equal hypnotizability who were not aware that they would subsequently be tested later in hypnosis.

Unfortunately, the subject's perception of an experimental protocol depends upon many subtle factors in interaction with the protocol itself. Frequently, minor changes in experimental conditions or in order of presentation will result in major changes in a subject's perception of the experimental purpose and consequently major changes in his responses.

The Study of Demand Characteristics

While it is possible to specify some of the sources of cues responsible for a subject's perception of an experiment, it would be a matter of empirical inquiry to determine precisely what subjects do in fact perceive. The investigator will often want to determine directly how the subject perceives a given experimental study.

The experimenter is, of course, not as interested in some aspects of the subject's perception as in others. He is specifically concerned with those perceptions which are likely to have a systematic effect on the individual's behavior during an experiment. It is this specific aspect of the subject's perception — the demand characteristics of the experimental situation — which become an important area to explore. In reading a protocol of a psychological experiment and thinking about how a subject might behave, one implicitly makes assumptions about how the subject perceives the situation. As we have tried to underline, all too often these implicit assumptions are incorrect. With sufficient experience — and sufficient knowledge about the kind of *details* about the experiment discussed earlier — the investigator may make some inference about how the situation is perceived. Colleagues, regardless of their seniority or experience, can never be the final arbiter of this question; only subjects who have been in the experimental situation can really elucidate how and what subjects perceive in the situation. The actor in the situation is likely to perceive cues differently in context than an outside observer trying to evaluate them. Consequently, subjects may fail to perceive what seems completely obvious to the investigator; at other times, they will easily see through the most byzantine deceptions devised by the investigator.

The Postexperimental Inquiry

The most straightforward kind of quasi-control procedure is the post-experimental inquiry. At the conclusion of the experiment, the subject's perceptions about the procedure are elicited in order to learn how the subject perceives the experimental situation, to answer the questions of what the subject believed the purpose of the experiment was, what he believes the experimenter hoped or expected to find, how he thinks other individuals did, and how he thinks he did in relation to what he believes to be the ex-perimenter's hypotheses.

In conducting an inquiry, it is necessary to keep in mind that subjects in psychological experiments tend to be aware that they ought not to catch on to some aspects of the experimental procedure, that if they indicate that they know too much, their data cannot be used. Since subjects tend to have con-siderable investment in having their data be useful, there is a tendency for them not to volunteer their awareness of the investigator's hypotheses, espe-cially if these have not been discussed. This tendency is, of course, rein-forced by a subject's reluctance to appear wrong.

It should be recognized that the needs of the subject in this regard tend to mesh with those of the investigator, who is by no means eager to learn that subjects actually caught on to what he assumed to be a clever deception or that subjects perceived the experiment as different from the way he in-tended. Consequently, there is a tendency for a "pact of ignorance" (Orne, 1962) to evolve where the subject answers the casual question: "What do you think the experiment was all about?" with "I don't know," and the investigator all too gladly terminates his inquiry. However, if the investigator persists, he will be rewarded — or punished, as the case may be — by learn-ing that most subjects form a very clear picture of what the experiment is about and why the experiment is being carried out, though this picture may or may not resemble the experimenter's actual hypotheses.[8]

A postexperimental inquiry, carried out with tact and persistence, com-municating to the subject that information is truly desired, while taking care, of course, not to shape his response, may yield a great deal of meaningful

---

[8] A number of recent studies have shown that inquiries may still fail to break down the subject's reluctance to admit to "forbidden information" (see Golding & Lichtenstein, 1970).

information. To carry out an effective inquiry, the investigator should strive to alter the subject–experimenter relationship and restructure it in order to make the subject a coinvestigator. The change in role from subject to co-investigator tends to have a significant effect on the nature of the communication. It is particularly helpful from this point of view for the inquiry to be conducted by someone other than the experimenter himself. A second experimenter does not need to alter his role relationship with the subject; rather he begins the interview with the subject as a coequal whose task now becomes helping the scientist to understand what was communicated to him by the experimenter, how he perceived the experimental procedures, and what might be done to improve the experiment in future work. Most important, perhaps, are the subtle, but often significant alterations in the nature of the communication which tend to take place when someone other than the experimenter discusses what occurred. In this different context, the subject can view his experience more dispassionately and may feel more free to discuss what he might construe as implied criticisms of the procedures or the experimenter. In conducting an inquiry, it is important to avoid any judgmental comments and rather to take the role of an individual seeking to learn and understand. As is the case in the therapeutic context, the more the subject is asked to explain and spell out what he means, the more likely that he will be in a position to communicate significant aspects of his experience. The more the interviewer is willing to accept ambiguous comments and such phrases as "You know what I mean," the less likely is he to learn what the subject really meant.

The inquiry procedure, even optimally carried out and objectified by the use of judges, still suffers from several limitations. The most important, perhaps, is that the subject's conclusions at the end of the experiment are determined by everything that has taken place, and it is very difficult to establish at what point in time within the experiment, or even the inquiry, the subject arrived at his conclusions. The relationship between behavior and the subject's awareness of a particular hypothesis is complex. Awareness may not be an all-or-none phenomenon; rather it may gradually evolve and it may even be partially shaped by the subject's observing his own behavior. On the whole, however, a particular hypothesis a subject may form about the experiment is likely to affect his behavior more after he has arrived at it. Consequently, it becomes very important to establish when in the course of the experiment, cues are available to permit him to form a particular hypothesis.

Solomon[9] has proposed the use of "sacrifice" subjects where the experiment is terminated at different points in time in order to establish the kind of

[9] Richard Solomon, personal communication, 1958.

hypotheses that are formulated at the various crucial points within a given study. Despite the cost of such a procedure, it is nonetheless extremely powerful in helping to clarify the nature of the cues which affect subjects' perceptions of an experiment.

The "Nonexperiment" Procedure

Another equally troublesome difficulty is the fact that subjects may derive their hypotheses about the experiment from their own behavior during the session. In order to avoid this difficulty, we have employed another procedure which was suggested independently by Riecken (1962) and which we have called the preinquiry or nonexperiment (Orne, 1962) in which all experimental communications are available to the subject.

In the nonexperiment, a subject is told everything about the experiment, given the experimental instructions, shown the experimental equipment, and is told about the treatment to which he would be exposed, but he is not actually exposed to any of the treatment procedures. For example, in the sensory deprivation study, he would be given the instructions, administered the pretests, shown the setup, put in the situation momentarily, and then told, "If you were a subject in this experiment, you would now be left alone for an indeterminate period — that is, you would not know how long it would be; actually, however, it would be 8 hours." He is then told, "Now, I want you to behave as if you had actually been in this experiment." He is then administered the posttests as if he were an actual sensory deprivation subject. In the nonexperiment, the subject comes from the same population and shares the same background information as other members of the subject pool who would ultimately participate in the actual study. Such a subject is not quite an actor in the actual experimental context, but he is considerably more than an observer. He is in an experimental situation, though not the identical experimental situation as an actual subject, and tends to yield information that goes beyond what can be surmised intuitively by the investigator in planning his experiment.

The nonexperiment is an extremely interesting procedure because it depends exclusively on the subject's ability to think himself into the situation. Again, the very kind of mental mechanism which tends to complicate human research is turned to advantage in this procedure. The nonexperiment could easily be conceptualized as an extension of the inquiry procedure, but it has the virtue of yielding data in the same form as those given by subjects who actually participate in the experiment. It is no longer necessary to make an inference about how a given perception might affect a subject's behavior — the subject himself makes that inference and provides the behavior. If preinquiry data are identical to those obtained by subjects in the actual experiment, an alternative explanation for the subject's behavior must be considered. Thus, the subject in the actual experiment might be responding in terms of his expectations rather than to the experimental variables. Such a finding would suggest that the experimental procedure was not adequate as a rigorous test. It is for this reason that we think of these controls as procedural controls which help design better experiments.

Simulation Techniques

A further extension of this principle can be seen in the use of simulators as controls (Orne, 1959). This technique, which was originally designed for use in hypnosis research but can be extended to other kinds of treatments, asks the subject to simulate a state, for instance hypnosis, for an experienced hypnotist who is actually blind as to the true status of the subject. Again, we are asking the subject to utilize his cognitive processes in the service of the control procedure, to try his best to respond to all the subtle cues in the situation in order to yield the kind of behavior a highly hypnotizable, deeply hynotized individual would give. To the extent that an unhypnotizable, simulating subject is able to do this without special training, we must conclude that an alternative hypothesis *could* explain the behavior. It thus indicates that the experimental test, designed to prove something as necessarily due to hypnosis, is not adequate. It of course says nothing about the treatment itself. Thus, the simulator may merely know enough to predict accurately how a given treatment would affect the subject.

The nature of inference based on simulating subjects' responses must be very carefully thought through since only counterexpectational findings can be expected to yield differences. Consequently, we will often find no differences in behavior between hypnotized and simulating subjects even though there are differences in the *mechanism by which the behavior is elicited.* On the other hand, when differences do emerge, we will have considerably more faith in the experimental conclusions based upon them. [For a more detailed discussion of the conceptual issues, see Evans (1971), Orne (1971, 1972), and Sheehan (1971).]

The Concept of Quasi-Controls

In order to carry out any experimental research, it is necessary for the investigator to translate his theoretical concepts into operational terms, which then define the intended meaning of the experimental procedures. For meaningful experimental research in any field of science, it is crucial that what is operationalized in the experiment validly reflect the more general theoretical construct being examined. There are, however, no fixed rules by which the validity of the operational definition is evaluated, and, at times, this appropriately becomes a source of controversy. For the most part, in the physical sciences the reader of a paper is able to evaluate the adequacy of the translation.

As one applies the operational approach to psychological research, however, a new set of problems emerges. For example, in studying physiological effects of stress, the technique of requiring subjects to count backward rapidly by sevens has often been used as a moderate stressor. In order to compare the physiological response of the subject in his resting state with his response under stress, physiological recordings are obtained, first during a "base line" period and then after asking the subject to count backward as rapidly as possible by sevens – the latter procedure being operationally defined as stress. In a recent experiment (Paskewitz & Orne, 1971), we were surprised to note that of nine subjects, two showed absolutely no objective evidence of stress when counting backward by sevens. These subjects reported that they were not troubled by this task, and, indeed, their objective performance was such that there was hardly any difference in either rate or accuracy when these individuals counted backward by sevens versus when they counted backward by ones.

While a great many techniques have been developed to make certain that differences observed in experimental situations are not random or chance events, very little, if any, attention has been given to the validity of the operational definition (Evans, 1971). It is obvious in this instance that for two of our subjects counting backward by sevens under time pressure was simply not stressful and that, to the extent that one is seeking to study the effect of stress on physiological responsivity, they should be excluded from the data analysis.

While most readers would agree in this instance, the more general implication would be that the investigator, defining a given procedure as a stressor, must ascertain whether in fact it serves the intended purpose for all of his subjects. If it fails to stress some individuals, they should not be considered in the same experimental situation as those who are in fact stressed. In other words, some aspect of the subject's response must *a priori* be used to ascertain whether the situation is for that subject what it was intended to be by the investigator.

There are a considerable number of research contexts where the subject's perception of the situation leads to radically different responses. In the example just given, the problem arose due to individual differences in numerical skills. More subtle, but equally serious, problems result from purely cognitive factors leading to differing perceptions of the experimental situation. In translating the work on avoidance conditioning with dogs to humans, Turner and Solomon (1962) used a simple manipulandum which required subjects to move a lever in order to avoid shock. Some subjects failed to learn and continued to accept shocks for very large numbers of trials. These subjects had been solicited for a shock experiment, and the initial experimental procedure included considerable emphasis on the level of shock that could be tolerated. It turned out that some individuals perceived the purpose of the study to establish whether they would be able to tolerate the discomfort of the shock, and they behaved accordingly, ignoring the manipulandum. Clearly, the subjects who learned perceived the experimental situation differently from those who failed to do so. A minor modification in the instructions, including the statement that it was possible for subjects to learn to avoid the shock, led to rapid learning with all subjects. The experiment, as originally conceived by the investigators, concerned the learning of avoidance conditioning in man, but the perception of some subjects defined it as an endurance study for them, leading to very different and initially somewhat surprising behavior. Once the investigators explored the subjects' perception, it became possible to alter the experiment, leading to far more stable and predictable results. This was possible only after the experiment was analyzed from the subject's point of view.

Another kind of problem occurs when the subject sees the experimental situation in a way totally different from the way it is perceived by the investigator. This was the case in the studies on antisocial behavior and hypnosis to which we have alluded earlier. Only after the use of simulating subjects demonstrated that unhypnotized individuals would be willing to pick up a poisonous snake and throw acid at an assistant, did it become fully clear how differently the situation was seen by the subjects and the investigators. Once this discrepancy was recognized and resolved, it became a simple matter to run other control subjects and demonstrate that compliance in this situation varies directly with the degree of conviction with which the instructions are given.

Deception as a Control Procedure

The problems inherent in how subjects perceive the experimental situation are implicitly recognized by all investigators. This recognition has led to the use of deception in psychological research becoming so commonplace. Subjects are deceived in the hope of finding out how they would really behave in a situation not confounded by their awareness of the variable actually under investigation. Typically, investigators take considerable pride in the subtlety of their techniques and are satisfied to present the outline of how subjects were deceived, going on to assume that this was actually the case. Obviously, these investigators would not have utilized the deception manipulation had they not believed it would make a difference. It seems remarkable, therefore, that both they and their professional audience often uncritically assume that the subject is in fact deceived (Orne & Holland, 1968).

In each of the examples previously cited, the meaning of an experimental finding can be understood only when the investigator evaluates it from the subject's point of view. This allows him to determine the validity of the procedures as operational definitions of the psychological process under investigation. In the study from stress research where two subjects failed to be stressed by the demand to count backward rapidly by sevens, these individuals differed from others in their ability to manipulate numbers. As a consequence, however, their perception of the situation was drastically altered. Thus, the operational definition of the counting procedure as a stressor was not valid for these particular subjects. In the conditioning study, subjects who perceived the experiment as a test of their masculinity were clearly responding to an entirely different psychological context from those who perceived the situation as a test of their ability to learn to avoid electric shock. Inquiry procedures clarified that situation and made it a simple matter to design instructions which assured that all subjects were in a learning experiment. In the study on antisocial behavior, simulating subjects were used to clarify that the act of using one's bare hands either to remove a penny from fuming nitric acid or to pick up a poisonous snake need not necessarily be defined by the subject as self-destructive behavior. Rather, these subjects showed that they clearly recognized the procedure as safe. Once the validity of the procedure as an operational definition of self-destructive behavior is questioned, our understanding of the previous experimental findings is radically altered.

In any deception experiment, it is clearly crucial to determine whether the deception manipulation was effective in order to evaluate the validity of the experimental procedure. Thus, if subjects are tipped off as to either the nature of the deception or to the fact that deception is part of the experiment, they ought to behave differently from those who lack such information. If they fail to do so, one may seriously question, in the absence of other data, whether it would not be best to assume that the original subjects might somehow have seen through the deception manipulation. Hence, the particular deception procedures are not likely to help in creating a valid operational definition (see Golding & Lichtenstein, 1970; Holland, 1967; Levy, 1967).

Several other relevant examples have been given earlier in this chapter, and many more will undoubtedly come to mind when the reader considers studies where doubts can be raised regarding the validity of the experimental approach. It would seem clear that, for the experimental technique to become more effective in psychology, it is essential that we consider this problem at least as carefully as that of statistical significance. It is particularly relevant to the ecological validity of an experimental study to establish whether it validly reflects the mechanism it is meant to explore.

Quasi-Controls as Procedures to Evaluate the Total Experimental Communication

The usual concept of control is intended to clarify the nature of the independent variables. However, the problems we have been discussing here all result from the way the subject perceives the situation, what the experiment communicates or means to him, and how he is affected by the demand characteristics. These issues are at a different level from those generally considered in texts on methodology. Clearly, the discrepancy between how the subject perceives the experimental context and how the experimenter intended for it to be perceived will be more serious in some research studies than in others. Further, the effects of the discrepancy, if any, will be greater in some situations than in others. While we can never be certain about the extent to which these factors may be confounding variables, we can and need to use techniques to estimate their possible effects.

We need to think in terms of controls built into the experiment to evaluate the effect of the experimental situation itself. These procedures are designed to explore how the subject perceives the situation and to determine whether his perception is that which the experimenter intended. Findings from these procedures will tell us little or nothing about the independent variables, and will help to shed light only on the extent to which the experiment is a valid means of examining them. These techniques are controls to evaluate the procedures of an experiment and the extent to which they validly reflect what they are intended to reflect. It is difficult to find an appropriate name for them. They could be considered "active controls" since they are concerned with the unwanted contributions to the experimental situation which the subject inevitably adds that are the result of the subject's active thinking processes. One might call them "validity controls" except, of course, that all controls speak to the validity of findings. Again, one might call them "procedural controls" because they test the adequacy of the experimental procedures, yet this seems hardly an adequate description. For want of a better term, I have called them *quasi-controls* (Orne, 1969). One would hope that, in addition to the quasi-control procedures discussed earlier (which include the nonexperiment, the use of simulating subjects, the use of subjects alerted to possible deception), other quasi-controls appropriate to special experimental problems will be developed. These control procedures need to be interpreted with great care because they include involving the subject in a special and different way from simply asking him to be a passive responder. They require responses from the subject as basic data to evaluate the communication of the total experiment.

When Are Quasi-Controls Needed?

For didactic reasons, a number of examples have been given where the subject's perception of the experiment, his beliefs about what constitutes appropriate behavior, and his perception of the research aims account for the major portion of the variance in his responses. Though these variables are important in some experimental situations, they have little or no effect on the outcome of others. Unfortunately, in the absence of quasi-control data one can hardly ever be certain whether this is the case in any particular experiment. Since clear instances can be documented in such diverse areas as conditioning, perception, and psychophysiology as well as social psychology where subjects' perceptions have played unexpectedly important roles, one may well ask to what extent an investigator needs to concern himself with these issues. Is it essential to set up elaborate quasi-controls in every study with human subjects? Such a course would increase the cost of research geometrically and slow research to a snail's pace. On the other hand, if the investigator assumes that these factors are unimportant, is he likely to be deceiving himself and wasting his time on laboratory artifacts?

There are a number of hints, however, which ought to alert an investigator, in the course of reviewing the literature as well as during his pilot research, to the likelihood that demand characteristics are important variables in the particular phenomenon under investigation. If the same procedure appears to lead to dramatically differing results in different laboratories, or, alternatively, if widely different procedures used in the same kind of context produce similar results whereas these procedures in other contexts do not elicit such findings, the subject's perceptions are likely to be of paramount importance.

During pilot studies, most subjects may yield data consistent with the literature, but a few produce totally different findings. Under such circumstances, it will be most productive to explore in depth the nature of the aberrant subjects' responses and the possible reasons for them. From this point of view, it is not important whether the number of subjects who behave appropriately is sufficiently great to yield statistically significant findings despite several deviant subjects. The purpose of exploring the reasons for subjects' aberrant responses is the likelihood of obtaining crucial hints about the nature of the demand characteristics in the situation. The question, of course, is to establish whether the deviant responses are a function of peculiarities of the subject or of alternative perceptions of the experimental situation. When the latter is the case, it is usually possible to alter the experimental results drastically by subtle variations in procedures and instructions. Furthermore, the findings from the experiment can be generalized only to those individuals who perceive the experiment in a particular manner which, in turn, may be contingent upon subtle and ephemeral cues. Similarly, a bimodal set of responses should alert the investigator to explore differences in subjects' perceptions. This is especially true when subjects split on such parameters as psychology majors versus others, previous experience with experimental studies, subjects run early in the experiment versus subjects run late in the experiment, IQ, and so on.

As investigators, we should seek to understand insofar as possible every response of every single individual. In order to accomplish such a goal we need to focus on how each particular subject perceives the experiment. It should be clear that such efforts to understand and explain responses have little or no place in the published account of an experiment; rather, they are intended to serve the vital function of helping to increase the investigator's sensitivity to alternative explanations of subjects' responses. Such an understanding is likely to permit the investigator to redesign his experiment in such a manner that the subject perceives the situation in a way that makes the operational definitions more congruent with the mechanisms they are intended to reflect.

Common Pitfalls in Attempts to Control for Demand Characteristics

With the growing concern about issues of demand characteristics, studies in some areas of psychology have attempted to deal with the problems in a variety of ways. Two procedures widely believed to be effective in controlling demand characteristics deserve mention because they simply fail to come to terms with the problems. Under the misapprehension that demand characteristics are communicated primarily by instructions, some investigators have tried to eliminate verbal instructions, attempting to treat their subjects as though they were laboratory animals. It is foolhardy to think, however, that simply because the subject is not told verbally why an experiment is being conducted or how he is expected to behave, he will therefore fail to interpret or to use the cues available from the experimental procedure itself as the basis for his experimental performance. No verbiage simply does not equal no communication! Regardless of what the subject is told or not told, he will inevitably form perceptions about the experimental purpose, which will, in turn, affect his responses.

Partially in reaction to the use of deception in psychological experiments, some investigators have made a special point of telling subjects precisely what is wanted and why. In some instances, they have made the unrealistic assumption that the fact of their honesty will assure how the subject perceives the situation. Unfortunately, some honest explanations about experiments are less plausible to subjects than some of the better deception instructions. At times, subjects find it hard to believe that the investigator is really interested only in what he honestly describes as his purpose. When this occurs, the subject's belief about what he is doing and his inaccurate perception of the experimental purpose will affect his behavior. The consequence is exactly the same as in an unsuccessful deception study: It is what the subject perceives which determines his behavior, and this need not be what the experimenter had intended.

Demand Characteristics as a Spoiler Variable

As one gradually becomes aware of the extent of the subject's active participation in experimental situations and how this may serve to distort and modify the effects of the independent variables, it becomes necessary to rethink the enterprise of research with human subjects. At first one tends to be appalled by the difficulties. The initial dismay may gradually turn into irritation, as students and colleagues are all too ready to base criticisms of serious research on questions of demand characteristics. It is always possible to raise doubts about whether subjects really perceived the situation as they were supposed to and, consequently, whether demand characteristics might not be a better way to account for the subject's behavior than the independent variable. Such criticisms when leveled glibly and without much thought become a source of considerable annoyance to those of us actively engaged in empirical research. A preoccupation with these problems may even serve to discourage colleagues from concerning themselves with substantive psychological issues.

Unfortunately, the investigator trying to answer substantive questions by carrying out laboratory research with human subjects must somehow deal with the infinite regress implicit in criticisms arguing that a given effect is due to demand characteristics. There can be no simple answer since any experiment, regardless of the caution with which it is conducted and the careful use of quasi-controls, can still be subjected to such criticisms. While there is little doubt that research with human subjects is far more difficult and complex than has generally been recognized, no adequate viable alternative to the experimental method is available. Field experiments, experiments in nature, the technique of the participant observer may all serve useful purposes, but none permits the systematic exploration of psychological mechanisms, nor do they provide for the kind of control which is potentially possible in the laboratory. The recognition that the experiment is a complex interaction and that subjects' cognitive processes may interfere with our efforts to investigate these very processes should not negate the potential usefulness of the experiment. An understanding of the concept of demand characteristics should ultimately allow us to design better experiments, permitting ecologically valid inference to the real world, because we have learned how to analyze the communication of the total experiment from the subject's point of view.

It does follow however, that it will be necessary to take the potential problems of demand characteristics into account in any interpretation of psychological research. Perhaps this will help us recognize that no single experiment can ever resolve major issues — that the effort to design the single perfect, definitive experiment is essentially futile. Instead, experimental findings need to be conceptualized as a useful source of relevant information concerning the psychological phenomena they purport to investigate. The controlled circumstances under which the observations are obtained help in their interpretation; however, certain inevitable limitations also stem from the context in which the observations are carried out.

When data from experimental studies appear to contradict repeated reliable observations in nonexperimental settings, further work seems essential to resolve such a paradox. We can ill afford to accept experimental data because "it was obtained under carefully controlled laboratory conditions" and reject other observations out of hand; nor is it appropriate to reject experimental data because of conflicting field observations. Science must be able to account for apparently contradictory findings, and the kinds of variables we have been discussing here are particularly likely to be responsible for discrepant observations.

The experimental investigation of psychological phenomena remains an exceedingly powerful and effective way of answering important questions. Nonetheless, it is essential that the limitations of findings from any given experiment be recognized. This seems particularly urgent if it is our intent to generalize our observations so that policy decisions in the real world can be based upon them. Under such circumstances, we should require a matrix of experimental data as well as congruent, systematic observations gathered in nonexperimental settings in order to feel reasonably confident about the ecological validity of our conclusions. If the concept of demand characteristics is useful only in raising doubts about premature generalizations from single experiments (regardless of how congruent they may be with our value system) to policy decisions affecting the lives of individuals, such an outcome would still seem highly desirable for psychology, for those who would apply its findings, and particularly for those who would be affected by the decisions.

Even though an investigator is careful in his research, tries to see experimental observations in the broader perspective of observations obtained in other contexts, and tries to use quasi-control procedures as they seem relevant, he may still find his experiments subject to criticisms arguing that a given effect is due to demand characteristics. How can he deal with such critiques?

While any experiment may be criticized on the basis of presumed demand characteristics, such criticism eventually boils down to a controversy about how the experiment is seen from the subject's point of view. Since it is far more difficult to specify how subjects actually perceive an experiment as opposed to the nature of instructions and physical stimuli, it is hardly surprising that it is more difficult to deal with. The concept of demand characteristics forces us to attend not so much to what is done to the subject, but rather to how the situation is perceived by the subject. Implicitly, all investigators make definite assumptions about how their subjects see the experimental situation, assumptions which are generally taken for granted and rarely challenged. A criticism based on demand characteristics challenges this implicit view and thereby provides an alternative hypothesis to explain the observed findings, which is not different in kind from a myriad of other alternate hypotheses which can be devised to account for experimental observations. Clearly, no investigator can be required to answer every possible alternate interpretation of his findings; he needs to concern himself only with plausible alternatives. Thus, if a critic argues that an effect is due to demand characteristics, he is implicitly stating that the experiment is perceived by the subjects in a particular fashion. Such an assertion is readily made explicit and should in the final analysis be resolved empirically, much as any other dispute about possible causal mechanisms.

The Peculiar Nature of the Psychological Experiment and How It Affects Replication of Prior Research

This discussion has consistently emphasized the importance of what is communicated by the total experimental situation to the subject and the significance of his perceptions of this total context for an understanding of his behavior. The experimental method, however, was developed in the physical sciences and assumes the object of study is passively responsive and that it is possible to specify all relevant variables that impinge on the object of study in a given experiment. In utilizing the experimental procedure in psychology, the major difficulty is the subject's status as an active participant rather than as a passive responder to stimuli.

Unfortunately, we do not have a viable alternative conceptual model for the experiment. It is all too tempting to criticize its use in psychology because the assumptions of the physical sciences are not satisfied. However, it is an extremely productive exercise to force ourselves to specify all relevant variables that may affect the experimental outcome – even though the subject is not a passive responder – and it is likely that the assumptions of the experimental method are not significantly violated *provided the subject perceives the total experimental situation in the manner in which the investigator had intended him to.*

It is worth noting that in each and every instance where the demand characteristics of the experiment appear to have been the significant determinant of the subjects' behavior (rather than the independent variable which had previously been assumed to determine the responses), there was a major discrepancy between the manner in which investigators had thought subjects perceived the experimental situation and the manner in which they actually did perceive it.

Despite the shortcomings of the experimental method as used in psychology, every effort should be made to design experiments so that the relevant variables can be objectively stated, and the primary role of quasi-controls is in helping to design better experiments. Specifically, they make it possible to evaluate whether the subject's perception of the experimental situation is isomorphic with how the investigator had intended it to be and therefore address the validity of the experimental procedure.

One special characteristic of human experimentation deserves particular attention. Not infrequently, very subtle and apparently trivial changes in subject selection, experimental setting, instructions, or procedure may cause major differences in the manner in which the experiment is perceived by the subject. Sometimes such changes can be anticipated in advance, but at other times the effects are puzzling and unpredictable. The tendency for communication implicit in the total experimental setting to be radically altered by some apparently trivial modification of procedure has, however, crucial implications for an understanding of replication.

In contrast to the physical sciences, detailed replications are rarely carried out in psychology and many widely quoted, frequently cited studies have not ever been replicated. When a noncontroversial finding is replicated, it is not seen as a particularly significant contribution to the field. On the other hand, a failure to replicate is also not readily published. The contrasting attitude in psychology, as opposed to the physical sciences where replication is seen as an essential and valuable enterprise, cannot be ascribed to the amount of effort involved in carrying out the research, since this has not prevented replication of major findings in other sciences. Rather, it seems related to the difficulty of coming to terms with the inherent problems of the experimental paradigm itself as it is used in psychology.

The most serious problem seems related to the implicit assumption that it is possible in psychological experiments to specify adequately all relevant variables in a scientific communication. However, due to the limitations of space, the procedure section is invariably cut to a bare minimum, and while the casual reader may find even such a shortened version pedantic and detailed, anyone seriously attempting to replicate finds innumerable questions where details of procedure are simply not spelled out.

A failure to replicate a psychological experiment is, in fact, usually a trivial observation which makes little or no contribution to the field, because this failure is likely to be due to subtle, unspecified changes in procedure. The fault is as likely to be with the attempted replication in not reproducing the circumstances under which the original findings were obtained as with the original study. The only way in which an investigator may have some reasonable certainty that he has created an experimental situation which truly replicates that of the original study is when, after obtaining answers from the author of the original study concerning the myriad of unpublished details, he repeats the study and actually obtains findings similar to those of the original paper. If he fails to do so, it becomes necessary to systematically study the experimental procedure, subject selection, amount of information available to the subject, and so forth, modifying these parameters in subtle ways consistent with the published description as elaborated by the author's commentary, until a situation is created where the original findings *are* replicated.[10] Only after this has been accomplished, is it possible to clarify the mechanisms by which these findings were obtained. Only then is it appropriate to show that varying the independent variable involved in the original study fails to affect the experimental results, whereas varying some other variable to which the original author had ascribed little or no importance is sufficient to alter the findings drastically.

For example, consider the antisocial behavior and hypnosis study previously discussed. It would have been meaningless to carry out this study without demonstrating that hypnotized subjects could be compelled to carry out antisocial and self-destructive behavior while other subjects, when asked whether they would carry out these behaviors, indicated that they would not. Only after the essential observations of Rowland (1939) and

[10] The asymmetry of positive versus negative findings in replications has recently been emphasized by Aronson and Carlsmith (1969).

Young (1952) had been replicated in fine detail, with the authors' clarification of the procedural nitty-gritty, did the experimental demonstration that simulating subjects would carry out the same behaviors become relevant and, subsequently, the demonstration that other subjects could easily be persuaded to do likewise. One can conceive of an experiment done in a way that would have made the safety precautions so transparent that subjects asked whether they would carry out the behaviors would readily indicate their willingness to do so. If this had been the case, other aspects of the demonstration would have been trivial and meaningless because it would have been very unlikely that a truly analogous situation had been created.

In our present state of development in psychology, then, the only meaningful replication is one where the experimenter is able to reproduce not only the conditions, but also the responses of the subjects. This is necessary as a means of ascertaining that the original situation had, in fact, been replicated; that is, it is not likely that the communication of the total original experiment has been brought under control without being able to reproduce the basic data of the original subjects' responses. Only after this can be accomplished is it possible to demonstrate that the determinants of the subjects' responses might not be what the previous investigator believed them to be, but rather something else. Such an experiment is, of course, more difficult to carry out than a casual replication. It forces the investigator to try to understand how a given finding might have been obtained and to come to terms with the likelihood that a failure to replicate is probably due to his inability to reproduce the relevant conditions (in terms of the total experimental communication). Such a level of understanding is essential, however, in order to be able to explain previous findings definitively and add significantly to our knowledge.

In our work, we have attempted this type of procedure and in several instances have been fortunate enough – after a considerable period of experimentation – to replicate the original findings of others and then to dissect the mechanisms which were involved (Gustafson & Orne, 1965; O'Connell, Shor, & Orne, 1970; Orne, 1959; Orne & Evans, 1965; Orne, Sheehan, & Evans, 1968). This has led us to a progressively greater emphasis on understanding the experimental communication from the subject's point of view.

There are, of course, disadvantages in requiring that findings be replicated. Since the likelihood of replicating erroneous findings reported in the literature would be small indeed – despite the most assiduous efforts to vary the conditions in a plausible manner – the requirement that this be done would tend to allow an incorrect finding to stand.

Perhaps even more important is the possibility that even if a finding is replicated by varying some of the subtle demand characteristics which could presumably have played a role in the original observations, one can never be certain that the mechanisms responsible for the data obtained in the replication are the same as those which were operant in the original study. Thus, even if an investigator is able to show that by approximating the situation and varying the manner in which the subject might have perceived the experiment he is able to manipulate the presence or absence of previous observations, he can never conclusively prove that these were in fact the mechanisms which accounted for the previously reported observations. He has, of course, documented a plausible and viable alternative hypothesis, and, hopefully, future work will permit the scientific community to decide between his conclusions and those of the original report.

Despite these limitations, this approach toward replication seems the best available compromise with the realities of psychological experimentation. Though it makes it more difficult to refute erroneous observations and it does not eliminate the possibility that similar data can be produced by multiple mechanisms, the proposed ground rules still seem worthwhile. Hopefully they provide a framework within which it becomes meaningful to build upon the work of others. Further, they spell out how critiques based on the concept of demand characteristics can be applied responsibly (see, for example, Page & Scheidt, 1971). In the final analysis, a realistic view toward the problems and virtues of replication will help psychology in its efforts to develop a reliable hard core of information that is generally accepted by the field.

Summary

In this discussion, an effort has been made to focus on what is communicated by the total experimental situation from the subject's point of view and to show the crucial importance of being certain that the subject's perception is that which the experimenter intends it to be. The significance of subtle factors affecting subjects' perceptions have been emphasized as well as how the experimental model derived from physics must be modified in order to make it appropriate to the study of psychological problems. Despite the discrepancies between how the experiment is ideally conceptualized in the physical sciences and the realities of experiments with human subjects, it remains the single most useful tool for the systematic study of psychological mechanisms. It is, however, essential that the Achilles' heel of the psychological experiment receive careful attention; that is, the extent to which any given experimental procedure serves as a valid operational translation of the psychological process the investigator hopes to study. Appropriate techniques, designed to clarify the validity of the experimental procedure, must be developed and used lest inappropriate and misleading conclusions be drawn from the data.

Since the major difficulty is a function of the subject's active mental processes which make him a participant in the unique interaction we call the psychological experiment rather than merely an object of study, we have tried to suggest special ways in which the possible influences of these active mental processes may be evaluated. Therefore, an effort must be made to specify not only what is done to the subject but, equally important, what is communicated to him by the total experimental situation. As we become more adept at recognizing the contributions which these variables make to our findings, the psychological experiment will become an even more powerful tool. Certainly, such an understanding is essential if we would hope to claim ecological validity for our findings and extend them beyond the confines of the laboratory.

Ultimately, it will be necessary to devote the kind of careful attention to questions concerning the validity of operational definitions that is currently paid to questions concerning the statistical validity of findings. As we gain a better understanding of these issues, the experiment in psychology will have not only the appearance of science, but will also serve psychology with the kind of effectiveness which has made the experimental method the hallmark of the physical sciences.

Acknowledgments

I would like to express appreciation to my colleagues at the Unit for Experimental Psychiatry, Mary R. Cook, A. Gordon Hammer, David A. Paskewitz, and Harvey D. Cohen, for their helpful comments in the preparation of this paper. I am particularly grateful to Frederick J. Evans, Charles Graham, and Emily Carota Orne for their detailed criticisms and many incisive suggestions.

The substantive work upon which the theoretical outlook presented in this paper is based was supported in part by Grant #MH 19156 from the National Institute of Mental Health and by a grant from the Institute for Experimental Psychiatry.

References

Adair, J. G., & Fenton, D. P. Subject's attitudes toward psychology as a determinant of experimental results. *Canadian Journal of Behavioral Science,* 1971, **3**, 268–275.

Aronson, E., & Carlsmith, J. M. Experimentation in social psychology. In G. Lindzey & E. Aronson (Eds.), *The handbook of social psychology.* (2nd ed.) Vol. 2. *Research methods.* Reading, Massachusetts: Addison-Wesley, 1969. Pp. 1–79.

Brehm, J. W., & Cohen, A. R. *Explorations in cognitive dissonance.* New York: Wiley, 1962.

Evans, F. J. Simulating subjects: Who is fooling whom? Paper presented at the meeting of the American Psychological Association, Washington, D. C., September 1971.

Evans, F. J., & Orne, M. T. Motivation, performance, and hypnosis. *International Journal of Clinical and Experimental Hypnosis,* 1965, **13**, 103–116.

Festinger, L. *Theory of cognitive dissonance.* Evanston, Illinois: Row, Peterson, 1957.

Golding, S. L., & Lichtenstein, E. Confession of awareness and prior knowledge of deception as a function of interview set and approval motivation. *Journal of Personality and Social Psychology,* 1970, **14**, 213–223.

Gustafson, L. A., & Orne, M. T. Effects of perceived role and role success on the detection of deception. *Journal of Applied Psychology,* 1965, **49**, 412–417.

Hilgard, E. R. *Hypnotic susceptibility.* New York: Harcourt, 1965.

Holland, C. H. Sources of variance in the experimental investigation of behavioral obedience. Unpublished doctoral dissertation, Univ. of Connecticut, 1967.

Hull, C. L. *Hypnosis and suggestibility.* New York & London: Appleton, 1933.

Lana, R. E. Pretest sensitization. In R. Rosenthal & R. L. Rosnow (Eds.), *Artifact in behavioral research.* New York: Academic Press, 1969. Pp. 119–141.

Levy, L. D. Awareness, learning, and the beneficent subject as an expert witness. *Journal of Personality and Social Psychology,* 1967, **6**, 365–370.

Masling, J. Role-related behavior of the subject and psychologist and its effects upon psychological data. In D. Levine (Ed.), *Nebraska symposium on motivation.* Lincoln: Univ. of Nebraska Press, 1966.

O'Connell, D. N., Shor, R. E., & Orne, M. T. Hypnotic age regression: An empirical and methodological analysis. *Journal of Abnormal Psychology,* 1970, **76** (Monogr. Suppl. No. 3), 1–32.

Orne, M. T. The nature of hypnosis: Artifact and essence. *Journal of Abnormal and Social Psychology,* 1959, **58**, 277–299.

Orne, M. T. On the social psychology of the psychological experiment: With particular reference to demand characteristics and their implications. *American Psychologist,* 1962, **17**, 776–783.

Orne, M. T. Demand characteristics and the concept of quasi-controls. In R. Rosenthal & R. L. Rosnow (Eds.), *Artifact in behavioral research.* New York: Academic Press, 1969. Pp. 143–179.

Orne, M. T. Hypnosis, motivation, and the ecological validity of the psychological experiment. In W. J. Arnold & M. M. Page (Eds.), *Nebraska symposium on motivation.* Lincoln: Univ. of Nebraska Press, 1970. Pp. 187–265.

Orne, M. T. The simulation of hypnosis: Why, how, and what it means. *International Journal of Clinical and Experimental Hypnosis,* 1971, **19**, 183–210.

Orne, M. T. On the simulating subject as a quasi-control group in hypnosis research: What, why and how. In Erika Fromm & R. E. Shor (Eds.), *Hypnosis: Research developments and perspectives.* Chicago: Aldine-Atherton, 1972. Pp. 399–443.

Orne, M. T., & Evans, F. J. Social control in the psychological experiment: Antisocial behavior and hypnosis. *Journal of Personality and Social Psychology,* 1965, **1**, 189–200.

Orne, M. T., & Holland, C. H. On the ecological validity of laboratory deception. *International Journal of Psychiatry,* 1968, **6**, 282–293.

Orne, M. T., & Watson, P. D. The motivation of subjects for traumatic experiments. Paper presented at the meeting of the American Psychological Association, New York, September 1957.

Orne, M. T., Sheehan, P. W., & Evans, F. J. Occurrence of posthypnotic behavior outside the experimental setting. *Journal of Personality and Social Psychology,* 1968, **9**, 189–196.

Page, M. M., & Scheidt, R. J. The elusive weapons effect: Demand awareness, evaluation apprehension, and slightly sophisticated subjects. *Journal of Personality and Social Psychology,* 1971, **20**, 304–318.

Paskewitz, D. A., & Orne, M. T. Cognitive effects during alpha feedback training. Paper presented at the meeting of the Eastern Psychological Association, New York, April 1971.

Riecken, H. W. A program for research on experiments in social psychology. In N. F. Washburne (Ed.), *Decisions, values and groups.* Vol. 2. New York: Pergamon Press, 1962. Pp. 28–42.

Rosenberg, M. J. The conditions and consequences of evaluation apprehension. In R. Rosenthal & R. L. Rosnow (Eds.), *Artifact in behavioral research.* New York: Academic Press, 1969. Pp. 279–349.

Rosnow, R. L., & Aiken, L. S. Mediation of artifacts in behavioral research. *Journal of Experimental Social Psychology,* in press.

Rowland, L. W. Will hypnotized persons try to harm themselves or others? *Journal of Abnormal and Social Psychology,* 1939, **34**, 114–117.

Sheehan, P. W. Countering preconceptions about hypnosis: An objective index of the involvement of the hypnotist. *Journal of Abnormal Psychology,* 1971, **78**, 299–322.

Shor, R. E., & Orne, Emily C. Norms on the Harvard Group Scale of Hypnotic Susceptibility, Form A. *International Journal of Clinical and Experimental Hypnosis,* 1963, **11**, 39–47.

Silverman, I. Role-related behavior of subjects in laboratory studies of attitude change. *Journal of Personality and Social Psychology,* 1968, **8**, 343–348.

Solomon, R. L. Extension of control group design. *Psychological Bulletin,* 1949, **46**, 137–150.

Turner, L. H., & Solomon, R. L. Human traumatic avoidance learning: Theory and experiments on the operant-respondent distinction and failures to learn. *Psychological Monographs,* 1962, **76** (Whole No. 559), 1–32.

Young, P. C. Antisocial uses of hypnosis. In L. M. LeCron (Ed.), *Experimental hypnosis.* New York: Macmillan, 1952, Pp. 376–409.

Zamansky, H. S., Scharf, B., & Brightbill, R. The effect of expectancy for hypnosis on prehypnotic performance. *Journal of Personality,* 1964, **32**, 236–248.

AUTHOR INDEX

Numbers in italics indicate the page on which the complete references are listed.

SUBJECT INDEX

A

Adjective, 4
Alexia, 92, 115
Ambidexterity, 91
Anthropogeny, 67–88
Aphasia, 89–91, 95, 114–115, 117
  therapy for, 118–119
Associations, 50
Attention, 50
Attention hypothesis for brain function, 111–112

C

Cerebral commissures, 92, 95, 114, 116, 119
Cerebral hemispheres, 89–122
Chaining, 128
Cognition, 68, 69
Cognitive dissonance, 166
Communication system, 128, 131, 134, 137, 142, 149
Concept formation, 76
Concepts, 83–84
Conditioning, 67–88
  communications in, 81
  semantic, 67–68
    and grammar in, 73–75
Configuring, 67
Corpus callosum, 90, 92, 93, 114, 116
Cortex, 92

D

Dichotic listening technique, 96, 107, 110
Dominant hand, 93
Dominant hemisphere of brain, 91–122
Dyspraxia, 92

E

Eduction, 67
Efficiency model of brain function, 107–111
Epilepsy, 95
Expectancy hypothesis for brain function, 111–112
Experimental situation, 157–189
  communication in, 157–189
  deception in, 166, 177–179
  demand characteristics of, 163, 171–175, 182–184
  experimental procedure, 170–171
  perception of by the subject, 166–171
Experimental subjects, 157–189
  solicitation of, 167–170
Evaluation apprehension, 165
Evolution, 67–88

F

Frontal lobe, 114
Functional localization model of brain function, 95, 113–122

G

Generalization, 71–73, 75–77
  along logical association categories, 72–73
  semantic versus phonetic, 71–72, 77
  sentential versus propositional, 75–76
Grammatical information, 30, 37
Graphs, 39
Gyrus, 114

H

Hemiplegia, 90
Hemispherectomized patients, 116

198

Split-brain patients, 90, 92–95, 113, 116
Strict localization model of brain func-
    tion, 89–92, 99, 107, 110–111, 113
Symboling, 67–88
Syntax, 82–83

T

Tachistoscopic techniques, 93, 96, 107
Temporal lobe, 91, 92, 114

U

Unmarked, 13–14

V

Verbal functions, 89–122
Visual half-field, 93, 96–122

W

Will, 9
Word blindness, 115
Word deafness, 115
Words, 2–4
    classes of, 2–4
    contents of, 2–4
    function of, 4